QUIET JUNGLE

—

ANGRY SEA

Dedicated to the memory of Doc, Bosun and Snowy;

To Titch who died at home;

To Ernie, Tombola and Dicky;

To my faithful friends, Lissy the wise and Lofty the sailor;

To Tiny, wherever he is;

and finally to The East Surrey Regiment, the finest
of them all.

QUIET JUNGLE

—

ANGRY SEA

My Escapes from the Japanese

DENIS GAVIN

Lennard Publishing
1989

The Publishers are grateful to the *Evening Standard*, Palmerston North, New Zealand, for the photograph on plate VIII; and to the Imperial War Museum for the arms of the East Surrey Regiment.

Lennard Publishing
a Division of Lennard Books Ltd.

Musterlin House
Jordan Hill Road
Oxford OX2 8DP

British Library Cataloguing in Publication Data
is available for this title.

ISBN 1-85291-062-3

First published 1989
© Denis Gavin 1989

Typeset in ITC Galliard.
Design by Forest Publication Services, Luton.

Cover design by Pocknell & Co.

Reproduced, printed and bound in Great Britain by
Butler & Tanner Ltd., Frome and London.

CONTENTS

1926 – 1942

These are the historical events surrounding the events of this book:–

With the succession of Hirohito as Emperor, in 1926, Japan resumed its previous policy of aggression against China.

In 1931 the Japanese Imperial Army occupied the province of Manchuria.

Two years later the League of Nations requested that Japan cease its hostilities in China, and Japan replied by withdrawing its membership from the League.

In the same year, 1933, Japan began to consolidate its gains in China, landing troops in Shanghai. Unable to resist the superior Japanese forces, China was compelled to sign a truce in May.

Following pacts signed with Nazi Germany and Fascist Italy, hostilities were recommenced in 1937 and a Japanese force quickly overran Northern China. By the following year they had advanced into Eastern and Southern China, successfully capturing Shanghai, Soochow, Nanking, Tsingtao, Canton and Hankow.

War was declared in Europe in September, 1939, and Japan concluded a tripartite alliance with Germany and Italy in 1940.

In December, 1941, Japan commenced its downward thrust into Indo China in earnest, invading Siam (Thailand), simultaneous with its attack on the American fleet at Pearl Harbor. Burma and British Malaya were quickly overrun.

By the 15th of February, 1942, the British naval base at Singapore was in Japanese hands.

FOREWORD

Denis Gavin, my brother in law, was born in a mining village on the outskirts of Newcastle-upon-Tyne. A member of a large family, Denis went to the local village school and gained a scholarship to Grammar School. Rather than go into the mines, which was then the only local employment, he decided to travel South. He worked briefly in York then proceeded to Cambridge and London, working as a barman. Whilst in London he became a supporter of the Socialist side in Spain, and decided to join the International Brigade in the Spanish War. He got as far as France where he had a disagreement with a gendarme regarding the ownership of a bicycle, and consequently spent a short spell in a French prison before being sent back to Britain.

Denis had always had a longing to join the Army but had understood that the fact that he had to wear spectacles made it impossible. However, in 1938 he was able to realise his ambition and enlisted in the East Surrey Regiment – a Regiment of which he was always immensely proud. On the outset of hostilities, he was sent with his regiment to Singapore and was there when the Japanese forces invaded. He eventually ended up as a prisoner of the Japanese, and the extraordinary tale of his escapes from the enemy is the subject of this book. After his third escape, he was flown back to the United Kingdom in an extremely poor state of health. Eventually he settled in Cambridge, but was very anxious to visit Australian friends made during his period as POW and, to accomplish this, he obtained a job as steward aboard an ocean liner calling at Australia and New Zealand. He was so taken with New Zealand he decided to make it his permanent home. There he married, and held a variety of jobs and finally was employed in the New Zealand Education Department. After the tragic accidental death of his only son at the age of 20, Denis involved himself with the Psychiatric Ward at the local hospital and worked there as a full-time male nurse. He later rejoined the Education Department and before retirement he became involved with organisations catering for 'down and outs', and helping to rehabilitate those discharged from mental hospitals. Denis was until recently a permanent resident in a War Pensioners establishment, where he devoted his time and energy to helping other residents in need.

Writing this book was always a driving ambition of his, and he was delighted when he learned that it would be published. His death in April this year was tragically close to its final publication, but he did at least have the satisfaction of knowing that the story that he told was about to be made available to a wide readership.

G.F. Wilkins, Cambridge,
1989

MY BROTHERS IN ARMS

Major H.M. Kilgour, RAMC	29*	Doc
F/Lt. Dykes, RAF	29	Dicky
LAC Douglas Bowler, RAF	26	Tom
Conductor F. Dainty, IAOC	30	Tiny
Conductor S. Lissenburg, IAOC	27	Lissy
Bar. Rawson, HKSRA	25**	Bosun
Sgt. Beaumont, HKSRA	26***	Snowy
Sgt. E. Forty, AIF	45	Ernie
Pte. V. Hudson, AIF	18	Titch
D. Eastgate, AIF	23	Lofty
D. Gavin, East Surrey	26	Gabby

*   Died Rangoon, Dysentery

**   Lost at sea

***   Died at sea from Malaria

Bowler was Hugh's orderly.

CHAPTER 1

CALL TO ARMS

8 December 1941. The Far East.

The bugle sounded and we were running. The first note was all we needed, we'd been waiting for it and we were reaching for our packs and rifles as the strident message echoed through the trees.

"Calling A !!!

"Calling B !!!

"Calling all the COMPAN-EE."

North, south, east and west the bugler summoned, and then came the clarion alarm with the urgency of its

"Get on parade!

"Get on parade!

"Get on parade!"

and the final "Double, Double, DOUBLE" of the bugle put more speed in our running for the platoon truck, already loaded and set to go.

"Get them aboard, Gerry!", I called to my Lance Corporal friend, and raced towards Bill Bateman, the platoon Lieutenant.

"Down to the gates Corporal," Bill yelled, "Follow Sergeant Hall and wait at the guardroom."

Within moments I had taken over from Gerry in the cab of my truck, and as he piled into the back we moved away, slipping easily into our place in the convoy just behind Sergeant Hall's truck.

"Tokyo, here we come!" Gerry yelled, and you could feel the exhilaration in his voice. Gerry was only a little man but he had a great heart.

"Look out – you yellow bastards!" big Edwards shouted with his gap toothed guffaw, and then, just as we were on the jungle road by the guardroom, I leaped off the still moving truck with my farewell, "Hold the fort Gerry!"

Bill Bateman was already waiting and he pushed a map into my hand. "We're going into Siam, Corporal," he said, "Right up to Bangkok." He spread his map for me and the three mortar Sergeants. I was the only Corporal with the mortar team. Sergeant Henry Hall was senior Sergeant, he was really Platoon Sergeant but he had a gun team also.

I admired Henry, and not just because he tried every way he could to get me that third stripe. Bill had also tried, and only because we were still a pre-war battalion of regulars, I missed it. I only had three years service in the army, and regular battalion commanders still didn't believe that sergeants could be made in less than seven years.

I liked maps and crawled in to get a good look at Bill's astoundingly detailed shoot of Bangkok. It was an army map, and my eyes widened as I realised that we really did have an intelligence service in the Far East.

There was an aerodrome there and one of our companies, "C" I think, was to capture it. Another company was to cope with the military garrison of two or maybe three Siamese Battalions. There was even a Japanese spy ring quartered in a brothel to attend to, and Jacko, the junior Sergeant, licked his lips. "That'll do me," he said, but Bill cut him down.

"We'll be with Battalion Headquarters" he said with his matter-of-fact formality, and closed his map.

"Any questions?" And when they had been asked and answered, we went back to our section to wait once more for the signal to move off. We'd already been waiting in our barrack rooms in Kitra, close to the Siamese border, for the last twenty-four hours and now we waited again nearly four hours more.

The date was 8 December, 1941, and just 600 miles north of us at Singora on the east coast of Siam (now Thailand) the Japanese had made an almost unopposed landing. We were at war, and the Japanese were heading straight for us.

'We' were the East Surrey Regiment, known to all simply as 'the Surreys'. I had joined up in 1938 at the time of the Munich Crisis when war with Germany seemed inevitable at any moment. The idea of being a sloppy Navy boy or a cissy in Air Force blue didn't appeal to me, so I joined the Army. Or, to be more precise, I joined the infantry. All those corps - the Medical Corps, the Service Corps and the rest - they wore the uniform, but to my uniformed mind, they weren't real soldiers. So Fortune's hand guided me to one of the finest regiments in the British Army, which by 1920 had already notched up over ninety battle honours, including Sevastopol, Ladysmith and the Somme. Now, I knew, we were about to chalk up another, which was to be one of the costliest ever for the regiment: Malaya.

I was with the 2nd Battalion and we arrived there in August 1940, having had an uncomfortable couple of years keeping the peace in Shanghai, where the Japanese controlled great tracts of the city and took pleasure in trying to provoke 'incidents' with the British and international community in its enclave. Our pride was boosted by our achievement in maintaining relative calm, but nevertheless we were glad to swap it for the reassuring invincibility of 'Fortress Singapore'. Its bright lights, bars, dances and air of general gaiety combined with the power of its huge guns and its newly built naval base to banish thoughts of the Japanese and rumours of war to the realm of fantasy.

For the locals, this state of blithe self-delusion was to continue for almost another year, but for us a move up the peninsula in February 1941 and a sudden dose of serious training opened our eyes to the real possibility of a Japanese attack.

We were part of the 6th Indian Infantry Brigade, which formed one third of Major-General Murray-Lyon's 11th Indian Division, and had been assigned the hypothetical task of defending positions around Jitra, just south of the border with Siam. As if to give a stronger note of realism to it all, we even staged a mock 'Battle of Jitra' in which the Surreys played the part of the attacking Japanese forces, unaware that this same scene was to be re-enacted before the end of the year, but on that occasion with real Japanese and a very real defeat for the division.

I even got into the elite among companies, H.Q., and as if Lady Luck had married me I made the crack HQ Platoon.

This was the mortar platoon, the 3" mortars, and for speed in action, clockwork precision in drill and loyalty my section had taken all the points. We even beat Henry Hall's, and he had trained Gerry and me.

Bill Bateman was without peer. As a Lieutenant and a ranker, he was tougher and knew more about handling men than any other three officers put together. He was one of those men you occasionally meet who had the ability to inspire, so that we would follow him through hell. And now perhaps we were waiting to do just that. The top section of the ace platoon in the elite company of the crack regiment in the finest service was waiting to serve its King and country: Britain had just declared war on Japan.

CHAPTER 2

BEDLAM, BAYONET AND BLAST

When it came, the move was an anticlimax. There was no race for the Siamese border, no speeding to Bangkok. Not even another bugle note. Instead, Bill came and told us we were going north, about four miles north of our barracks to the trenches and entanglements we'd been digging for months.

It had been generally anticipated that the Japanese would land somewhere on the east coast of Siam and try to work their way down the peninsula towards 'Fortress Singapore'. To thwart this a counter-operation, code-named 'Matador', had been conceived. We were to beat them at their own game by marching north - violating the neutrality of Siam on the way - and lying in wait to oppose any seaborne landings. That was the plan.

As the Japanese bull charged ashore, the 'Matador' stood still and waited. We were not going to attack anybody. The era of defence had started and, for the last time ever, we moved out of our jungle camp, with the barrack huts already crackling in the flames of the demolition gang. Nothing was being left to chance and if the enemy was to break through our lines, we didn't want to leave a welcoming note.

Slowly, and just a bit subdued, we advanced northwards. By nightfall we had dug new trenches, our mortars were set up and our 10 lb bombs were stacked neatly in the gun emplacements. We'd dined royally on stolen chickens and eggs and even had huts to sleep in, as the positions were in the centre of a village from which the inhabitants had hurriedly fled.

I should have made sure of a good night's sleep as there hadn't been much rest the night before. But I was the worrying type, who liked to make sure of things, and I spent too much time making a nuisance of myself at battalion headquarters, pestering for information and then studying the local terrain from my map.

As I liked maps, I enjoyed working out the ranges and bearings of every possible target within our hitting range of sixteen hundred yards. I catered for everything, except that my mortar didn't have overhead clearance from a coconut palm in front of us and when we got a call into

action next morning I splattered coconuts all over the area.

I was quite calm and precise in getting my section into action on a map reference target, and when the number one raised his right arm in the 'on' signal I set them off.

"Rapid ———— Fire!"

The first bomb hit the cluster of nuts at the top of this palm but was itself high in the air when it burst like an ack-ack shell. It was a very confusing situation, with coconuts crashing everywhere and ack-ack shells bursting overhead and none of us knew for a moment what was happening. As the second bomb followed the first, we still didn't know what was wrong.

Then Bill cut right through me with his scathing "Overhead! Corporal!" I didn't like to be told, especially as I had spent three months as mortar instructor for Malayan command.

Still, we had the gun out of the emplacement in the open and firing within sixty seconds. Gerry chopped the tree away and as we got back into the emplacement, we got the cease-fire order.

We never did find out what we were firing at, but at least we knew that somebody thought there were Japanese within a mile of us. This didn't help much, as the day dragged on without further action and we in bewilderment began to wonder what was really happening and where everybody was.

It was our Division's job to stop the Japanese from forcing a way down the west coast. The defences, which we had been constructing since June but had still not completed, were supposed to hold back the might of Japanese armour which we heard had crossed the border on the 10th and which was now heading directly for us. The combined power of four Battalions of the Punjab regiment, the 1st Battalion of the Leicesters and three Battalions of Gurkhas made up the rest of the Division just a few miles to our right, but as we peered through the darkness from our forward observation position, it felt as if our little company alone would be defending Malaya against the invaders.

The Japanese divisions were probably swarming round us and we might already be cut off. Every possible disquieting thought and rumour visited our company. In this mood I took Gerry with me for a walk to see if we could find someone outside our own lonely little island.

We followed the track which wandered towards the road which was our way out, and just before the track broke clear of the jungle to partly open country we came upon one of our machine gun posts. A despatch rider cycled past us as we stood talking to the post commander. He cycled

towards the road quite unhurriedly, and was passing a stand of palm trees, when seven little men in uniform materialised from the trees and stood gazing after him.

We took them in casually. They turned round and examined us, then, almost simultaneously, horrified realisation came to both parties that each was facing the enemy.

The Japanese dived into the jungle, the British machine gun clattered and I frantically flapped my arms in the 'action' signal to the observation post for relay to my team. Gerry tore back to give the range and direction and the whole four guns of the mortar platoon shelled the jungle for five minutes until it didn't look as if a bird could live where the enemy had gone to cover.

I thought it would look grand to call for a volunteer to come with me to see what we could see and the wretched Gerry called my bluff.

"Me and you Gabby," he said, using the form of my second name everyone in the Army had used since Shanghai days. I'm not really 'gabby', but no one ever called me Denis.

So Gerry and I took off but I decided it was smarter to lie down and listen before we got to the danger spot, so we found nothing. We found plenty when we got back to our guns though. Everybody was running hither and thither and most of them were yelling out orders or information. A frantic order to withdraw had come through. The Japanese were reported to have overrun our positions north of Jitra and their tanks were carving a route through the half-finished defences which the division had erected either side of the main road to our right. We had been ordered south as divisional reserves but we had no trucks, and anyway the enemy was said to be on the road in force, so we had to carry what we could, destroy what we couldn't, and make our way over ten miles of sodden paddy field, and rubber plantations. It was a slithery, sloppy, exhausting ten miles for us, burdened with full marching order plus one part or another of the mortar and bombs.

Darkness had fallen by the time the gun commanders reported to Bill Bateman at Battalion Headquarters on the south bank of the Sungei Kedah at Alor Star, ten miles south of Jitra. It was now 12 December, and in four days of war, without having set eyes on a single Japanese, we had lost a thirty mile strip of Malaya and the Division had suffered a major defeat. Further withdrawals were on the cards and as soon as our forces were safely across the nearby bridge, we were to blow it up and beat a hasty but orderly retreat south to the village of Gurun.

There were only two mortar sections complete now, mine and Sergeant Jackson's, and Bill gave us two positions for the night. As senior sergeant, Jackson took the nearest position and when he ordered me to

go nearly a mile away my nerves, badly frayed by two restless nights, gave way. I hit him. Twenty-four hours earlier no one could have persuaded me that I was capable of any kind of insubordination, and now I had knocked down a senior NCO. But Jackson let it go, and my gang trudged wearily away. A few minutes later I was screaming at an insubordinate Edwards, and shoved a round up the breach of my rifle and was going to shoot him. So far I hadn't been much good as an NCO.

A few hours' sleep that night worked wonders, but food was becoming a problem as we only had unpalatable biscuits, and hunger and weariness were battling for supremacy. However, the feeling of urgency seemed to have gone with the night and I took the opportunity on an apparently peaceful morning to clean myself in the river by the bridge.

The shattering roar of the blasted bridge galvanised me and I didn't even put socks on under my light shoes before I was speeding back to my men. They were ready to fly, but I was calmer now and we stayed until we got word from Bill to pull back to Headquarters, now well below Alor Star. Thirty-five miles gone.

Later that morning, Bill sent me and my team to give a hand to an Indian rearguard who were nervous and liked the idea of artillery (which of course we weren't) to support them. This rearguard of two companies was spread out about two hundred yards each side of the only road leading south, and was quite secure until one of them blazed away at what was probably only a butterfly. Immediately the two companies started a battle with a non-existent enemy in a copse in the middle of a wide expanse of paddy fields. I knew it was empty because an Indian sergeant had just come from there.

We finally got them to stop firing but couldn't persuade them that no enemy lurked there until I walked across the paddy and through the copse myself. When I got back to where my team should have been, they had piled into the truck leaving the mortar and bombs and were speeding south. Furious, I flagged a despatch rider to go after them and got a scorching, agonising burn on my bare ankle from his red hot exhaust pipe. I still hadn't put my socks on.

The rider stopped at Headquarters while I, fuming, made my report to Bill. It was another ten miles south before I caught up with them. This time I didn't scream, but I did shove a round up the breach and the team came back without demur.

As it turned out the flight was not their fault. An Indian Officer had told them that the Japanese were only twenty yards away and that the orders were to scram, but just the same the desertion grieved me. Funnily enough, it was from this moment that my team became my followers, and even in danger they still stayed with me. They'd started to think I was tough, and they started remembering incidents like Gerry and me going alone after those Japanese soldiers, about me hitting Jacko, about the copse where the Indian rearguard was and even my firm stand with big Edwards.

Now they came back with me to salvage our mortar, which we got without incident, although the Indian rearguard, and in fact all allied troops, had disappeared from the area. We took it back to Headquarters, where Bill told us to settle down and get some rest.

Rations still weren't organised and rest was still hard to get, so we were completely worn out next morning, when, just before dawn, we were bulldozed into a rifle and machine gun platoon for service as a rearguard ambush.

Most of our Brigade was still intact, but the remainder of the Division had been badly cut up at Jitra, many of the survivors being forced to take off into the jungle to save their lives. The few that were left had been collected together south of Gurun to act as reserve, while we and 1/8th Punjabis flanked the main road to the north in an attempt to hold back the Japanese long enough for the formation of a defence line further back.

The rearguard action we were on was supposed, I believe, to make the enemy pause long enough for the formation of a defence line to the south.

Always blasted defence!

Still, we got to our position which was a good one, and somebody in our group wiped out the first Japanese soldiers who came plodding along the road. For an hour after that there was the incessant sound of grenades or machine guns, so presumably we were holding the enemy at bay.

Then suddenly there was a shrill blast of a whistle, repeatedly assailing our ears, and then the shout "Withdraw!" Without further ado, we turned and ran helter skelter through the woods. I felt thoroughly ill when I stumbled out of the woods to the road and into the gleeful arms of a crazy Royal Artillery Lieutenant who was happily laying another ambush for the Japanese.

He had already assembled a mixed collection of Gurkhas, Punjabis and British soldiers in position astride the road, and had two anti-tank guns trained on the crest of the road about 200 yards away. He assigned to me a tree to lie behind and there we waited until the enemy came, four abreast, pouring over the crest towards us.

The Lieutenant held his fire until it was almost too late, then he let loose a flood of tearing destruction, converging lines of unbelievable devastation. In a moment the road was swept clear except for the dead

8

and the dying, and then there was an unearthly silence for about twenty minutes before the enemy air support arrived overhead. Then I discovered that my great friend Gerry Hawkins had strolled off into the jungle towards the Japanese lines, just looking for trouble.

He had been my close friend for three years. We were two of an inseparable trio and I think if I had known that I would never see him again, I would have tried to stop him. For I never did see him again. His body presumably fell into the leaves somewhere for the ever-scavenging ants to devour, but the ants can't destroy the picture I have of him, a picture of a man gifted with humour, and whose chuckle was always so welcome. It was a terrible taste of death for me, and I realised how the war was capable of taking away those I cared for.

At this terrible moment, enemy planes hopped along just above the treetops, and I'd swear the pilot was throwing bombs or grenades at us. Although they didn't shift us, they did keep us down, out of sight. All, that is, except a little Gurkha who planted himself solidly in the middle of the road waiting for the plane to make a third run. He had a Bren gun with him and I remembered having been told that a Bren gun couldn't be fired without its bipod or tripod stand.

The first plane came down the road, machine guns rattling, and the Gurkha took aim. We watched him as the plane zoomed closer. I never noticed him fire but suddenly the plane distintegrated and burning petrol and plane showered over us. The Gurkha looked as if he was on fire for a moment and then he rolled over towards the ditch and the Lieutenant and two others rushed over towards him. The other plane disappeared from the scene but the Japanese 5" mortars opened up and in their uncanny way they got our range. I was unlucky - I got something in my good ankle, I think it was shrapnel. It was only then that the RA Lieutenant gave up and his whistle shrilled out the signal to get the hell out of it.

I went out perched behind the shield of one of the anti-tank guns, and with both trucks and guns jammed with men, off we went out of battle again, leaving the sound of warfare behind us.

We stopped a few miles down the road amongst bivouacked troops, and when I recognised my beloved Surreys, I limped away from the motley crowd, glad to be back once more among my own.

I should have gone to the first aid post to get a dressing for each of my hands, my burned and inflamed ankle, and I wasn't at all certain that I didn't still have a bullet or piece of shrapnel in the other foot. I should also have got some food into my aching stomach but I was just so overwhelmingly tired that I did nothing except find my section and sink down to the sodden ground beside Edwards. Not even the drizzling rain stopped me from passing into deep sleep.

Bill Bateman woke me. A lesser man than Bill would have given up the attempt to rouse me but he always finished anything he started.

"We're making a counter attack Corporal," he said, and I groaned while he went on to rouse the others. I rolled under a bush but Bill found me on his way back and woke me again and I knew that I didn't really have any chance to skulk or hide.

"Come on, Corporal," he said and there was nothing to do but obey when he used that tone. I followed him to the roadway where our Brigade Commander, Brigadier W.O. Lay and our Regimental Sergeant Major were marshalling all available forces.

Everyone who could hold a rifle was in the column they had already formed. They were ready to trudge forward, to halt and turn back the Japanese and pick up the hundreds of our stragglers somewhere to the north of us.

I was near the head of the column when it moved off, but I soon managed, with my limping, burning ankle, to drop back. I would eventually have been near enough to the tail to drop out unnoticed, but we got into the battle area before that.

Then I heard the machine guns open up at the front and soon afterwards the Japanese mortars got cracking. As I listened to the shrapnel pattering like falling stones through the leaves my heart completely failed me.

I couldn't face the fight and I didn't have the guts to turn and run away. Despairingly, in anguish, I turned for help to my oft-forgotten God.

He heard me! He calmed me! He took away my fear and a great unafraid peace descended on me. Even my leg stopped burning and I strode forward with an exhilaration I'd never known before. I had a smile in my heart and a joke on my lips as I passed those blessed comrades of mine and chaffed them (with the licence of camaraderie) as sluggards.

I passed Brigadier Lay and was passing our Sergeant Major, Teddy Worsfold, still leading his men as if he was on the Barrack square, when he stopped me.

"Far enough, Corporal," he said and turned to deploy his column to the left and to the right for the final swoop through the woods to the waiting enemy.

"Come on, Corporal," Teddy said and off we went together through the trees. I got my first enemy at 200 yards from the top of an ant-hill, but as I gazed at the still figure I had to make my peace with God all over again, and even then I still didn't feel quite so good.

I was still all set to die and the roaring torrent which barred our way five minutes later was not enough to turn me from my goal. Henry Hall, Teddy Worsfold and a varied half dozen others looked speculatively at the mere fifteen feet of water, from our bank, while I plunged in, rifle, bandolier and all, and for a few minutes they watched me drowning.

I did drown, gulpingly and chokingly, past the point of lost consciousness and still don't know how I found myself clinging to an overhanging bush across the stream. I didn't even know I still had my rifle until I tried to use my other arm to pull myself up, but I did know the final depths of physical misery as my abused and wretched stomach revolted and heaved while I lay on the bank. Unfortunately, this was the enemy bank. The movements on the other side of the bushes were not from my friends and the head which suddenly appeared with startled eyes staring at me was certainly not that of an Englishman.

The head was withdrawn with a shrieked warning. A background of further frantic shriekings spread through the woods to be followed by the sounds of a helter skelter screaming race for safety as the waiting Japanese force fled in an abandoning desertion, leaving machine guns and ammunition where they lay.

I was still lying face down when Lieutenant Quarrell of my regiment arrived by my side. He was first across the stream after me.

"Coming, Corporal?" I staggered along after him through the woods now empty of the enemy. Empty they might have been, but our artillery and mortars didn't know that. As their fire rained down on us, we made a dash towards the road alongside the river at Gurun, right up to the menacing tank whose clanging and clattering didn't drown the shouts of the crew. We got to within twenty yards of it before we were spotted. Young Quarrell was nearest and had just called out to me, "Got any grenades, Corporal?" when all of its bellowing fury was loosed at us and he was plucked up and hurled back by one of the cannon shells.

I stared at the wall of death which separated me from the Lieutenant, while behind me too death and destruction were cutting a swathe through the rest of the battalion holding out on the river's edge. I was weighing up my own chances of survival when suddenly an almighty explosion erupted the other side of the tree behind which I was sheltering and sent me flying into oblivion.

The Japanese screams were still ringing in my ears as consciousness began to return; but the tank was smoking and silent, and two orderlies were coping with young Quarrell's injuries.

The burning bloody mess on my neck was frightening, until my fearfully questing hand could find only scratches. Then the pain of shrapnel-peppered legs but I still found only scratches and I couldn't believe the evidence of my hands.

Scratched or not, I'd had enough. I wanted some hot soup, I wanted a clean bed. I wasn't really running away, I'd come back later, but I must have some hot soup first. In this new search I turned away, scorning cover and only half conscious of the machine guns clattering around us.

I heard Lance Corporal Freddie Hughes's cry of horror.

"Christ Almighty, look at his bloody head," and I guessed he meant me. I heard Henry Hall tell me to get down, and then I heard and saw the ambulance which my bloody appearance had caused to come skidding towards me. Poor Henry got seven machine gun bullets in his stomach a few minutes later.

Two of our regimental bandsmen were orderlies on the ambulance and I tried to make my excuses to them as we sped towards the regimental aid post. I was still trying to justify myself to the doctor and to Bill Bateman in the aid post as oblivion descended on me again.

CHAPTER THREE

THE JUNGLE WARFARE TEAM

I was rested and well when I awoke next morning but there was a cloud of unhappiness over me and a worrying shame in my heart. Why had I failed myself? I would have given my two stripes, treasured though they were, for the chance to re-live the events of last evening. I would have stuck it out instead of breaking under the strain, especially as the strain, viewed through rested, sane eyes did not seem so great after all. We'd been at war for about a week and only the last two days had really been hectic, yet here I was, a leading NCO skulking in a casualty clearing station which was full of casualties with appallingly serious injuries. I would have given anything for an honest-to-goodness wound to serve as balm to my spirit.

My shame was complete when later that morning, ambulances whisked us from the battlefield to the field hospital. The Japanese had rallied from our thrust and were once more streaming south, but by the time they smashed through the Surreys to the field hospital, a long train load of wounded was snaking its way down the peninsula to the serenity of Seremban. Many, of course, did not live to see Seremban: the little Gurkha, for instance, who'd shot down the Japanese plane just the day before, incredibly distant as that day seemed now. He died quietly and without complaint; in fact, no one even noticed him die; somebody just happened to notice he was dead. Henry Hall just managed to reach hospital in time to be buried with the machine gun bullets still in his stomach.

As I lay on my bed, news came of the terrible toll that one week of fighting had taken of the battalion. We had been reduced to just ten officers and 260 men and could no longer be regarded as a fighting unit. The survivors, apart from those still struggling through the jungle behind Japanese lines, had re-assembled further south at Ipoh and had been slung together with the remnants of the 1st Leicesters to form 'the British Battalion'. It was hard to imagine such a hotch-potch unit ever functioning efficiently, let alone possessing any *esprit de corps*, but the two battalions combined to give a strength greater than the sum of their parts and went on to achieve a legendary status all their own in the weeks of hard fighting which lay ahead.

I fretted in my morose isolation, my mind on my regiment two hundred miles to the north; and the fact that somehow I'd acquired a reputation for fearlessness didn't help. Nothing could help me except another chance and I was in this frame of mind when the final blow came. I'd lost one pair of spectacles in that wretched river, and had one lens somehow splintered in my spare pair, and now the medical board decided that I could not be considered fit for any draft back to the front until I got new glasses. In the chaos of war no one could tell me how I was going to get a refit. I had been laid up for several days, and I was in the depth of despair when Tony Cater and Nobby Howard came to see me in the Hospital.

Nobby and Tony were two captains in the East Surrey regiment, and they were looking for recruits in a new project conceived by Malaya Command who had commissioned a major of the 8th Punjab regiment to find and organise a band of men, to do battle in the jungle. I believe that many other bands were formed, although we never met any. This Major decided that the Surreys with their background in jungle training and experience in war could provide his team - and Nobby and Tony were on the look out for the men they needed.

My morale got a real boost when I found that I had been selected. In two days I was, in quick succession, appointed Lance Sergeant, then promoted to Sergeant and was out of hospital. The spectacle issue had been lightly and successfully brushed aside and I sallied forth to meet my new comrades.

I already knew them as it happened - Len Avery, now sergeant major from sergeant and Joe Hocking, promoted sergeant from corporal. I used to give him hell when he was a junior lance corporal in my company, and I found myself still jumping on him but with mock ferocity.

Nobby reminded me of the cartoon character 'Ol' Bill', principally because of his moustache, though he could never see the resemblance himself. I still don't know if he was the bravest man I met or whether he was just mad. He collared me as his partner and caused me more missed heartbeats than did any of the enemy, although now that I think about it I wouldn't have swopped him.

Tony Cater who grabbed Len Avery seemed very cold-blooded. He struck me as emotionless. He and Len seemed to be a good pair, however, and were good friends. These then were my comrades in the new jungle warfare team. Under direction from Malaya Command, we made ourselves as much like brigands as we could and were ready for war.

War now turned out to be parading and strutting about, all for the benefit of awe-stricken troops, on their way to honest fighting, who were supposed to need a pat on their back and a boost in morale, before they went to face the foe. They had to be talked to by 'heroes', which meant us. They were to be given the chance to see the kind of fighter who could make mincemeat of the Japanese army. Then they were supposed to be filled with a contempt for the Japanese and jungle which would hurry them north, eager to come to grips with the enemy.

We lived in comfort and luxury far, far away from any sound of war and even had a car, a little truck and a motor bike for our added comfort. If the war had gone differently we would doubtless have rapidly scaled the ladder of promotion to goodness knows what dizzy heights, and finished up with a row of medals without ever again seeing the enemy, except in captivity. Fortunately we were spared some of the parades.

Meanwhile, however, I gradually realised that really we were doing a good job well and were giving those poor tremulous reinforcements hope that had not been in them before we came.

Many of the reinforcing infantry had recently landed in Malaya, almost fresh from the village green, and had weird and wonderful ideas about both the enemy and the jungle gleaned from comics, penny dreadfuls, and the cinema.

Many of them would scarcely leave the centre of the road when, as often, it was flanked by jungle. In their minds, this abounded with tigers and rampaging elephants, and teemed with deadly snakes. A patrol to men like these would be nothing but a nightmare. With their comic strip idea of sword-brandishing, screaming oriental fanatics, many were beaten before they started. The old-soldier habit of telling tall stories had not helped them much either. This was the situation when we entered their world.

One such occasion was when we were directed to an English country regiment on its way to the front. Two hundred yards short of our destination we parked our transport and donned our brigand disguise. I had a light khaki drill uniform, sweat stained and baggy, rubber shoes, gaiters and a bush hat. These were sewn with skull and crossbones, and childish as it seems now it gave us just that much additional value. I had a water bottle and a parang (the Malayan knife) on my belt, a bandolier of ammunition and my Tommy gun cradled in my right arm - thus clad I was ready for introduction.

Driving up to HQ would have been too easy. The regiment knew that the Jungle Warfare Team was coming, and half expected us to swing in through the trees. We couldn't disappoint them too much, so we separated to come in at different directions. It was not too difficult for me to reach a sentry before he knew anything and to put my hand on his shoulder to attract his attention. The poor fellow nearly jumped out of his skin but before he had time to shoot me - this was always a hazard -

I'd spoken, just briefly but introduction enough:

"Where's the cookhouse, mate?" was all I said, but within an hour the whole regiment knew that the Jungle Warfare Team had stepped right out of the jungle into their midst.

I made my way to the corporal's mess, knowing that the sergeants would find their way there. Still uncommunicative, I lined up for dinner which I ate voraciously, looking up only when I was fumbling for a cigarette.

I grinned to myself as I noticed that the tables in my vicinity were full and the others further away were not and with a "Thanks mate," took a cigarette from one of the proffered packets, inhaled deeply and spoke profoundly and deeply. "That's good."

The ice was broken and I was no longer isolated. "You blokes are moving soon, aren't you?" I asked and was told not too happily.

"Yes, to Ipoh."

"Ipoh," I said, "Ah!" as if my mind had turned nostalgically to the place of my dreams. "Gee, I wish I was there now."

Immediately, the floodgates were opened as they sought news and information. Did I know Ipoh? What was it like? Was there jungle there?

"Oh, yes, the jungle is thick around Ipoh," I said, "Just as thick as it is here in fact," and they were rocked. In the last few days they had got used to their present environment of trees and bush. It hadn't occurred to them that they were actually in the jungle until I explained that they could not find jungle much thicker than this anywhere. This raised another question. "What about the tigers?" I had to laugh. "Tigers," I snorted, "You'll never see a tiger in Malaya - I haven't and I've been here a year." I explained that the tigers were not only few and far between but were usually hundreds of miles away from any form of civilisation.

Elephants and crocodiles were dealt with similarly. I believe that there were crocodiles in some rivers but I'd never seen one and certainly the Malayans had no fear of them. They used the river continuously, wading through the fords or bathing in the shallows.

Snakes had been my hobby in peacetime, and I told how I caught them with my hands in the flooded paddy fields. The corporals, reinforced now by many sergeants, looked doubtfully at me.

"Of course, they're not poisonous you know," I explained and then told them of the only two poisonous snakes in Malaya, the king cobra, deadly but rare enough almost to be a museum curiosity, and the tiny silver krait or bootlace snake, a really lethal little thing, but not big enough to strike above the ankle, and I showed my protecting gaiters. All the terrors of the jungle were reduced to their proper size. Only the enemy had to be dealt with now and here was where my own personal experience after crossing the river was invaluable. Undoubtedly, an enemy force had been stampeded by one man or rather by the sight of one man and that alone was the most heartening thing they could have been told. I told them of Shanghai where the Surreys had also met the Japanese when we were stationed there and how in our Shanghai he was 'just another wog'.

This expression was one I loathed, but it was language which the average soldier understood and the phrase was appropriate to a figure that could be pitiful, but never fearsome.

Meanwhile, in different parts of the camps the rest of our team were doing the same as I. Two days later this poor untrained country regiment went north and they went almost lightheartedly, poor devils - very unlike the crowd that was afraid to walk in the jungle and almost ready to stampede at the sight of a little Japanese soldier.

I have an idea that it was the dissenting voice of Nobby that got our role modified and it was decided that not only could we tell the troops what to do, but we could go north for a few days with each unit and show them how to do it. The idea was that one of us would accompany every patrol that went out until the men and officers were more or less at home in the jungle. But after a while, when the regiment commander wanted information quickly we found it easier to go and get it ourselves.

We ran into an appalling battle one night. We had been sent to get information about enemy troops in one area. All our vehement declarations that there were no enemy were useless against the evidence of the sounds of battle, including heavy artillery from our reinforcing units in the rear. The battle lasted all night but we knew that it was all from our side and that the nearest enemy was twenty miles away.

I was with Joe Hocking, though usually when I was with Nobby, Joe was with 'Fishy', Major Finlayson. In all our time together, Nobby never once relaxed. I think he would have addressed me as 'Sergeant' if he was ministering to my dying needs and he would have expected the 'Sir' if I was offering him his last drink of water.

I don't believe he knows even now what my first name is and come to think of it, I didn't know his, all Howards are Nobby in our regiment, maybe in the whole army. He was in fact Captain (later Major) Eustace Aubrey Howard. Anyway, when we retired from the job of morale boosting and found ourselves detailed by Malayan command to do various nasty jobs, Nobby grabbed me as his partner. Captain Cater had already grabbed Len Avery and Fishy had taken Joe Hocking so Nobby and I were stuck with each other.

He shaved daily, was always properly dressed and never got ruffled, although I do remember one occasion when his imagination was just as vivid as mine.

Nobby had been assigned to a brigade which badly needed to close the gap in its defence line for one night. He took me along and my mouth opened when he grandly declined the offer of a platoon of thirty good fighting men to help him.

"My sergeant and I can cope," he said, and told me later that he did not want to be hampered with noisy, blundering incompetents.

So, my Tommy gun and Nobby's silly .45 went to stop the breach. He claimed that we would be able to hear any movement in the area which wasn't really big, and we could demoralise the enemy who tried to go through. This was alright at first then I sensed that someone was following us and by listening and waiting, we soon placed the cunning tracker.

Nobby motioned for me to squat down and he leaned against a tree with his pistol drawn to outwait the enemy who was equally patient and cautious. The next sound we heard was a twig creaking away to the right then a little later we heard him again, further out. We followed the sounds in a semi circle, each sound being just where we expected it to be. He was finally in line and dead in front of us.

He was waiting for us so Nobby decided to follow his example and we made our whispered plans before Nobby started his circling movement.

"I'll make enough noise for him to hear me," he said and off he went, crashing through the jungle like a browsing, meandering elephant. Then he was ahead and started to move forward so that we'd get the enemy between us. Nobby expected me to be right on top of the waiting man and to keep him covered and I didn't let him down.

I was less than fifteen feet from the crouching form when Nobby had started his advance but I had no intention of doing anything hasty. I wasn't going to be like any of those trigger-happy rookies who'd fire at a butterfly or a lizard. I was cool, calm and collected and I held my fire right up to the moment I saw the man point his rifle at Nobby - then I set the night reverberating and clattering with the merciless hammering of my Tommy gun.

We waited until every last echo had given way to a deadly silence, even the frogs and crickets were quiet, then Nobby strode forward, torch blazing and we saw the enemy - an old, and very dead, tree trunk.

It took a while for us to believe it ourselves and until we started remembering that the noises were always just where, and when, we expected them.

We saw another example of frayed nerves that night and had a bird's eye view of the enemy's probing tactics. Nobby and I had got ourselves into a position where we could see what was going on from both sides and he suddenly spotted a pattern in the desultory exchange of shots.

Those Japanese soldiers were probing for gaps, their guns methodically worked their way along the British front until some trigger-happy sentry's nerve gave and he loosed off a burst.

Then the enemy fire moved to the next section and gradually they drew fire from every part of the allied front except for the strip patrolled by Nobby and me. They tried repeatedly and must have decided at last that there was a gap through which they could push an infiltration force.

Nobby was quite happy about this. "We'll set an ambush," he said.

We seemed to have our share of anticlimax because nobody came that night. Instead, we warned the company that relieved us next morning, and they caught a whole column of Japanese soldiers boldly marching through what had been a 'gap'.

I hope this changed the opinion of some Japanese tactician who did not rate the British intelligence very highly.

Certainly Nobby always went in boldly, like the time when we had to occupy and attack, if necessary, Fort Pasir Laba.

Fort Pasir Laba was a complex of rock and concrete built into the hillside on Singapore island, and contrary to general belief, the guns could be turned to face the mainland. The Malayan regiment which manned the fort must have annoyed the Japanese, because they pin-pointed it and plastered it with a ferocity and thoroughness which the Malayan regiment couldn't take. This was evident to anybody who saw the debris afterwards, it included a big gun with its barrel twisted like a bent hairpin.

The Malayan regiment stampeded and took to the woods, and by the time Malaya Command got the news the fort had been unoccupied for hours they hoped it remained so because an enemy landing had been reported in the vicinity. Malaya Command wanted the fort back and panic orders went out to assemble a regiment to man it, though, first of all it had to be got back from the enemy (if they had it).

People were still impressed by the Jungle Warfare title of our gang and a lot of exaggerated and unfounded stories had spread, so we were called in to help. Fishy told Nobby to cope and his "Come on sergeant!" pulled me in.

A company of Punjabis had been assembled to storm Fort Pasir Laba and they were handed over to Nobby, who through an interpreter told them to pile into the convoyed trucks at our disposal. Nobby had been told that speed was the essence of the project so he proposed to drive straight up to and into the fort. This would be easy if there were no Japanese about, but the Punjabis saw the dangers and started to climb out of the trucks. Nobby stalked up to the leading truck and planted his lanky, ungainly body on the front mudguard and drew his pistol. It worked, and the Indians climbed back into the trucks.

Then the Indian Colonel ordered Nobby out of the way. He, as CO was not expendable. But, before the troops could clamber out of the trucks again Nobby solved the problem. "My Sergeant will volunteer," he said.

I had thought Nobby's original idea quite good and was comforted by the thought that Nobby would be the first to cop it. Now that I was the 'Aunt Sally' it was horrible, and I felt that my Tommy gun and I were completely futile. Every bend in the road threatened a roadblock, or an ambush just around the corner. Even where there were no corners, every foot of the menacing jungle which flanked the road added another year to my life and I was a nervous wreck by the time we drove, unopposed, to the hilltop fort.

We stayed there until the relieving regiment arrived and in the meantime replenished our stocks of revolvers, Tommy guns, grenades and rifles from the armoury and food, cigarettes and supplies from the general store.

I got a swag of Malayan dollars out of the petty cash box but I didn't tell Nobby about that.

CHAPTER FOUR
BATTLE OF SINGAPORE

Although Malaya suffered from a mixture of ideas about how it might best be defended, the island of Singapore enjoyed some solid investment in the improvement of its defences. 'Fortress Singapore', as it came to be generally known, had acquired a mythical reputation for invincibility. This helped maintain an air of relative calm among its population in the early days of the campaign, despite repeated and heavy enemy air raids, and lulled us all into a feeling of confidence that, once on the island, we would be safe. */348267/*

The campaign in Malaya had gone badly for the British from the start, and in just five weeks the might of the Empire had been forced to retreat down most of the country's four hundred mile length. By the end of January 1942 there were few remnants of the three divisions still involved on the peninsula, the island's population had nearly doubled and the enemy were amassing their forces across the Johore Strait which flowed between Singapore and the mainland. The only physical feature connecting Singapore and Malaya was a mile-long stone causeway joining Johore Bahru to the northern tip of the island, carrying a railway and the pipeline supplying the island with a quarter of its water requirements. During the night of 30-31 January the final evacuation of troops across the causeway was completed and at 8.15 am on 31 January this last link with the mainland was sent skyward as the charges planted by Indian and British demolition teams were blown.

Even though the island now stood isolated, there was still no real fear about the outcome of the war. In fact it was almost a relief to be on the island with a hundred thousand other defenders and know that all we had to do was form our perimeter and just knock off the enemy as they tried to cross the water. The island was teeming with troops of every description, ack-ack guns were in almost every available space and as far as we knew we lacked nothing except tanks and aircraft. We lived on the fat of the land and even had a little truck loaded with choice food which we'd picked up from abandoned food dumps. By this time we had seven vehicles including a motor bike and two luxurious limousines, also picked up from abandoned dumps, where we had acquired Tommy guns, revolvers and unlimited grenades. Some of us even had bed mattresses. Len Avery had

21

a captured Japanese machine gun very similar to our Bren but much lighter; I had a beautiful Japanese sword and we had about six captured rifles. In fact, we were affluent, leisured and serene - for a week.

Then on 8 February, just one month after they had landed at Singara, the illusion blew up and unbelievably the enemy was on the island. Seven days before, General Percival, the General Officer Commanding, Malaya, had announced that the 'Battle of Malaya' had finished and the 'Battle of Singapore' had begun. Suddenly I realised what he meant. The first shock numbed us and then common sense was regained. After all, there were enough of us to stand shoulder to shoulder almost, and certainly there were more than enough of us to deal with any presumptuous Japanese. Our team was back in action, mainly on reconnaisance patrols.

We were also called in to advise on various matters, such as the incident during the last few days of the fighting, when a unit was having problems with its 3" mortars and Fishy sent me with Joe Hocking to sort them out. The problem was a Japanese machine gun which was doing a lot of damage and three mortar teams had been trying to silence it for the last two hours.

The action was at the golf links, to the north west of the city, with the enemy at the far side and British troops on the near side. No man's land was the fairway and was sprinkled with the bodies of both sides, reminder of a patrol clash during the night. Somewhere in the trees at the other side was a machine gun which only opened up occasionally, but always devastatingly. Obviously the gunner had a clear view and could not be too far in the trees.

I got the mortars to repeat what they'd done a dozen times already, and plaster every inch of the edge of those trees to a reasonable depth. The enemy gunner opened up again, so I got two Bren guns, a Vickers and a Lewis to spray the tree-tops. The gun kept on firing, so that we could almost pin-point the sound.

We sent thirty shells into that spot and when we stopped he was still at it.

I climbed a high tree and searched the terrain until I knew every branch of every tree on the other side. Suddenly, "Rat-a-tat-tat!" went the gun into my tree and in that moment I had him. I could have kicked myself for not guessing beforehand. I'd been on an East Surrey camouflage and concealment course once, and had seen a demonstration by an instructor who completely disappeared by stepping in front of, and merging with, an ordinary bush in the middle of a field. There were no bushes in the fairway so the enemy must be in the grass - right out in the open where nobody expected him.

I told the company commander and we got the mortars ready again and then we started on the fairway in front of the trees. I don't think we got him, but we certainly scared the pants off him and had the satisfaction of seeing not one but three gunners, running for their lives to the trees.

This finished my job and I stopped only to share a mug of tea and a cigarette with the company commander. Then something else happened which gave me another insight into the Japanese character.

An Indian soldier near us suddenly went hysterical and started wailing cries of grief. He sobbed and panted "My poor brudder!" "Oh, my brudder!" His brother was out on the fairway, and had been one of the motionless corpses, only he wasn't motionless now. He was sitting up and I put my glasses on him. He held his head in his hands and you could see the intolerable agony he was suffering.

Our man was still wailing. I can't bear agony like that and I growled "Shut up! Shut up!" He shut up momentarily and his tear-filled eyes pleaded with me, "Help my brudder! my poor brudder!"

It crossed my mind that even the Japanese might respect a stretcher bearer, only there weren't any stretcher bearers about and in a moment before I realised what I was doing I had stripped off my equipment and was groping in my haversack for a white towel which I'd looted from somewhere or other. I waved it from behind a tree for a minute or two, and then stepped out and waved it above my head. Then I stepped back and tied a handkerchief on my arm and stood out again.

It seemed alright so I walked three paces on to the fairway and stood there with the white flag high above me. Slowly and deliberately I went forward and I felt a sudden warmth and kinship for the Japanese. I was a hundred yards clear of cover when the bullets sprayed the ground in front of me and I dived to the shelter of a slight hollow.

There was only one burst and when I calmed my beating heart and raised my head nothing happened. I got up slowly and stood there waving my towel to assure everybody I was harmless and then the moment I took a pace forward the bullets sprayed in front of me again and I sprawled to my cover once more.

I lay there, considering, and it seemed to me that the machine gun was in the British lines and it also seemed that they did not want me to go forward. Perhaps they had misconstrued my flag of truce so I turned and showed my arm-band and I pointed to the wounded Indian who was now lying down.

I hoped I'd made my point but when I turned to go forward again I found I hadn't. This time I didn't dive for cover but stood still. The machine gun stopped and I shook my fist at the whole blasted British army. Then they started again ten feet in front of me and moving towards my feet.

If I'd been a hundred per cent hero I would have stood my ground and called somebody's bluff but I wasn't. I backed off. The firing stopped and I tried again. Somebody was getting really angry and the bullets whipped the grass by my feet. Then I panicked and ran back to the trees.

The Indian was completely motionless again and was probably dead. I went home disgusted with myself because I never managed to be a complete hero.

Home at this time was on the warm sands of the ocean beside the Seaview Hotel, that luxurious colonial resort of the old days. Malaya Command wasn't bothering much about us at this time and we were left mainly to our own devices. The reports were varied, ranging from one story of how the British army had landed in Malaya, cut the Japanese forces in two and was now advancing on Singapore, to another that we were about to throw the Japanese into the sea and clean them up ourselves.

The troops on the island were almost in a state of anarchy. Groups stampeded from their positions in the line and no commander could ever be sure that his flanks were still secure. British regulars usually stayed put, especially those who had years of discipline behind them like the Surreys and the Leicesters.

As well as the chaos of the siege, and the carnage inflicted on the densely populated native quarters by constant aerial and artillery bombardment, there was the hopelessness of using new troops in a war which needed specialists, or at least experienced men.

These troops were trigger-happy as well and I know that I felt a lot safer behind Japanese lines than I did wandering about British installations. Many of them had phobias about fifth columnists and about passwords, and I had a narrow escape one night from one of our own crowd.

I'd been detailed to have a look at forty-three alleged Japanese spies who had been taken prisoner one afternoon. I worked out my route from the map and set off on a bicycle, finding the bullock-cart track leading to Battalion Headquarters. I rode up loudly whistling 'Roll out the Barrel', it was dusk so I thought an identification like this would be helpful.

However, the bloody idiot guarding HQ picked this as a typical enemy infiltration trick, and the first warning I had was from a hail of machine gun bullets loosed at me from the side of the track.

I still don't know how they missed me and even the language from the ditch into which I'd hurled myself still didn't convince them. "Friend or foe?" yelled the Corporal in charge.

"I'll give you bloody friend when I get out of here you stupid, flat-faced, ignorant bastard!!"

"What's the password?" he said and I snarled, then tried to calm myself. After a while I called out "Hey you!" and I got a warning reply, "Keep down or we'll let you have it!" "Where's your officer?" I demanded and only got "Mind your own business!"

I had to pause again to calm myself then I said "Listen mate and listen carefully,' I've got a bag of grenades here and I've got a Tommy gun and if you don't get an officer quick I'm going to start on you."

I heard somebody say "He sounds English," and I roared "Of course I'm bloody English you flaming stupid nits!" (Or words to that effect.)

"All right," said the commander, "Come out with your hands up."

"Not on your blasted life," I said. "You come over here or I'm going to start throwing grenades. One! Two! Three!"

"Hold it," he called, and I heard his footsteps approaching. I was so mad I nearly did let him have it when he arrived and I was madder still when I got to HQ to look at the forty-three Japanese. There were Chinese, Malaysians, Indians, Tamils drooling with betel nut chewings, and even two Eurasians - but no Japanese. I left with the parting shot, "Why the hell don't you lot join the bloody Japs and give us a chance?"

The situation in Singapore became more demoralising and Military Police units set up road blocks to stop deserters getting away from the battle lines and into the town. Malaya Command stopped giving us orders and left us completely to our own devices, so one day Len Avery and I took our little truck and set off to see if we could find our old regiment.

We careered round for a while in what we thought was the battle area although there wasn't really much happening until we were stopped at a road block and questioned by a very suspicious Lieutenant. He had a right to be suspicious because he told us we'd just driven from the enemy lines.

Ten minutes later the same thing happened when we ran into a platoon of Indians led by a havildar, who were waiting for the Japanese to come down the road we'd just used. When we found that most of our search had taken place in enemy territory we gave up and returned.

We still hadn't seen the Japanese.

CHAPTER FIVE

DEATH OF A FORTRESS

This was Singapore in the last days of the siege. It had lasted only two weeks, one of apparent passive complacence and one of chaotic noise and movement. The noise was almost continuous, with Japanese aircraft always droning somewhere overhead, the whistling of artillery shells, and then later, as the battle came nearer, the violent eruption of mortar bombs.

By Friday 13 February, 1942, it just had to be accepted that Singapore was doomed. The Japanese had encircled the entire suburbs at a radius of just five miles from the centre of the city; drinking water and water for fire-fighting had practically disappeared, deserters and looters were roaming the streets of the town and general morale was at rock bottom. God knows how it had happened, why our superior numbers had not swamped the Japanese army, or why we had spent the whole ten weeks of war on the run.

The Jungle Warfare Team was finished; Fishy had gone back to the command of his old Indian regiment and we decided to go back to the Surreys. By nightfall of 14 February, we had it from a reliable source that the Surreys were near Tanglin barracks and it was settled that we'd go there next day.

I was very nervous by this time and not a bit keen on the whole idea. I lay awake for hours thinking about it. I was scared about what was going to happen to us all when the enemy took over, as take over they certainly would - we'd had it! Going back to our regiment was just a stupid gesture which would do nobody any good. I tossed and turned and finally drifted into uneasy sleep with my mind made up. I would run for it, back to the mainland, to the jungle where I would be safe and secure. Once I got to the mainland I knew I could make rings round the Japanese and I knew enough Malay to make my way to Siam and from there to Burma and safety. It might take a while but I had no doubt that I could do it.

I hinted at breakfast next morning but it was obvious that Nobby and Tony would never tolerate desertion. They truly were 'Officers and Gentlemen', so I stopped hedging and changed the subject. Breakfast over, Nobby and Tony were to make one trip into town for news and then we'd take off for the last time as freelance brigands and revert to type once more as units of the East Surreys.

Len Avery, Joe Hocking and myself went to say goodbye to the only civilian friends we had in Malaya, a Chinese family of three generations. Our visit exposed us to the horrifying plight of the starving civilian population of Singapore.

For the first time on any of our visits to the family we were not offered food or refreshment. Usually we had started with, at least, a fruit drink and a dish of tropical fruit. I will always remember my first meeting with this family when we were between tasks in Malaya and on leave in Singapore. I had wandered away from Len and the others as I was feeling a little melancholy as I so often did when I was near the sea and thought of home and family at the other end of the ocean.

I heard the sweetness of young voices singing a hymn in a garden and I can still see the smiling face of an American missionary who saw me standing among the trees listening. I was dirty, sweat-stained, unshaven and an obvious brigand but the young girls in the garden had swarmed around me and I had been feted as I had never been, in war or out of war. I had finally departed with a promise to return which I did, over and over again whenever we were in Singapore. It was a Paradise to which I introduced Len and Joe. Then, one of the younger family members gave me a pair of spectacles which miraculously suited me and I would have done anything for the whole family.

I had always tried on glasses since I lost mine, but I could not believe my luck when the world suddenly jumped into focus. If there had been any hope that the young Chinese could get a replacement for himself I would have tried to buy them from him. There was no hope and reluctantly I passed them back to the owner. He would have none of it however, and pressed them back into my hands and the whole family implored me to accept. They finally said that it was not only a personal gift but part of their war effort and so I must take the glasses, so with this thought to mitigate my selfishness, I put them on.

It was this same family who now, shamefaced and apologetic, could not offer us refreshment. We finally found out neither they or their neighbours had even vegetable peelings to eat.

This was the kind of situation that we, experienced looters, could cope with - and off we went. Trucks were not difficult to acquire, nobody liked driving with the sky never empty of planes. We already knew the location of a food dump, so with little time to spare, we worked quickly and within an hour Len, Joe and I each had a truck load of cases of tinned vegetables, fruits, meats and milk, sacks of flour and sugar and even some chocolate and tobacco. We filled their attic to overflowing with almost enough food for the entire occupation.

I wonder if they will ever read this - and I wonder what happened to them.

We left our friends with some joy mixed with our sadness, but as we journeyed through the town, the full picture of chaos and devastation unfolded and a sense of desolation swept over us. Everywhere was rubble and wreckage, and we got the impression that Singapore was indeed destroyed. There were broken wires, leaning telegraph poles, shattered cars and trucks, many of them still burning, and piles of rubble everywhere.

The sight of the shuttered and silent shops in what had once been a thriving metropolis tore at our hearts, and as we left the town behind, exchanging the battered chaos for the withered destruction of woods and groves, the sense of disaster increased.

We stopped near swarming troops and a siren started though the sound was discordant and wrong. There had been no sirens for a week because there had been no All Clear for a week, but as the rising crescendo reached its peak and settled down to its long drawn out message, the air was filled with foreboding. The sound went on and on, longer than any All Clear had ever done before. Suddenly we noticed that every last man of the swarming troops was still and the tense immobility of the listeners conveyed the message to us. There was a finality here and, when, after an eternity of motionless waiting the drawn out wail died down to silence, we knew the end had arrived.

Then we heard the other quiet. The guns were silent, the shells no longer bursting and only the single shatter of a distant machine gun emphasised the stillness.

It was six thirty in the evening of Sunday 15 February and the surrender of 'Fortress Singapore' had been signed. We had known this moment would arrive but the sudden finality of it filled us with a foreboding and a despair which had no solace. Grief was there too, grief for the shattered sight of the British Lion, imperial and grand, unbeatable and invulnerable, master wherever the Union Jack went. Now, we were slaves to a new master. With our grief came fear and with that came determination, determination not to stay as a slave. Nobby and Tony could do what they liked, Len and Joe could do what they liked. I was going back to the jungle and even if I had to stay in the jungle till the British came back, I'd be better off there. With the sense of urgency I tackled Joe who unhesitantly said "Yes". I asked the officers' batmen who were all for escape, and finally I broached the subject of escape to Nobby and Tony only to find to my horror that they were in no hurry to do anything.

The thought of inactivity at this stage left me aghast, but I was a bit dubious about persisting as Nobby, as an officer, might easily have ordered me to stay put and disobedience would have meant court martial sooner or later. So I shut my mouth and organised the others. Len was Sergeant Major and I should have put myself under his command but in this matter I knew what I was going to do and it was just a matter, in my mind, of the others tagging along if they wanted to come.

I told Joe and the three orderlies to lag behind us and then drop out and make their way to a rendezvous on the dockside. I asked Len, on the motorbike, to lag furthest behind but to follow us so that he'd be near when we stopped for the night. I made one more plea to my two officers that we do something quickly, but it was hopeless and at the next opportunity I slipped away from them to join the patiently waiting Len - and off we sped to the docks.

The waterfront was swarming with hundreds of men bent on escape, parties had been leaving every night since 10 February. Other people were looking for boats and we soon realised that this was not going to be an easy task.

I should have had the courtesy to let Len, who was a Sergeant Major, do the organising, but I was impatient and fretful and I despatched Len and the orderlies in search of supplies while I took Joe with me to get a boat, somehow, by fair means or foul. I got a sampan, broad in the beam and sound, even if it was only nine feet long. I planted Joe in it with my Tommy gun while I went after the oars which it lacked.

I eventually had to get into the harbour and swim after oars, going from one craft to another until I had six short and stumpy paddles, not oars, but they were better than nothing - and back I went to the boat where the cases of tinned food I'd demanded were already arriving.

Len, however, had disappeared, last seen streaking towards the city on his motorbike, on goodness only knows what quest. Besides this, the officers' orderlies had had afterthoughts about our project. They had been listening to yarns about mines, machine guns and Japanese naval forces and when I saw how they felt I released them from our pact. They almost fell over each other with relief and tried to help Joe and me stow things away. It was while they were doing this that Joe went off on a chore of his own.

My helpers wandered off after leaving me their water bottles. With no sign of Joe I was left alone until three drunken soldiers descended on me. Friendly and maudlin they squatted on shore and were drunkenly enthusiastic about escape. Before they changed their minds I got them aboard, promising myself that I'd line them up when they were sober. And there we sat waiting for Joe.

The cold sea air had a sobering effect and the four of us sat, huddled and mostly silent, with the overhanging pier, dark and threatening above us. We waited for Joe and the silence was only broken when one of the other three started grumbling and once more my cry of "Joe! Joe Hocking!" went resounding along the docks.

Finally, even I began to wonder if it was any use waiting longer while my newly recruited crew chaffed and fretted. They, of course, hadn't my bond with Joe. Joe was my very last link with my Surreys, the last link with the joyous camaraderie of my regiment. The Surreys of recruit days, years before at Kingston, Colchester, the Surreys of Hong Kong, Shanghai and Malaya. The Surreys which contained the only real friends of my life, Gerry Hawkins, already dead, Len Nunn soon to die, Henry Hall and a host of others, friends of sportive days, comrades of an inglorious war.

We waited for Joe until the early hours of the morning of the 16th and then, after one last lingering search, we had to go. We wanted to be well away from the island by dawn, and if we stayed longer it would certainly be easy for some patrol boat to pick us up and bring us shamefully back to the slavery we all dreaded.

I settled my crew midships, took my place in the stern, slipped my paddle in the water and smoothly and easily we slid forward towards an uncertain future. From the shadow of the pier the sea had looked dark and sheltering. But leaving the protecting shadow we were aghast to find our course brightly lit by the glare from the burning oil depots on Singapore and the tin-smelting plant on the island of Pulau Brani which our forces had deliberately blown up to prevent them falling into the hands of the enemy. The flames cast a lurid glare over the water so that we felt we must be at the mercy of any trigger-happy machine-gunner who looked our way. We knew they would be at the narrow mouth of the harbour and we almost turned back. However, thoughts of what we'd be going back to were worse - so we went on.

I put Little Jock (one of my crew so christened to distinguish him from one of the others, also a Scot) in the prow of my sampan to look for mines which probably never existed, although Little Jock saw several. He would have seen the Loch Ness monster if he'd thought about it, but anyway despite his mines we crept safely forward to the headland. We passed the narrow mouth of the harbour and then miraculously we were at sea. We were clear and free and now for the first time we rested and looked back at burning Singapore. The town certainly looked as if it was burning, not in one sweeping destroying blaze but burning with silent flames. Everything was quiet from where we were, and as we looked at the scattered fires and huge pall of smoke over the island, our thoughts silenced us.

Singapore was dying and there, on that burning island, were so many of my friends. I had also had a thousand comrades of war who now lay

ANGRY SEA

stinking and unburied in the jungles of Malaya, or were just corpses left to rot on the route of the retreat as even the scavenging ants abandoned them.

CHAPTER SIX

THE THOUSANDTH MAN

On the docks in Singapore, our original gang had the idea that we'd get a boat to take us to the mainland of Malaya and then travel overland. However, word was out that there was a well defined and organised escape route to Sumatra starting from a point just outside Singapore. Destroyers, gunboats, cruisers and in fact everything was laid on Dunkirk fashion. We believed this so firmly that, in the night, we even crept up to a huge battleship which turned out to be an island. As it happened there were no waiting boats at all but we had been directed to the west and to the west we made our amateurish, laborious way. We progressed from paddles to oars at one island, we learned to use the tides and not battle against them on another island. We followed the blazed trail of three thousand escapers to Sumatra. We picked up a stranded Aussie on one island and lost him to another boat on the next island and then finally following the trail we came to Singkep, which we christened Ration Island.

Ration Island was just exactly that, an island halfway in the hundred miles of sea separating Singapore and Sumatra. It was stacked high with escape rations all nicely sealed in tins labelled '1 man for 5 days', for 'two men' and 'up to four men'.

We didn't need any rations but authority decreed we must take rations and so, we took them. Authority also decreed that we take two or more passengers, so apparently this was also a collecting place for boatless escapers. Goodness only knows how they got to the middle of the Malacca Straits without boats in the first place but we took two anyway.

One of these passengers was Lissy and I got my first glimpse of him when I was making my way through the drizzling rain towards my boat. Little Jock and Big Jock (who wasn't big) were happily boiling pork and beans on one of the hundreds of camp fires in the trees, so Lissy was alone when I met him.

He was a miserable-looking, shrunken specimen of dried up humanity, wretched and huddled under a protective groundsheet in the prow of the boat. I couldn't see much of him except a pair of beady eyes and a hawk nose and I was not at all favourably impressed when he held out a limp arm wearing, I noticed, a warrant officer's crown and said: "My name's Lissenburg, Sandford Lissenburg, Indian Army." When I'd introduced myself, he volunteered the information, "Most people call me Lissy."

I had no intention of calling him Lissy, and disliked him or rather was contemptuous of him from the start and could not possibly have thought that, within two days, I would be quite content to leave my boat and my destiny in his hands. I was prepared to follow any course he advised, to do what he wanted, without any reservation at all, and to admit that he was a better man than I, in every way. More than this, he was to become one of my two best friends. It was from the other friend, strangely enough, also on Ration Island, that I learned much about Lissy. He scarcely had his equal as a sprinter in the Indian Army, he had been railways representative in the previous year's all India games and had won a place in the javelin, discus, pole vault and long jump. He was almost as good, despite his size, at the shot putt but his real prowess was on the hockey field. Hockey, of course, was the national game of India so to be considered good a man really had to excel. Lissy certainly did. Later I saw him dribble his way through an opposing team and it looked almost as if the ball never touched the ground. He was like a juggler, tossing the ball on his stick, over heads, to the right, to the left and even circling with it until he was just exactly placed and then, wham!, the ball was in the net of the opposition goal.

Lissy was more than an athlete, he had the mind of a chess player, or a general, he had a wisdom and a knowledge of people, and better still he had an instinct which kept him right. And he had the virtue which above all endeared him to me: he was loyal to whatever friend and cause he took on and was indeed 'The Thousandth Man'.

'For the thousandth man will stand by your side to the gallows edge, and after.'

He was quick, perceptive, and humorous. The whole night's watch was not long if Lissy was by your side. Sometimes conversation was no more than casual remarks, but there was a pleasant aura of camaraderie when you were with Lissy, whether he was just making occasional observations, telling a yarn or discussing some abstract philosophy.

He united our gang, he had Little Jock eating out of his hand on the first day, and even had Big Jock and Frank working quite willingly at the oars.

After Ration Island, the sense of urgency was gone and indeed we began to wonder if we ought to make the most of our situation and have a real holiday, on the beautiful, calm, sun-drenched seas. Perhaps, instead of going due west to Sumatra, where organisation and service lay, we could meander down the coast towards Java and even on from there to Timor, and in fact, to Australia. We had plenty of food and could easily restock at any fishing village. With this prospect, who would have wanted anything to do with war?

But we had only half a day of this thought before the solitude got to us. Deciding that we were gregarious creatures after all, needing not only our own kind, but our own race, we turned once more to the west.

We had been directed due west until we hit Sumatra, down the coast to the Indrigirri river, and up which we were to go to a town called Perigiradja, where 'The Organisation' would take over. This 'Organisation' gradually took on a personality. At first, we thought of it as something all-powerful, but remote, then later it was just muddling. Finally, the 'Organisation' became a malignant, infuriating, restraining busybody. We had got away from the enemy, beat the sea and the mountains but the 'Organisation' almost got us.

Anyway, we hit Sumatra with a real stirring thrill. We rowed towards a tiny dark cloud on the horizon, which then stretched north and south, taking on height and density, and assumed colour, as a thick, green jungle, sweeping down from the mountain to the water. Almost as an omen we were welcomed by a very old fisherman and his wife, who came from their hut among the trees. They cooked us an appetising meal of rice and curry, and we relaxed happily, with black coffee and cigarettes.

As our hosts had no sugar, we used our own. Their eyes popped when they saw us ladling sugar from a four gallon tin. Actually, 'authority' on Ration Island had given us this as a five-day ration of mixed necessities. We gave the tinful to the old couple and they thought it was Christmas. They couldn't believe that so much sugar existed, much less that it was theirs.

When we got back to the beach to embark again we observed that our goodwill was being repaid. The old man was just finishing the rigging of the most beautiful mast in the world. We were indeed progressing, paddles to oars, and now to sail. We didn't know anything at all about sails and sailing, but we began to learn, the hard way of course. The wind was never quite where we wanted it - often it was just a few hundred yards to our port or starboard beam. We rowed to the place where we could see the breeze ruffling the water and then found we were in a calm, and the breeze was at the place we'd just left. Finally, we got sick of chasing the wretched thing and just went our own way and minded our own business. Then, of course we got a wind, but not until the tide had turned against us and we were battling hopelessly with oars and sail. Then two Malays took control of our destiny.

Apparently they were looking for idiots like us, and in two minutes one of them had rigged the oars so that one man could wield them from a standing position. Without any apparent effort, he took us surging onward, right to a little village tucked deep in a bay, just north of the Indrigirri and swarming with Australian and other British escapees. It was dark when we tied up under a ramshackle wooden pier, so we slept. Morning revealed us a motley collection of junks, sampans and even a raft, all from Singapore. One boat did catch our eye. She was a beauty - like a lifeboat, and as if she could go anywhere. We couldn't help comparing our humble little sampan with this imposing creature.

Jock, Big Jock, Frank and an Australian who'd hitch-hiked a lift from us went ashore while Lissy and I sauntered to the local coffee shop for breakfast and news. We leisurely returned to our berth just as the rest of our crew were finishing unloading our stores. I was quite calm as I asked, "Going somewhere?" and they turned, not guiltily, but with shining faces.

"We're fixed, Sarge," said Little Jock, "Yon boat'll tak' us if we gie 'em the grub," and he pointed to the dreamboat. My heart leapt and then I suddenly felt melancholy as I looked at my little boat again.

"I think I'll stay," I said and without hesitation Lissy replied, "I'm with you, Gabby," Lissy, incidentally was one of those who swore that Gabby was a fully descriptive name.

The others were disconcerted and it was Big Jock who said, "Och weil, we'll gie ye some rations," and at that I was no longer calm. "You'll put the whole bloody lot back!" I shouted, and they were shocked. There wasn't a fighter among them and they started whining. In the end I gave them just enough to get them a berth and they were gone, except for Little Jock.

"Ah think I'll bide wie ye Sarge," he said and so we were three, a little subdued maybe, but with a renewed bond of camaraderie in us. We were lying in the boat when a bearded face looked down on us from the pier edge. There was something familiar about it, and then I heard the cry: "Hey, Jimmy! Look who's here!"

I sat up, startled. A second face appeared and I yelled with pure glee. "Jimmy Jewell! John Freeman!" and I shot up to the pier to pump their arms in joy. They were East Surrey comrades and not only that, both had joined the army in the same week as I. We'd gone through our recruit training together, had soldiered and sported in our garrison town of Colchester, travelled and served in Hong Kong, Shanghai, Singapore and Malaya and that bond of kinship which classmates, squadmates and first loves carry through life was always present.

Jimmy was an archetypal little Cockney. He'd wheedle the bone from a dog if he wanted it, and I lost twopence for cigarettes every mid-

35

week we were together during training. He wasn't quite the world's worst soldier, but he was certainly a strong contender. His boots were enormous, and he could have doubled for Charlie Chaplin. He had an uncanny knack of putting things on the way they should not be worn, and our squad sergeant used to look at him hopelessly. "Has your mother any more like you at home?" he'd say, and Jimmy would grin at him. It was that boyish grin of his which was irresistible. I've never met a man in any company who didn't like Jimmy. His friendship with John had started with mutual laughter. They had landed in their first barrack room in adjoining beds, had moved together and now here was the evidence that they'd come through the war together. Two absolute opposites, yet absolute inseparables.

John Freeman was the kind of bandbox soldier that inspecting RSMs couldn't help approving of. Without any real effort on his part, his buttons, belts, bayonets, boots and body all shone. His uniform always fitted and he drilled like a guardsman. I hadn't been in touch with them so much after I got my first stripe, but I think I would rather have met those two than anybody.

I introduced them to Lissy and Jock and as they and Jock came together I realised that he was the only possible third to this pair. They were a trio from the first meeting, thieves, rogues and vagabonds together, all with the mischief never far away. John and Jimmy had got this far from Singapore on the boat to which we'd lost our crew, but they had a tale of woe to tell about her and a foreboding about their future on her.

"Come with us," I offered and they almost whooped.

CHAPTER SEVEN

THE OTHER 'THOUSANDTH MAN'

We told them we'd just lost our crew to their craft and at that moment Jock and Frank came slinking back. Their faces fell when they met our new crew and they didn't even broach the subject of their visit but slunk back to their chosen lot.

The two Surreys had not eaten particularly well for some time, so all five of us went back to our coffee shop to feast royally on curry and rice, banana fritters and coffee. Lissy incidentally had about 700 dollars in brand new notes, spoils from a payroll which should have been burned in Singapore. They were Malayan dollars but were as negotiable in Sumatra as the Dutch guilder. We feasted, then sailed away with the tide, in happy camaraderie for the first time since Singapore, three East Surreys, a Scots signaller and a warrant officer in the Indian army.

We should have followed the coastline of the bay where we lay, but as this would have meant a thirty mile journey up and down the two sides of the peninsular separating us from the Indrigirri, we took a chance in cutting across the base of the peninsular. A shallow and narrow stream which existed only at high tide took us right into the beautiful peaceful depths of the Sumatran Jungle, and if time had not been an important factor we would have lingered. But the stream was negotiable only at high tide and we finished the last few hundred yards dragging and pushing the boat in through deep, slimy and very evil smelling mud, left by the receding stream.

But we made it, and spent that night in a bamboo village stuck on rickety looking stilts far out from the shore. These villages, over salt water, were completely free of insects and sleep away from those beastly, marauding and voracious mosquito swarms was heaven indeed. We realised, after our most refreshing sleep since Singapore, how restless our nights had been.

The next night wasn't so good. We got ourselves stuck deep in a mangrove swamp and were stranded on a steep bank of grey slime when the tide went out. The mud was alive with miniature dinosaurs and other prehistoric monsters which kept popping up and sucking back all night. Only the incoming tide in the morning ended the nightmare and took us on our way again.

We hit our goal of Perigiradja on the third morning, only to find that it wasn't our goal after all, it was only another marker on the route and would we please continue to Tembilahan. The 'Organisation' had apparently got itself overburdened with a much greater exodus from Singapore than had been catered for, and it had contracted its shuttle service across Sumatra.

A little relaxation was a most attractive thought so we gave the three blood brothers two dollars each to go ashore and enjoy themselves, leaving Lissy and me with the prospect of a companionable stroll round the town. It wasn't really a town, except by comparison with the lonely outposts we'd been frequenting lately, but it looked good to us and we stepped on a shore already alive with bearded, nondescript men scarcely recognisable now as soldiers of the British Army.

I was not to have Lissy to myself however. He was no sooner ashore than he was pounced upon by a gigantic blonde creature with a pug face, the shoulders of an ox and the grip of a gorilla (as I found to my cost when he was introduced to me).

This was F. Daintee of the Indian Army Ordnance Corps, generally known as 'Tiny', six feet four and one half inches, and I looked at him with ill-concealed resentment. He monopolised Lissy over coffee and cakes. I was scarcely in the conversation and Lissy almost forgot I was there. They occasionally threw me an odd remark but apart from that I was just the hanger-on to two friends. I could cheerfully have murdered the pair of them, especially Lissy who should have shown clearly that it was I who was his friend and that this big brute should leave us alone.

Apparently, however, they were from the same unit. Tiny was also a warrant officer, and he and Lissy had escaped from Singapore together up to Ration Island where their own boat had sunk and the authority there had re-allocated them to different ones. Fortunately his boat was leaving soon and I was not a bit sorry to see the last of him, as I thought. By this time he had found a passage on a hundred and fifty ton junk which a corporal of the Hong Kong and Singapore Royal Artillery had pirated in Singapore. This corporal, incidentally, was reputed to be the toughest man on the escape route. He bossed the whole crowd on his junk and was known far and wide as 'The Bosun'. I hoped he was big enough and tough enough to hammer the daylights out of Tiny, if necessary.

The sight of Jimmy, John and Jock resplendent in clean green uniforms, wearing white Panama hats and smoking cigars, restored my good humour and the story of their jaunts cheered Lissy and me.

First, as soon as our backs were turned they'd sold a sealed, four gallon tin of water for five guilders to a black marketeer who thought it was petrol. Petrol, of course, was unobtainable to civilians. The black marketeer had whispered surreptitiously to Jimmy, pointed to the tin and said: "How much?" Jimmy had promptly answered: "Ten dollars," and the black marketeer had shaken his head. "Five," he said and just as quickly Jimmy answered, "OK."

Then Jock had started, he picked up a useless Tommy gun which the sea air had corroded and he had asked: "How much?" and had been asked in return "How much, you?" From here the conversation had followed its pattern. "Thirty dollars," from Jock. "Ten," from the black marketeer and "OK." quickly from Jock.

At this stage Jimmy felt he could sell some ammunition so he grabbed a box of revolver ammunition which wasn't even the same calibre as the .45 Tommy gun and offered it. "How much?" "Twenty-five dollars." "Five dollars." "OK." and off went the black marketeer quite happily with a tin of water, a useless Tommy gun and ammnunition which didn't fit it, while the three friends, rich and in the mood for spending, had sailed ashore for fresh conquests.

Cigarettes were the first goal, but they were horrified at the exorbitant price demanded by the keeper of the general store who was bent on exploiting the unique demand caused by the influx of refugees and escapers. Straw hats were about the only things in the shop which were cheap, so Jimmy haggled over the price of one straw hat while the other two pinched a carton of cigarettes each from the huge stack on the floor.

Later, they repeated the process when John bought a hat, then Jock, and then they even went back to get hats for Lissy and me. They'd probably have bought all his hats or run him out of cigarettes, but he got suspicious so they went off for a meal. By this time their pirate instincts were thoroughly aroused so they pinched three uniforms from a clothes line in the yard of the police barracks. They were proudly wearing them until Lissy broke the news that they were police uniforms.

We left pretty soon afterwards. Tembilahan was definitely the end of our unaided progress by river. Already the current in these upper reaches was too strong for comfort, but now at last the 'Organisation' took over. First of all they officially registered us as Mr Lissenburg's party prior to allocating us a passage on one of the two invasion barges being used as ferries to the next stage, Airmolek. At Airmolek there would be trucks to take us to Sawahloento where the trains were still running to Padang on the west coast. Padang was port of embarkation for India or even home so now at last our troubles were over. Or were they?

At Tembilahan we stripped our boat of all we could carry and Jimmy promptly sold it for twenty dollars. Then we cooked a huge meal of surplus food and shared it with whoever was near. We met Tom Cahill there, a colour sergeant from my company who had been badly wounded in Singapore and was being evacuated. He left soon afterwards and got to Padang and safely to India.

That tough man, Tiny, tagged onto us here and parked himself with our party when we boarded the invasion barge. Bosun was still on his junk which was packed with men and was towed by one of the barges.

Off we went on the most uncomfortable stage of our journey so far, twenty-four foodless and drinkless hours of battling against an ever-increasing current before we were emptied, in a drizzling rain to the chilly, still foodless, discomfort of Airmolek.

They dumped us in rubber sheds, crammed with sheets of dried rubber which really made comfortable beds and even better, they seemed to repel the mosquitos. A good night's sleep, a clear sunny morning and an invasion by hordes of native pedlars selling every possible aid to comfort made things look differently and we felt more content. For one day, anyway.

Then those morale-breaking rumours started, that there was no transport, the Japanese were closing in, we were being cut off from Padang, we'd been forgotten by the British and every other unsettling conjecture possible was voiced. Groups of men began to disappear, not content to wait any longer, despite the orders given by the 'Organisation' that no man or gang was allowed to travel independently. Any who did were not only to be refused help from the 'Organisation' but would be left until everyone else had been evacuated from Padang.

Our three rogues delayed their departure half a day hoping Lissy, Tiny and I would join them but Tiny was negotiating with authority for written permission to travel, and the boys couldn't wait.

Now we were a trio, two Indian army warrant officers and one East Surrey sergeant and from then on we travelled together. We left the 'Organisation' at Airmolek, hitched a ride a little further up the river, hitched another ride to Taloe and could have got to Padang on the same truck next morning. We'd made a rendezvous with the driver but the blasted 'Organisation' arrived in a long convoy of trucks and got the civil authorities to veto all free lifts and for a while we were stuck in Taloe.

It looked as if we'd rot there, because the rains came and made an impassable barrier of the Koeantan river we had to cross twenty miles ahead of Taloe. The Japanese had landed at Palembang on the southeast coast on 14 February, and by the next day held sway over the whole of the southern half of the island. They were advancing rapidly north and were due to hit us any day. So, Tiny left the 'Organisation' again and dragged five of us twenty miles to have a look at this impassable river.

Tiny had somehow taken the reins from Lissy as naturally as Lissy had taken over from me; but my respect for this giant was growing and I was just as ready as Lissy to follow him. I was coming to like his easy good nature too, and he and Lissy were no longer a pair. We were a trio. Tiny had been heavyweight champion of the Indian Army and his mind and Lissy's were almost a perfect match. I was in the best company a man could get, although what bound them to me I don't know, I could have beaten up Lissy with one hand, I hope, but Tiny could have done the same to me so I wasn't bringing anything to the team in that respect. I might have voiced some opinions sometimes but I don't remember any that were worthwhile.

Still, none of this mattered, we were three and we were a united front against the world forever, each of us was to each of the others:

'The Thousandth man

And the Thousandth man will stand by your side

To the gallows side and after,

His wrongs your wrong, his rights your right

In reason and out of season

Stand up and back it with all your might

With that for your only reason.'

Perhaps this poem, a favourite of Tiny's, gave the story of our bond. I knew that my instinct for loyalty was strong and perhaps Tiny liked this one virtue. He dragged us along with all our gear to have a look at this impassable river but one glance at the swollen rushing cataract of water was all any of us needed to agree with the world 'IMPASSABLE'. All except Tiny, of course.

When, three hours later, Tiny had the whole six of us wet, shivering but safe on the other bank we were fit for nothing but sleep. We were limp and emptied, and the range of mountains towering in front of us could wait until tomorrow.

The fat, smug Dutch town official, with the title of Controller, agreed with us and ordered us to stay put. The 'Organisation' had asked all Controllers to detain stragglers. It was early afternoon when we got this order but by dusk we were at the top of the mountain road which wound its way from the foothills. Even Lissy and I were cursing Tiny by this time. The man was just incredible in his powers of physical endurance and, even more incredibly, he drove us along, long past the point when we had reached our own limit of endurance. There was a rest house on the top of the mountain with hot, sweet coffee, a meal was being prepared and beds were waiting. Life held nothing but luxurious promise for us until we heard the roar of a powerful car coming up the hill behind us. Tiny bounded to the road which we'd left for the sanctuary of the rest house, leaping down like a mountain goat. By the time we reached him he had intercepted the car and was trying to arrange a lift for our party.

There were two very bitter Dutchmen in the car. Their world had crumbled with the fall of Singapore, the fortress of the East, the sentinel over the East Indies. They were bitter and hopeless, would soon be homeless, and they felt that the blame lay with the defenders of Singapore.

They certainly didn't feel like helping those who had failed to die defending Singapore and we didn't really have much to say for ourselves. Anyway, there was no chance of more than one of us fitting among the piled up jumble of personal possessions in the car. Grudgingly they conceded that they might take one of us to a village at the foot of the mountain where we could try to get a car to return for the others.

Two of our party were officers who'd tagged on to us in Taloe and one of them suggested that two officers might be suitable company for the colonials who were bound for Padang. I think that Tiny in that one-second pause, weighed up the chances of them coming back to pick us up and then he said something which bonded me to him till my dying day.

"One of you in the car," he said to the two officers and then: "Get your gear, Gabby and off you go with him" Finally, to me, privately, he said, "Come back if it's possible: if it's not, good luck."

By the time we'd reached the village the Dutchmen had mellowed somewhat and were even prepared to take us through to Padang. They told us the prospect of transport was hopeless and it would have been easy to be persuaded that it was up to us to save ourselves. This was why Tiny had sent me and it was this that I admired. He trusted me and we got off at the village, though my companion was grudging, and we set about finding transport.

There wasn't any, not even a bullock cart, not until the last east-bound bus of the war rolled in from an outlying village to wait for morning and for the last stragglers to flee before the Japanese sealed off any escape. These last stragglers, due to leave in the morning, contained the three-man police force of the village but even in the face of this opposition I commandeered the bus. I didn't actually have to draw my revolver, but my hand was on it as I insisted, "My friends must be picked

ANGRY SEA

up."

They gave in, but wouldn't lose sight of their bus, and eventually I took the police force, driver and passengers back up the mountain. Even Tiny had almost given me up but I still remember his expression and handshake when he saw me.

CHAPTER EIGHT

THE GANG GATHERS

Sawahloento was the next stop. As the wilderness of eastern Sumatra gradually merged with the civilised and populated west, it really looked as if the end was in sight. Sawahloento even had a large railway station and was policed and administered by Europeans.

The officers were despatched to a hotel and we other ranks to a less pretentious, but no less comfortable, railway shed. We were fed royally on eggs and stew with plenty of new bread, butter and coffee - perfect peace was ensured with the information that the journey to Padang would be completed on the morrow, by train. This was a welcome change to the twenty-four hours spent on the bus which had given us our fill of cramped travel.

The day was spent in resting and sight-seeing with an early turn-in, ready for the journey by train.

At 5 a.m. next morning to everyone's amazement, the refugee column which had been left in Taloe began to arrive by truck and by mid-morning the town was swarming with ragged and bearded Australians and other Britishers. The 'Organisation' had caught up and immediately took charge.

They cancelled our arranged passages to Padang, formed a roster for evacuation and put Tiny's gang at the bottom of the roster. As it happened this would delay us only one more day, but left us in a worse position for evacuation from Padang to India than we had been in Taloe. Even Joe, Jimmy and Jock who had been picked up by the 'Organisation' on the wrong side of the river had a place on the roster higher than ours.

Despite the 'Organisation' we were aboard the first train to Padang and almost as an anticlimax on 6 March were carried into the great Sumatra port just like ordinary travellers. The sight of the open sea, beyond which lay home and safety, gave us a thrill, which I'm sure would not be in the hearts of ordinary voyagers. Here was journey's end, our final goal and behind us lay the strain of war and escape. We could not go any further, not with the barrier of 1,500 miles of ocean to stop us, but then we did not have to go further. We were back in civilisation, law and order and could leave our destiny in the hands of our country.

44

ANGRY SEA

'The Organisation' was our country's administrator at that time and they began to administer, with a vengeance. Order and discipline were required with the commands to surrender weapons, shave, (no one did) and generally behave. The 600 odd refugees were split into three camps, and camp officials were appointed in each. Tiny, Lissy and I stuck tight and found ourselves allotted to the Chinese High School while the remainder of the gang disappeared elsewhere. There seemed to be nothing left to do now except eat, rest and mooch about the town.

All of these things were made easy by the Dutch who provided a team of good ladies to cope with the food temporarily, and also produced one and a half guilders per day for each man. Tiny didn't get much chance to rest because almost within minutes of selecting bunk space in the school he was pounced upon by a hefty Air Force flight lieutenant who had been appointed camp commandant. This was J.O. Dykes or 'Dicky', and he needed a camp sergeant major.

This duty would be a difficult assignment faced with a motley crowd of undisciplined toughs and apart from his gigantic bulk, Tiny had the kind of face that marked him out as the man for the job. He, in turn, tried to detail Lissy as Orderly Sergeant, but we laughed at him and in reprisal he made me Police Sergeant.

The duties were, in fact, practically non-existent except for a daily appearance at the improvised orderly room with defaulting troops, if any. These could only be lectured at anyway, and although I actually did have a prisoner for a few hours, he got away, much to everyone's relief. He was a renegade Australian who had been in Padang at least two weeks and had forgone all his chances of evacuation for the pleasures of causing chaos in the town. He was successful and two nervous native police arrived at the Chinese High School with an appeal for aid. Tiny collected me and off we went to one of the town hotels where the sight of the entire staff collected outside was not reassuring.

We entered, and were aghast at the wreckage marking the trail of the truant. We found him sprawled asleep on a settee and Tiny kicked him to his feet. The Australian, named McDonald, was six feet two inches himself, and he measured the bulk of Tiny towering over him. Despite his size Tiny looked unprepared and McDonald kicked suddenly, and viciously. But he'd never met anyone as quick as Tiny, who caught the foot in mid-air and with a heave lifted him right off his feet to send him hurtling backwards. He was up again in a flash, but Tiny hit him about six times in a baffling flurry of hands and arms and McDonald was down and out.

He was still out when he was dragged feet first to the hotel entrance and only sat up in dazed bewilderment when he reached the foot of the steps down which he had been flung.

Even after Tiny had left him alone in my custody at the school there was no more trouble from this subdued Australian. No lock-up was available so he had to be kept in open arrest under my eye. Within two hours he was drunk again and to my astonishment I had to take a flask of brandy from him which was still full. A few hours later that night he disappeared, to my relief, and no more was heard of him.

The first few days in Padang passed pleasantly enough now that our escape from Singapore was complete. We were once more a functioning organ of the allied forces, or at least we were the responsibility of the allies. All we had to do was relax and wait for movement orders which would come as soon as the expected destroyers arrived in Padang to take us off.

Lissy and I particularly grew fat and contented with good sleep under mosquito nets, first class food, guilders in our pockets and a thriving town at our feet. Tiny, of course, was tied down by his duties, but he still had Lissy and me daily reconnoitering the beaches, wharves, and the riverside craft of the port. He always believed in making sure of things and he even had us join the Dutch army (just in case) or at least the section of the Dutch forces which planned to fight its way, if necessary, to the north of Sumatra.

Tiny intended to leave nothing to chance until his feet were firmly planted on his Indian homeland, and he badgered Lissy and me into exploring every bay and beach of Padang. He even listed the details of big canoes we found. It was our description of a diesel barge tied up on the bank of the Padang river which most excited him, and the day after we told him about it he packed us off to the river with instructions to make friends with the crew.

As we'd previously exchanged greetings with the crew we knew they were disposed towards friendship. But there was nothing friendly in the eye of the man with the black beard who was squatting on the deck of the barge and obviously in charge. He had a blond sergeant and a Malayan named Ibrahim with him and I thought we had no chance of getting a boat. The one in charge was 'Bosun': no one seemed to know him by any other name and I knew he was too tough for me. Only yesterday, I'd seen him knock down an Australian after a few angry words, and he'd attempted to have a go at the whole gang of Australians who were with him. His reputation had spread all the way from Singapore. He had shanghaid the huge junk which had ended its journey at Taloe, ruled the whole crew with the hand of a Captain Bligh and been in more fights than anyone else I had met so far. Not one of these had he ever lost. He looked almost as big as Tiny and certainly more ready even than our own giant to beat anyone in his path. So we slunk back with our tale.

"He's too tough for us to meddle with, Tiny," I said, but the skipper only smiled.

"You don't really know me yet, Gabby, do you?" he challenged, adding more forcefully, "Six Bosuns won't stop me when I want something."

Tiny went after Bosun and at once the two men clicked. They were two halves of a whole and each half instinctively measured the value of the other and found a force to respect. They joined hands and forces. I think that this union of the mightiest of the three thousand escapers in Padang gave us the foundation of a gang which could tackle anything.

Bosun brought his blond sergeant friend whom we cherished from the beginning. He was 'Snowy' of course. He couldn't be anything else with that hair, and how he came to pair off with Bosun was impossible to guess. Snowy or Sergeant Beaumont of the Hong Kong and Singapore RA was as gentle as Bosun was rough and as unassuming as his friend was forceful. He was even blond as compared with the very blackness of Bosun's hair and beard. Perhaps the bond was regimental because Bosun was really Corporal John Rawson of the same regiment but anyway they were as close to each other as Lissy, Tiny and I were.

Ibrahim, the Malayan came in with the two gunners and to complete the gang Tiny introduced Dicky Dykes, the Flight Lieutenant who was acting camp commandant. Dicky, besides being in a key position for news and liaison, was another natural leader with his own record of personal achievement behind him. He was, among other things, a trained navigator and had, in fact, navigated a lifeboat from a torpedoed boat through ten days of hardship in the Atlantic. He was lithe and powerful and another giant of six foot two and a half.

We began to look like a gang of giants with only Lissy as a shrimp of 5'8", but even Snowy and I at just under six feet were insignificant compared with the others.

The next to join our group was Sergeant Douglas 'Lofty' Eastgate. He was a friend of Bosun's, an Australian from Melbourne and the only real sailor of our bunch. He had been bombed on the evacuation ship which was bringing him out of Singapore, and had covered the escape route in spite of a long jagged shrapnel wound across his thigh. Despite his sergeant's stripe Lofty was only twenty-three years old, and didn't at this time look any more than the open-faced, golden-haired young man he was.

There probably wasn't another man among the escapees in Padang who had Lofty's instincts and knowledge of sails and seas, and certainly no one else of his age who was as fearless.

Lofty had a cobber who was as small as Lofty was big. Victor 'Titch' Hudson, an Australian private, almost made Lissy look big, and Titch brought with him just that right mixture of cheekiness, cockiness and unquenchable good spirits to endear him to every heart. He was my idea of an Australian cockney, or rather a cockney sparrow from Sydney, and the only trouble with him was the way he idolised Sydney. The authorities who inscribed Rabbie Burns's lines, *'Breathes there a man with soul so dead who ne'er to himself hath said, this is my own, my native land'* on Sydney bridge must have been like Titch.

Tiny now had the cream of the Chinese High School in his gang and we had every ingredient we needed except one, the services of a doctor. We probably would have done without a medico had it not been that Dicky Dykes had been at Edinburgh University with a man who was working among the sick evacuees in Padang. This was 'Doc', Major Hugh Kilgour, the greatest of all in a gang of leaders and mighty men.

He wasn't great to look at, in fact he was more weedy than Lissy, and he was always in good health though he looked like a weasel or ferret. He hadn't any athletic powers. In fact, he had nothing except his quiet old eyes and even then they were expressionless enough to be fish-like most of the time. It was only on acquaintance that the quiet understanding and sympathy of the eyes became comforting. By the time you became friends with this man it was an allegiance which could not be bettered, even by the power of Tiny.

Doc naturally received the respect due to him as a Major and a Doctor, both factors recommending him as a candidate for our gang. But he was unimpressive enough to have been skipped over had it not been for his association with Dicky, who knew his worth. Doc had to be persuaded to join us and would not commit himself to a definite undertaking while the sick and wounded of Padang needed attention. Already he had refused passage on several evacuations to India and Australia because of the dearth of doctors, and it was only the influx of adequate Dutch medicos from the diminishing allied territory which gave him, in his mind, the moral right to make his own plans.

Doc had an orderly, Douglas Bowler, a Leading Aircraftman and another big man, with a hideous scar running like a sword cut from his mouth across his cheek. The wound was still open and undergoing daily treatment but Bowler was as active and untiring in his duties as medical orderly as Doc was. The name, Douglas Bowler, in the services of course, could only become Tombola and typical service irrelevancy had dropped the Bola, so, he was 'Tom'.

Tom was big, as I have said, and with his big frame came the most placid disposition of our gang, and an all-tolerating outlook on life. He had an optimism that never wavered, and could adapt to the worst conditions with his conviction that things could have been worse, and would soon be better. The only trouble was, his optimism was so great that he never felt it really necessary to better his own lot. He left it all to fate. However, he was with Doc and with Doc he came to 'Our Gang' where he at once gravitated to the other airman, Dicky Dykes.

An ample night's sleep always left us somewhat indolent, although luxuriously so, and even a leisurely breakfast usually taken with Tiny and Dicky left many hours of idleness before lunch. Tiny and Dicky always seemed to be confined to camp by duty, so we, as well groomed as a sparse wardrobe would allow, sauntered out to roam the town where Lissy's charm soon made friends at the coffee shops.

I'd always enjoyed wandering round the bazaars and the non-European quarters in the East. I liked smiling to the people and being smiled at, even though conversation was mostly impossible. Now, with Lissy, real fraternisation was possible. I've never met anyone like him with his ability to learn a new language, or to make friends even before he knew the language.

Of course he spoke Malay well, besides Bengali, Tamil, Urdu and some other Indian languages, so Padang was easy. With Lissy there were no barriers of formality or reserve, and the citizens of Padang we met loved him. We could meet strangers one day and the next we'd be visiting them as friends. We had at least half a dozen real social centres where we were made welcome. Even the horse buggy drivers, the equivalent of the rickshaw pullers of China, stopped and greeted us.

Wandering about Padang, with its shops and cinemas, seemed part of a wonderful holiday and one of the greatest pleasures was bickering and buying in bazaars. Lunch at the camp topped the contentment of the morning and an hour or so of drowsy chatting in the shade passed all too quickly.

Sometimes these semi-siestas were shared by Australians and other Britishers attracted by the trio who were the real core of the gang, and many tall tales of Australia, England and the war were exchanged. Often a story which sounded truthful and revealed courage and determination tempted us to include the narrator in our gang. But prudence told us we would quickly end up in a large, conspicuous, unwieldy, and eventually doomed group, instead of our small compact force. But the aura of friendship gradually spread and made the stay, or the return, to camp, more and more pleasant.

In the afternoon Lissy and I usually went walking by the sea. We knew every cove and curve of the shore and could almost have drawn a scaled map from memory, including times and reaches of tides and eddies. Even the fishing boats drawn on to the beach became landmarks. We noted the grim, but no less familiar, position of every pill box and barbed-wire obstacle for miles. We always returned to the river as our best hope and in time we knew every barge and launch on its banks and were on waving terms with all the Malayan and Chinese seamen in the area.

By the 15 March, news had come through that Java had fallen a week earlier, the same day that the Japanese had made a landing on the northern coast. By the 15th they had occupied most of the major strategic points on this massive island and were beginning to tighten their grip, as the Dutch showed a marked reluctance to fight and the British troops could muster little resistance to the apparently invincible and inexhaustible army of Nippon. The scene in Padang had gradually changed, and the air of gloom and desolation which had been so evident in Singapore had crept in. Many of the previously thriving thoroughfares were almost completely shuttered, and even the main streets were less lively.

The beginning of the end was evident to us one day when our favourite fat eating shop proprietor had no sugar for our coffee, but it was not this that had chased the wrinkled smiles from his round face. He had heard the news that the Japanese were only thirty miles away and he so alarmed us we fled in unaccustomed haste to Tiny. He was calm. A council of war was called, and after much discussion, we decided to stay in Padang until the last possible minute and then take to the jungle and hills outside the town. From there we would make our way south along the coast, until we could see a way to use the easier and quicker sea route.

CHAPTER NINE

TO THE HILLS AND THE SEA

We had left our retreat too late, and realised this only when a police squad arrived to act as guards over our camp. The Dutch had declared Padang an open town and were preparing to surrender it and us to the Japanese. A mixed bag of 3,000 refugees, escapers and even deserters who'd got clear of Singapore, 3,100 miles away, had merely exchanged imprisonment there for imprisonment in Sumatra.

As Lissy and I were not in the camp when the police arrived, we considered for some time whether we should leave there and then, or whether we should do something about Tiny. We couldn't quite see what we could do for him by letting ourselves be imprisoned. On the other hand we couldn't see him without going inside so, after a thorough reconnaissance to see which guards might have to be coped with later on, we walked back into our prison.

Tiny wasn't surprised to see us, he said. He had his plans all set and was only waiting for us. "Get all your gear packed" he said, "you're getting out tonight as an anti-looting squad".

My eyes lit up in memory of the last time I'd been on an anti-looting party just before the jungle warfare team started operating. Eight of us had had a deserted town on our hands for nearly twenty-four hours in Malaya, we knew the British would never come back to it and we were there only to discourage a too-speedy occupation by the Japanese. As soon as we'd set up a road block to the north of this town all we had to do was change the three man post of the road block and apart from this the town was ours.

We had a meal in the leading hotel, set up a table with snowy linen, shining silver and sparkling glass, even burst open a wine and spirit store to get the drinks and in our dirty, stinking uniforms we dined off the best, in style. We didn't bother washing up afterwards, just shot it up and went foraging. A big optical firm was one of the first places I went after but though I worked my way through tray after tray of lenses I could get nothing to suit me. Then I helped shoot up the shelves of liquor in the wine and spirit store. Four of us did this. We stood back to back in the middle of the store, each with a Tommy gun and at the word "Go" we

51

let those bottles have it, until the ricochets and splitting glass got too dangerous and we ducked out. Still I got what was left in bottles by firing two grenades from a cup attachment on my rifle through the big glass windows. The devastation those two grenades did among that glass was an eye opener to us.

It still hadn't occurred to us to do any real looting but then we burst open a jeweller's shop and loaded our transport with everything that caught our fancy. By the time we'd been in three jewellers' shops we were throwing most of our original haul away to make room for better stuff. I had six wrist watches on each hand and about two hundred in my car. The fever got me and from then on I couldn't tear myself away even for a meal.

Eventually I finished up in the southern end of the town with the Japanese in the north. I was cut off altogether and had to leave my loot except for what I carried. Mind you, the enemy weren't too concerned about going after stragglers, they were too busy on a looting spree themselves.

And now I was to be on an anti-looting squad. The looting was non-existent in Padang and it was only in theory that anti-looters were needed. The native police didn't know this and just watched somewhat dubiously as I went to the space in front of their guard-room and in my best East Surrey barrack square voice bellowed "On parade anti-looting squad."

Out they tumbled, Lissy, Titch, Bosun, Snowy, Tombola, Lofty, booted and belted and almost looking like a squad of real soldiers. Tiny and Dicky as Camp Commandant and Sergeant Major came out to inspect us, then I saluted Dicky, with my tongue in my cheek and marched my men away, even giving the native guard an 'eyes right' and a nippy salute as we passed their unsuspecting eyes. Tiny knew that the native police had been so long under Dutch colonial law they were not at all sure that they had rights over any Europeans, even though they had been sent as guards over us.

Tiny, Dicky and Doc looking very officious, still exploited this relationship and duly reported to the guard room next morning on their way out, to inspect the various and completely non-existent patrols. Just as easily as that they strolled down to the docks to our rendezvous and our gang was completed.

Almost completed, I should say, as we picked up the last one on our way out of town. He was an Australian, one of nature's lone wolves, a man who had made his way from Singapore and who was now prepared to carry on alone to Java and Australia. Lofty and Dick both hailed him as a fellow Australian and he also greeted Bosun somewhat dubiously which was not surprising as he was the man who had been flattened by Bosun in camp on the first occasion we saw our stalwart in action.

He was Corporal Ernie Forty. Like Lofty he was from Melbourne, veteran of two wars and, at least as far as we knew, had been everything except a bushranger between the wars. He was Australian and woodsman to the core, a man who could whittle a pair of shoes out of a piece of bark or make a fire in the rain with wet wood.

He was our final recruit and a welcome and useful member. He and Bosun were ever afterwards the best of friends, although Ernie never liked Tiny and was a constant thorn in our skipper's side. This kept Lissy and me from ever developing so close a camaraderie with Ernie, since our first loyalty was to Tiny and his friends were our friends.

Having met and accepted Ernie we plodded on, eager to shake the dust of Padang from our feet and by midday were well clear and in the foothills to the south. Escaping from the Japanese didn't seem to be very difficult. This was the second time most of us had slipped out of their hands, but it was not as easy to decide on our goal as it had been in Singapore. However, we no longer had the 'Organisation' to cope with, we hoped it had become a prisoner itself now.

There was a village in the foothills twenty-three miles to the south and we sent Ibrahim and Doc to find out from the headman where we ought to go from here. They returned, not with the headman but with a very haughty village priest who would not even help us with good advice. Poor Ibrahim was quite cowed by him and meekly accepted the order that he detach his sacred body from the presence of the infidels. He was not to travel with us another foot and would we please 'get the hell out of it at once', without Ibrahim.

We wouldn't 'get the hell out of it' Tiny said, until we were good and ready, in fact, we didn't feel like tackling the mountains until we'd fed and slept. This statement added some alarm to the priest's indignation and Tiny exploited this. "We might just wait here for the Japanese", he said and that did it. Already the Japanese reputation had put the fear of the devil into many villages and they were very afraid of the consequences of being found sheltering enemy troops. So we were fed, grudgingly but adequately, and offered two guides to take us round the mountains instead of over them.

All of this conversation went through Ibrahim, it was his last job for us and even before we started on our trek he had been banished from our presence and disappeared from our lives. He had travelled from Malaya, but meekly accepted the order given him here in Sumatra to leave us and remain in the village.

The journey ahead of us was predictable, just plain, thirsty, exhausting foot-slogging across the lower slopes of the hills running down to the sea.

At the beginning I had picked up the pack which Doc had brought along and which was almost as big as he was. But I clashed with him, and he had laid a restraining hand on his pack, "It's all right Gabby, I can manage". This sounded too much like martyrdom and I lost my patience.

"Don't be silly, Doc. We'll be carrying you and the pack before the day's finished."

"I can manage all right." He was quiet but determined. I said roughly: "Heck Doc, I'm stronger than you!" but the restraining hand still hung firmly to the pack and even a quick definite tug pulled the little man with it but did not loosen his hold.

"Oh all right, take the darn thing!" I growled with disgust and some aggravation. From then on I asked sarcastically every few miles, "How are you going, Doc?" and each time came the same response.

"Fine thanks, Gabby".

"Still not too heavy?"

"It's not heavy, really".

The wretched pack was heavy, as I well knew, but by evening I had come to grudgingly respect this martyr. The whole crowd were tired and no one was more glad than I that I didn't carry the pack.

By evening we had made our weary way round the foot of the mountains to a fishing village on the banks of a small river, tucked cosily under the shelter of the hills. This was Sungei Painang and for the second time in our travels we ran into unveiled hostility, possibly because our guides reported unfavourably on us, or maybe the villagers were already mentally acknowledging their new masters and turning on the old ones.

But we were tired and hungry and had already cast our avaricious eyes on the varied collection of sailing craft moored in the river. Tiny decided that we'd stay overnight to investigate the possibilities of this forgotten corner of Sumatra.

The headman was uncompromising in his refusal to let us have a boat at any price, and very ungraciously gave us the use of a broken-down deserted old hut for the night. The housekeeper charged us excessively for the food which we nevertheless thoroughly enjoyed. We sat in the cafe luxuriating in the atmosphere of smells and warmth which would have caused every nose to wrinkle in disgust a month earlier and we ate the dried fish, which we would have found loathsome, with real gusto. Later, when we were sitting outside our new home, smoking and dreaming, with eyes to the sea and the other side of the ocean, our minds and conversation turned to the real homes which seemed so far away from this lovely Sumatra village. But Lofty wasn't thinking of home, he had fallen in love with one of the boats in the river, and, fired by his enthusiasm, we made a further offer to buy it. This was refused just as ungraciously as our first.

Bosun, with my support, was advocating that we take the boat by force if necessary, even if we had to hold up the whole village at revolver point, but Doc was dead against this line. We argued that anything we took from enemy country was legitimate and, in fact, almost duty, but Doc wouldn't have it so. He pointed out in his quiet old way that the Japanese might never come to this out-of-the-way village, and even if they did, they would not necessarily harm the natives. We ought not to deprive the poor native villagers of any part of their livelihood, even if they were unfriendly. Poor Doc, he was always putting himself in the other fellow's shoes, although I still had the feeling that he was too good to be true. I hadn't quite got over the pack episode but subsequently I did and learnt that he was absolutely straight. Of course Dicky sided with Doc, and even Tiny was coming under his influence so Bosun and I were overruled. At least we agreed to sleep on it, but Bosun had already confided to me that he was going to have a boat by hook or by crook.

Even before breakfast next morning, Lissy and Doc (our interpreters) were away again trying to negotiate. We guessed at the outcome when our meal was suddenly interrupted by a shout from Lissy.

"Hey, Tiny, hey! Come here!"

We ran towards the two dealers in boats excitedly.

"How's the money, have we any more?"

"No more Dutch money. Why?"

"Those blighters will sell that boat now but they want 750 guilders for it, and we're 100 short."

Ernie dived into his pocket. "Here's 10 dollars," he said, and every other pocket was turned inside out. Dicky produced more Malayan dollars and scarcely stopping to count them Doc and Lissy ran off clutching the collection.

By the time we had reached the spot where the newly acquired boat was moored, Doc, having got what he wanted, was after extra and was pressing the Headman to accept more dollars - this time for food.

"Makan ada ini?" he asked, but the Chief again negatively waved his hands, "Tiada."

Doc was politely incredulous. "Tiada maken? Tiada nasi?" (No food? No rice?) and an angry shake of the head was more emphatic.

"Tiada." Tiny took charge now and idly swinging the revolver which he had drawn, he held the nervous attention of the no longer arrogant headman. "Tell him we're going away now, but we must have some food."

Doc interrupted. "Sayaya pulang ka-rumah, makan mau," and the chief hesitated, thinking.

"Piggi mana?" (Where going?) he said at last. And Doc pointed vaguely across the sea. The fellow laughed outright scornfully, but he broke off short and held up his hands in surrender as Tiny stopped twirling the revolver and pointed the muzzle towards him.

Within the next two hours our boisterous and exuberant gang inspected the boat from stem to stern and loaded her with the meagre supply of rice, eggs, dried fish and 'gulch', the Malayan sticky substitute for sugar. There was food for barely four days, and all the threats in the world had no more effect than cajolery and attempted bribery. There was simply no more food available and that was final.

"Well," Tiny said, "that certainly won't get us to India."

"What about trying for more tucker at another village?" Lofty suggested, but we were all against that.

It was now 17 March and over a month had passed since the fall of Singapore, but now that India had become the next target everyone fretted with impatience at any wasted minute and I voiced the general opinion when I stated, "I vote we get away to blazes out of Sumatra."

Tiny, as usual had already made his plans and only let the discussion run on to suit himself. "We'll take off for Siberoet," he said. "The name means island of good fortune, so we should be able to stock up there."

We all crowded again to look at the map which was already so familiar and gazed at Siberoet. There it was almost opposite the village to the west, and the hundred miles separating us did not look very formidable. But there was nothing reassuring in the meagre looking sixty miles of island which was Siberoet.

"Looks easy to miss," said Lissy, tracing what was a really imposing expanse of unbroken sea stretching for fifteen hundred miles to the southern tip of India.

"Fiddlesticks!" Lofty said, "We'll be able to see it in three days," and this seemed to help matters.

There was also a chain of islands right up to the most northern point of Sumatra stretching north from Siberoet. They seemed too close together to be missed.

As the incoming tide raised the boat slowly clear of the mud where it rested it began rolling at its moorings. Impatient to be clear of Sumatra but also with some fear of what might be ahead, the gang obeyed Tiny's command with alacrity. "All aboard."

Lofty had already inspected the boat thoroughly and had spent some ten minutes explaining certain necessities to the rest of us. Not one of us, except possibly Doc, had the least idea of handling or manoeuvring boats, and until lessons could be learnt, Lofty held not only our welfare, but possibly our lives, in his hands.

The boat was twenty-seven feet long stem to stern, and with a beam of eight feet looked somewhat squat and ungainly. The tapering mast of an astonishing thirty feet, set between midships and prow, helped to counteract the squatness and made a more pleasing appearance. The long, heavy outriggers, flapping like giant outspread wings transformed everything, and while in motion they were graceful as one or the other cut the water - in rest they made the boat look awkward.

The sail was furled on a twenty foot boom at present lying almost the length of the deck, with the hoist rope hanging limply from a pulley at the masthead. The gaff itself to which the hoist rope was attached was a ten foot spar with over a dozen bamboo rings in its length, holding the sail. The mainsheet running from the boom was lashed to a capstan on the small after deck by the tiller. This tiller was a single wooden arm detachable from the rudder, which answered to a finger touch during motion but at rest taxed the full strength of one man.

The after deck was big enough for two men to lie full length with only their ankles over the edge of the cavernous yawning hold. This was no more than four feet deep, but reached right forward to the mast and, although at this stage it was open to the elements had a canvas cover to draw over the whole gap. The absence of a keel of any sort made the boat ideal for shallow waters and indeed it drew no more than eighteen inches.

The outriggers, of course, gave the equilibrium of a keel but also made a greater spread of canvas possible as the five hundred square feet of sail would have capsized any other type of boat. The four wire stays which held the mast in position were lashed to them making it look somewhat like a huge tent pole surrounded by guy ropes. Lofty explained these wire stays; when the sail was set on a starboard tack then the port stays must be tensioned and braced more tightly; on a port tack this was reversed.

The mainsail, he promised, would be tricky until we were better trained, and indeed he would have been wiser to have stuck to the jib sail first. That was a beautiful, graceful, triangular strip of white canvas, running from the mast head with the base of the triangle fastened to the tip of the bowsprit, pointing its way five feet above the prow, and also to the base of the mast so that it could be pulled in close to the wind or let out full before a following breeze.

Both the jib and mainsail were furled as we took our places in the boat, two men to each of the four huge oars provided. Not even the sullen mood of the crowds at the waters edge could dampen our spirits. The cheery waves and shouted adieus of Titch and Tombola produced only a scowling disapproval, while the jeers of Bosun and myself brought a resentful flow of muttered imprecations.

"Stand by," Tiny yelled and four oars were raised.

"Go!" the skipper roared, and amazingly synchronised four oars dipped and pulled as with Lofty's guiding hand the prahu sped easily and smoothly into deep water towards the open sea beyond. There was a soft offshore breeze, and when Tiny hauled up the jib we could feel the easing of the pull on the oars. The breeze held, and there was a sense as of the boat pulling on its leash to surge forward with increasing speed.

"Steady boys! Hold it!" Tiny called and we stopped rowing and laughed gleefully and clapped each other's shoulders and stood up and danced, and still the boat raced forward.

"India! Here we come!" Lofty yelled, "Mainsail," roared Tiny, "Aye, Aye, Sir!" piped Titch as we sprang joyfully to our allotted stations.

One man each to an outrigger, sitting astride with legs dangling, ready to loosen and tighten the mast stays respectively. Two men on the mainsheet ready to haul away at the mainsail and Lofty at the tiller with his eyes glued to the set of the jib while three stood by to let out the boom of the sail.

"Right! Up she goes," called the steersman and "Heave! Up!" - pause - "Heave! Up!" shouted the rest of us.

The boat heeled over to starboard as the breeze filled the sail and the starboard outrigger rolled and dipped down to the sea to leave a trail of foam in the water behind. There was a lurching and tossing for a moment then Lofty caught the wind and the white sail billowed and strained when the boat settled, and we turned for the narrow exit of the bay. Before running into the open sea, exactly as we had done when leaving Singapore, we all turned for a last look at the beach behind us which already seemed at an incredible distance. Even Lofty at the tiller, answering easily to a touch, turned around.

It was his loud cry which brought every eye ahead, and for a moment all stood aghast at the sight before us. We had sped forward so smoothly that unheeded, we were almost on top of the small island which nearly blocked the narrow exit from the bay. Already, even we landsmen could see that we couldn't slip through the channel to port, and nobody knew what to do or how to slow the boat, until Lofty called "Stand by to go about."

A flood of curses and directions followed, and there was scurrying and flying in all directions, but untrained and undrilled, we were beaten before we started. Tiny yelled and Bosun called, "All set," as they got the stay on the back outrigger to starboard but Lissy and I were still struggling frantically with the other stay which for the first and last time had been fastened with a landsman's knot. Lofty's eyes were hopping in all directions as he tried to watch the island, and, easing the boat away glanced occasionally at the sail, drawing in ever more dangerously to the wind, while he also kept tags on us tearing and pulling in complete futility.

"Look out," he yelled as Doc, Titch and Tom on the mainsheet drew the sail in just a little more, so that it was almost parallel to the centre of the ship. We were practically on the island now and Lofty had no choice as he veered round still further.

"Get down", he shrieked as the wind got behind the sail. The other side filled like an exploding rocket, the boom and sail whipped from the starboard tack hard over to port. Lissy and I were still struggling with the stay when the heavy boom hit it and we were jerked violently off our perch almost into the water below.

There was a whip-like crack as the back of the boom snapped, and then the white sail was flapping and sagging like a broken wing. We rolled and pitched to the open sea, and wished that we were back in the placid waters of the bay. When we had lowered the mainsail, the jib, too low to catch the breeze above the high island, also flapped idly and emptily and without steerage it was like being on a cork, tossed effortlessly on the very crest of everything.

It seemed as if fate would turn us back to Sumatra even now but every heart aboard was against retracing one single foot of the way. Once again the oars came out while Dicky Dykes came to the rescue of the boom. Painstakingly and patiently Dicky sat alone and unaided paring, preparing and finally completing a wonderfully neat, sound job of splicing.

CHAPTER TEN

FISH AND SHIP

The main sail went up again, more soberly this time. But as the breeze freshened to send our little dove racing forward, sobriety departed, and we sang and capered as we sped forward, homeward bound and going there fast. Then the rain started and the chilling drizzle subdued most of us and drove us below to what should have been cosy shelter under the protecting canvas we pulled above us.

But the canvas was rotten and wherever we huddled the trickling leakages found us until we were all thoroughly soaked and shivering. All the canvas did was help to thicken an atmosphere already heavy and nauseating with the pervading fish smell which had started just after we loaded the boat in Sungei Painang. Some of our dried fish had slipped into the bilge water and was absolutely rotten.

We couldn't find it in the rising water without bailing everything dry and this was impossible with rain coming in from every direction. Besides that we were seasick and nobody wanted to do anything but lie down and die, except Lofty who sat by the tiller, bared to the wind and rain, singing with joyous exhilaration. He stuck to his post at the tiller all day with Doc relieving him for short spells while he bailed out the flooded hold where we lay. Lofty thrived and exulted in the situation, but though we should have been grateful for his boisterous good cheer he collected more curses than blessings from most of us, especially when he came blundering below, glistening with rain and bringing the cold air with him.

"Gee, I'm hungry!" he said, "Don't we get any grub?"

Ernie had been appointed cook and turned away from him with a shudder. Lofty sniffed the air.

"That fish smells good to me," he said and Titch retched. "For cripes sake get out you big ox!" he shouted. The fish had really blossomed by now and every head was aching and swimming in the foulness of the hold.

Lofty stood up to scratch himself. A characteristic of Lofty was his habit of simultaneously scratching his ribs at each side. He banged his head on the canvas cover and sent a deluge of collected water cascading on us and Bosun snarled at him, "Get the hell out of it, you blasted idiot," as he rolled out of the path of the worst deluge.

Tiny weakly turned over. "Bale some water out, Lofty," he pleaded and the big Australian kicked his clumsy way over legs and bodies to the bailing tin.

He stuck to his bailing and steering, his singing and his cheerful but resented comments until nightfall. By this time even he was a bit green and the rest of us couldn't have cared whether the boat filled or sank, we were too miserable even to do anything about the bilge water which swished around us.

Night ended that dreadful day and brought some fitful sleep with only Lofty, Doc and Dicky taking turns at the tiller. Thankfully, none of the rest of us knew enough to be trusted with the ship in rough seas.

Dawn disclosed a choppy expanse of sea with only our lonely bobbing cockleshell, puny in the vastness. Then the sun came up in a clear sky and ten sailors crawled weakly into its warming rays with wan faces, pale and ghastly against the blackness of unshaven whiskers. Life began to creep through Ernie first and he got a fire going in his fireplace, fashioned from a kerosene tin. He even cooked an unsavoury mess of rice and fish which that wretch Lofty ate with gusto. Water was all that the rest of us wanted but already Tiny had clamped his huge controlling hand on our supply and would allow us only a very meagre ration.

We had been at sea for only two days but already the hardships and minimal diet were wearing us down and we longed for what we imagined would be the peace and comfort of a prison camp in Sumatra.

The sun warmed us and the habitual restless questing of Bosun sent him to the bows, eyes straining and squinting. He stared long and hard, then called out, "Lofty! What's ahead?"

Lofty stood up and started to scratch his ribs and immediately fell off balance and clutched to steady himself. It took all of us a day or two to realise that there would never be a time even in the calmest of seas when the rolling bobbing boat would allow anyone to stand up unsupported. Anyway our sailor boy clambered forward, supported by the mast and searched the horizon ahead. We were all staring and straining our eyes at the long low clouds lying here and there on the edge of the rim where sky met sea. It didn't seem possible that we could have left Sumatra almost a hundred miles astern since yesterday morning but as the clouds joined, darkening and taking on colour, we had to believe that we were rapidly closing up to an island so big that it could only be Siberoet.

Our gallant little craft went straight ahead and without changing course even half a point, we hit the exact centre of a small entrance to a spreading bay which was sheltered and peaceful.

CHAPTER ELEVEN
PIG ISLAND

We glided into a lagoon. The surface was very calm, with the jungle encroaching on the water, perfectly reflected everywhere on the perimeter. The place was remote from both sea and land, with only the distantly booming breakers to mar the silence. Our battered boat slid over the surface, still under the momentum which carried it in right to the wooded edge.

Almost before the boat was tied up we swarmed ashore, all except Dicky, who was already in the grip of the malady which was later to sap his energy and leave him useless and lethargic. He lay unconcerned on deck, but we revelled in the feeling of dry land beneath our wobbling legs.

It was young Titch who first noticed the two almost naked black figures standing in a background of shadow just a little darker than they were. "Oho!" he called, "We've got visitors."

The figures didn't move, and Lofty voiced our first concern. "Is there any more d'yer reckon?" he whispered and every eye probed the other shadows.

"Can't see any signs."

"Are they carrying anything?"

There didn't seem to be any immediate danger, and Doc raised his voice.

"Tabeh!" he greeted but not a movement or murmur was made. Lissy tried unsuccessfully. Titch took a hand.

"Tubak ada?" (Got any tobacco?) he ventured, but the two just looked blankly at each other, and Titch looked discouraged while they broke into a wondering and completely unintelligible gabble. Titch hadn't given up hope.

"What's the word for grub, Doc?" he asked and was duly enlightened.

"Hey, boys!" he called imperiously to the open mouthed blacks, "Makan ada?"

So as to leave nothing to chance the little Australian pointed to his mouth, rubbed his protruding stomach and repeated his query.

The natives suddenly grinned and one pointed to the stomach while he said something and both laughed while Titch scowled.

"That's nothing to go by, you black bastards" he remonstrated, using the usual Australian endearment. Inspiration struck and he suddenly fished out a dollar and managed somehow to look like a sword swallower who had turned his attention to dollar bills. However, light dawned on the previously unresponsive pair, two black hands reached for the dollar and two native heads nodded vehemently as they both gave a long drawn out "Ah!" and then decisively, "Uh!" which was obviously meant to be "yeah, sure."

They half turned away and with beckoning arms bade somebody or everybody to follow.

"I reckon they're OK," Ernie said, "Me and Titch'll go."

Titch was not completely happy when he disappeared in the shrubbery but he was hanging onto Ernie's arm. They still had their guns, and anyway they left as much trepidation behind them.

It seemed an eternity afterwards when the two Australians returned, smiling, jubilant and with the stomach of Titch even more prominent than when he left. A cortege of natives strung out behind, escorting a squealing pig slung upside down by its feet on a bamboo pole carried on two powerful shoulders.

Titch and Ernie, especially Titch, were like blood brothers to the whole of their unsavoury following by this time, but the feelings of the rest of us were summed up by Lofty's "I'm not a bit keen on this mob."

"I reckon we'd better watch the boat and not get too far from it," Lissy added.

Tiny agreed. "You and Gabby get on board and keep a gun in your hand."

Lissy and I were indeed glad to put some distance between us and the 'Pig Islanders' and made haste to the seclusion of the ship. From there the activity about the pig was indistinct but it was explained to us afterwards when most of the pig, later pork, had vanished.

Apparently there was some difficulty about butchering the pig for which, amazingly enough, Malayan dollars had been accepted. Doc was the only possibility and he received the suggestion that his medical degree qualified him as a pork butcher unfavourably. Anyway there was some difficulty about the slaughtering and so Titch took charge and despite the language barrier conveyed to his warriors by signs the need for a fire, a butcher and a cook.

Those who had not previously rated Titch at his true value opened their eyes wide at the speed with which his requests were obeyed and a few indignant, then terrified squeals soon gave way to a sizzling and pleasant aroma of pork.

But Titch's value went down again later when it was found that his wretched sign language had been taken by the horde of natives as an invitation to a feast on pork. When Lissy and I gazed in horror at our tiny ration brought to us by a shamefaced Ernie we cursed the little Australian with heartfelt fervour.

However, accompanying the few charred bristles was a large portion of fat flavoured rice and we ate our fill of the appetising mess. A second bowl of rice liberally mixed with juicy banana slices and abundant black coffee took away the resentment - and we lit cigarettes contentedly.

Doc had not wasted time and even on board was levering information from his childlike friends. While we dozed happily under the stars he gave us his news.

"We've hit Siberoet all right, these fellows also call this Siberoet."

"Where's the town?" Tiny asked.

"As far as I can make out," Doc cautiously said, "we're on the north of Siberoet and the town of Siberoet is down on the south end."

"Any chance of stores here?"

"Not a hope, there's only a small village this end."

"Well, I suppose we might as well get to sleep and kick off at dawn."

"What about this mob?"

"I wish to hell they'd clear off, just look at the blighters," Lissy said.

The whole horde were perched like vultures round the deck, silent now and in the starlight, they seemed to be glowering at us. Even Titch thought they looked ominous and I was frankly alarmed.

"The beggars look as if they are going to jump us any minute," I said and added to Titch "They're your pals, cobber."

"What about making them go?"

"Get your guns ready," Tiny warned as Titch got ready to ask his friends politely if they'd leave.

Titch scratched his head for a minute, perplexed by his problem, trying to be polite and not to antagonise the natives while at the same time telling them they weren't welcome any longer. The job would have been difficult enough without the language barrier but this fool decided to rush in. He cleared his throat "Uhurum."

ANGRY SEA

The blacks turned a barrage of eyes on him and he was unnerved. Titch concentrated on his original two.

"You fellows, all," his sweeping hand embraced all and black heads craned left and right to see "all". The point was obviously made but Titch failed for a moment. How could he say, 'go', 'scram', 'vamoose' or anything like that with courtesy?

Inspiration came and he pillowed his head on his hands and pointed to us and then again to the natives, ending lamely as if he was shooing the chickens home to roost. But they were not really chickenlike.

"You all go," he pointed to the woods and then a number of horror stricken black faces reproached Titch and then a babble of resentful chatter broke out.

"This is it," Lofty said.

"All set, watch out," Tiny agreed.

Suddenly the chatter stopped and one man held the floor. It looked as if he was haranguing for the onslaught and then suddenly a grin appeared, then a laugh was heard and in a moment the whole jolly crowd were grinning and laughing. They straightened, stood up, waved, and in a flash were gone.

There was nothing to remind us that the villagers had ever been here except the receding sounds of their passage through the jungle. We sighed thankfully and moved towards our resting places.

Lissy and I were dragged out at 2 a.m. and feeling refreshed already we saw the night out without waking the others, sitting together in the stern and chatting desultorily on rambling topics as odd thoughts came to one or the other of us. The glow of pipes and cigarettes through the foliage ashore showed the presence of other watchers, but dawn came and the pipes vanished together with the smokers.

A gloriously refreshing swim in the warm waters of the lagoon gave a good, but not really needed, stimulus for an ample breakfast of rice and bananas and once again we were ready for the road.

We got the *Venture*, as we had named our boat, around on the jib and had her pointed towards the narrow entrance when a large unwieldy-looking junk, although smooth and swift in action, glided effortlessly through the gap. It slid over the centre of the lagoon and in one graceful movement, skidded about to face seaward and came to rest.

We had watched the junk enter the bay with some trepidation until it slowed past us, and then our trepidation gave way to curiosity and speculation as to what kind of people were aboard. And speculation as to the possibilities of a junk in so much more capable hands than ours. Bosun

65

had been going to take a barge and crew from Padang and now he saw the possibilities in a similar project.

We even got our revolvers ready to board the boat as we slid more closely towards it to investigate. But it was a mixed screaming and shrieking from children and women aboard that sent us helter-skelter for the peace of the open sea.

Doc drily pointed out to us that only a few weeks previously we had all been uniformed upholders of law and order.

"And now we're ruddy pirates," said Titch.

All that day a following friendly wind bowled us merrily south. As night came the lights of Siberoet twinkled over the starboard beam. At least we took it to be Siberoat, and so when later the lights were snuffed out one by one, we lowered the sails and dropped anchor in a vain attempt to prevent drifting, until morning would show the best way in.

In the morning light the town looked big and imposing to eyes used to small villages. We approached warily. The huts took shape set back from a long wooden waterfront landing-stage with a mass of waving humanity moving colourfully on it.

Dicky had the binoculars and was optimistic. "I can see no uniforms," he drawled, then added, "They're pushing out to meet us."

The small canoes swarmed around but the paddlers did not attempt to climb aboard only waving and smiling and gesticulating to show the course.

Tiny made up his mind. "OK, in we go."

In a few minutes many and willing hands had lashed the outrigger firmly to the wharf. Bosun and I, nimble on our bare feet, were first ashore along the outrigger arms and we gazed happily at the friendliness which was evident everywhere.

Drinks were provided for everyone and then we were almost dragged to an eating shop a few yards away where bananas, biscuits and coffee in hopeless confusion disappeared into nine capacious stomachs. Doc and Tiny had had one drink and then disappeared in search of the headman and while we were stuffing food wholesale, they had made real headway. He was benevolent and hospitable.

We got the first inkling of their activities when a voice addressing us in halting uncertain English brought us all spinning round to the speaker.

"Excuse plis! Excuse plis! Will you to come to follow me."

This was Besu. Besu of the infinitive, Besu who never would deal with a split infinitive. Wondering, we fell into step with him and left the waterfront behind for the pleasantly shaded seclusion of the village suburbs.

In fact, his name was Immanuel Loembantobing, and his father, David Loembantobing, bore the title of Malay Commissioner for the Dutch. But to us they were Besu and his father the headman.

We found Doc and Tiny comfortably installed on the verandah of the headman's house, and we dropped into the most heartwarming hospitality and kindness of all our travels. From the benevolence of the headman, to his brother, the village doctor, already blood brother to our Doc, and reflected in the frankly smiling wives, sisters and daughters in the vast residence.

Tiny had the chance to whisper imperatively, "Behave yourselves you blokes and don't speak to Doc unless he speaks to you," he cautioned. "Doc's their little tin god so don't spoil it, show some respect for your betters." He glared at me, "That means you!" He switched his glare to Lissy and Titch. "And you two! Understand?"

The skipper obviously meant it, so, we understood.

There wasn't much chance to find out what was happening about us yet, as we had been brought from the waterfront for a hurriedly prepared banquet. As soon as we'd smoked a cigarette we were led inside to a banquet room almost filled by a long table sagging under its load of meats, fruits, hot steaming rice, curries, sauces and drinks.

An hour earlier we would have sold our boat for such a feed, now our stomachs were already bulging from our orgy on the waterfront and we gazed in horror at the ordeal.

"I'll bust if I touch another mouthful," I groaned and Tiny waved a huge fist in front of my nose.

"I'll bust you if you don't," he snarled.

We slunk to our places.

Tiny and Doc attacked everything in sight eagerly, the skipper only pausing now and then to glare at Lissy and me.

"Eat, you gluttonous bastards," he warned.

We ate, we controlled the impulse to retch, we ate again until we were finally allowed to stagger to the shelter of an empty barracks compound which had been prepared for us.

CHAPTER TWELVE
POLYNESIAN ARCADIA

From the beginning the citizens of Siberoet took full charge of our comfort and welfare. The halcyon days of the early restful period in Padang returned, with good food, plenty of leisure and a sense of security and peace which carried our thoughts far from war and the enemy.

The accommodation allotted to us was clean and spacious with full evidence of the order and hygiene of the Dutch troops and police who had vacated the barracks when the emergency on the mainland called them away.

Siberoet, the town, had been the administration centre for the island of Siberoet, and under the Dutch had been prosperous and peaceful with much of the nominal authority in the hands of Besu's father.

Besu's family, along with the remainder of the town, were Polynesian. A placid, timid and peace-loving race who rolled contentedly through their lives so long as they had their Dutch masters. Now, however, with no white law-enforcers on the island an uneasy situation had arisen and was becoming daily aggravated by the jungle dwellers who were neither Polynesian, nor peaceful. They were the true natives of Siberoet, the Dyak, and their appearance was fearsome. The flat ugly faces, with a perpetual saliva of betel juice dripping from their mouths were repulsive, and the eyes, dull and humourless, added to their unprepossessing looks.

They dressed like the savages out of Robinson Crusoe. Cloth had never replaced the grass girdles of their ancestors and the only difference in attire to distinguish women from men lay in the additional grass around the bosom. The men, one and all, carried what looked like arrow quivers but we assumed they were blowpipes.

The Dutch had never tolerated anything but docility in any of their East Indies colonies, and the Dyaks had come and gone from jungle to town on their trading missions unobtrusively and with apparent goodwill. Gradually, however, as they became used to the absence of restraining police, the jungle men began to raise their heads to a more arrogant poise, and each day saw them becoming more bold, until they were receiving more than double value for their goods from the intimidated town tradesmen.

ANGRY SEA

Larger numbers were frequenting the village, and the frightened townsfolk had been living for weeks with the threat of an eruption from the jungle. Our arrival had brought the Dyaks smartly to heel again and the timorous townspeople breathed a sigh of relief. Besu showed this relief and translated the hopes of his family to us on the second day of our stay.

"You all to like to stay, to live Siberoet?" he asked.

Even Doc was never able to teach Besu to use anything but the infinitive of his verbs. He was cautious as he answered. "Yes! We do like, Besu."

The boy's eyes lit up. "You like to stay forever?"

Doc hesitated, not wanting to commit himself to what was obviously impending. "Well! No! Not forever, but for a few days."

"Plis! You doan to go India!"

The boy was pleading and Doc tried to be gentle. "Why! Besu! We must go back as soon as possible."

"My fader, to look see you OK!" he insisted. Doc tried to evade. "We have no money!"

Then Titch butted in. "Excuse me, Sir!" Doc's nod gave the permission to proceed and Titch continued. "Does he really want us to live here?"

Besu plunged in. "Yessah! Yessah! Always!" He threw in for good measure. "Plenty food!" and as an after-thought, "No to work," and then with final inspiration he beamed, "You to like good girl?" He looked about him. "One! Two! Three - eleffen pretty girl."

Lissy grinned. "There were ten pretty girls .... "

"Shut up, Lissenburg!" and Tiny's huge searching arm cut the song short.

"What's the catch?" Titch asked, "Wine, women and song if we stay, is it?"

Besu could understand English better than he could speak it, and he protested. "No catch!"

He pointed to the jungle. "These fellow Dyak, no good, you to stay, they not to make trouble."

"Oh!" Doc said, "I see! It looks as if we'll be worth our keep as a restraining factor to the Dyaks."

"Yes! Yessah! That it! Jungle boy no to make trouble, white man here."

Doc reflected with some sympathy, "These poor beggars must miss their Dutch police rather badly and we must have been a real godsend to them." Tiny agreed, and Doc turned to the black boy. "Look, Besu. . Japanese soldiers will come here soon."

"Oh, that OK!" An arm gestured embracing the jungle, "My fader to fix place to live there. Japan no to find."

"Anyway Besu," Doc continued, "when the Japanese come, the Dyaks will do you no harm."

Besu had not thought of this angle and new hope came to his eyes and then he had an afterthought. "Maybe Japan not to come?"

"They'll come all right," Tiny reassured him, "and pretty soon - maybe tomorrow."

Almost as if to fulfil his prophecy, at that moment a shout went up at the compound gate. One of Besu's people came breathlessly in and we were now upright and alert. A flow of apparent invectives was shrieked at the headman's son and he turned to Doc.

"Prahu! to come here," he announced, and consternation filled his listeners.

"Japanese?" but a shrug showed that so far this was not known.

Seen from the landing stage, the huge barque approaching seemed to be swarming with men, but who they were, or what their intention was, could only be conjecture.

The ship slowed about and it was evident that it only had a single mast and was not a barque at all. Rigged with a jib up for'ard and a huge jury mast just astern of the main mast, it had appeared at first to have three masts.

The movement to go about was awkwardly executed and a murmur went up from the thronged natives at the water's edge.

"I bet we looked like that, too," Lissy said cynically, and Tiny caught at the possible inference.

"Maybe they're escapees, like us."

Dicky had the binoculars focussed, but his contribution did nothing to allay fears.

"They're uniformed anyway," he said, and that decided Tiny.

"Doc!" he snapped, reverting immediately back to his role of skipper, "Get cracking on Besu will you, and get a couple of guides ready for the jungle." He swung round to the others. "The rest of you! Get back to the compound and put your traps together!" His finger pointed at me. "Get my gear and scoot back here with it."

He looked regretfully at the little boat which was to have been our salvation. "I'm afraid we've had that, for the moment."

Dicky's eyes were still glued to the binoculars as Tiny finished speaking, but keen native eyes are ahead of binoculars and a murmur was already spreading through the ranks.

"Inglia!"

The boat had started another tack and Lofty exclaimed, "They're no sailors, anyway."

"I can see bush hats on deck," said Dicky slowly, and it was true. The villagers started cheering the oncoming vessel, and five minutes later a crowd of bearded refugees were swarming over the landing stage.

Tiny grabbed a stripling, 2nd Lieutenant.

"I'm Dainty!" (He didn't look it) "Sub-conductor Dainty," he said, "Indian Army."

The rather nervous reply was, "How do you do. I'm Trelawney."

Handshakes were exchanged all round and the formal 'How was the trip?' 'Where did you come from?'

"Oh, we sailed straight out of Padang after the Japs took over, came right out in broad daylight and not a soul challenged us. Might just as easily have gone back in again, too."

He pulled a wry face at the memory and went on, "We bust the mast soon afterwards and had the devil of a job to save the sail."

Tiny's eyes took in the massive girth of the main mast and whistled. "Yes, you'd have a fair sized job on your hands with that."

Trelawney grunted. "It wouldn't have been so bad if we could have got all hands going. There are twenty-seven of us, you know, enough to carry the boat, but we had no show of getting the whole gang cracking."

Tiny's eyes lifted in polite surprise and Trelawney unburdened his sorry tale of woe. He supported one party aboard who were under an autocratic English army captain and consisted mainly of junior officers. However, there were two other parties led by men who had completely thrown off the yokes of service allegiance, and, as often happens, they went out of their way to defy authority.

"We determined to bring them to heel in the beginning," Trelawney said defensively, "And the whole lot ganged up on us, the leader of the other two parties came to us and told Captain Marsh to forget 'that old army stuff.' They had their hands on their pistols and the whole unsavoury bunch were standing by ready for trouble." He finished bitterly. "That was an end to law and order."

An unholy din rose at this point and he held up a hand. "Listen to the blighters, and just look at that bunch."

A trio of unwashed ruffians were shouting at a trembling storekeeper and demanding tobacco. Bosun swung round and his mouth tightened.

"Come on Gabby!" he said, already on the move as he grabbed my arm and together we strode forward purposefully.

The frightened native had his hands held out uncomprehendingly to the rascals but he gave a nervous grin when he spotted Bosun and myself.

We two big rescuers were standing with hands on hips as the trio swung round and then Bosun's thumb gestured.

"Beat it!" he snarled.

The burly ruffian in the centre took in the figure before him and curled his lip insolently.

"Beat it!" Bosun's tightly drawn mouth and slitted eyes looked menacing but the trio were not daunted.

Tiny, in the background was holding back his gang and there was a little grin on his face. He knew Bosun.

The burly one moved towards Bosun and his mouth twisted, "Look chum!" he growled, "What about keeping your nose out of this?"

"You going?" Bosun's voice was quiet now, the calm before the storm.

"No chum! We ain't going nowhere," he took another step forward and Bosun exploded.

Wham! His right fist moved forward with his whole body and the ruffian seemed to hurtle through the air as his head jerked back.

He hit the ground and lay still, but neither Bosun nor I heeded him. I had moved, almost as fast as Bosun and as the other two sailed in I took the first one on my lowered shoulder and sent him crashing down to join his leader.

Bosun took his time with the third man and cut his face to ribbons as he worked on him while I stood over the other two and tried to kick the one who was still conscious to his feet for more punishment.

ANGRY SEA

The first casualty was just getting up, groaning when Bosun ended the fight and all three, sullen but subdued, took Bosun's ultimatum.

Doc found it difficult to explain to the islanders how our gang could so easily be fine while the 'twenty-seven' were such obvious ruffians and yet all of us had the same nationalities. The only thing he could say was more or less that all nations had good and bad and anyway these people could not be judged because of the unique circumstances in their flight.

It wasn't by any means a complete explanation but it could have settled the hand of the 'twenty-seven' as far as supplies and fittings were concerned. With Tiny and gang ranged with the townsfolk they would have been forced to leave Siberoet without hope of obtaining help anywhere except on the Japanese-occupied mainland.

Doc, however, used his powers of persuasion and turned the tide for them. In fact most of the labour was diverted from our boat with a view to equipping the other quickly so as to get rid of the unwelcome crowd with all possible speed.

The only stipulation made to 'the twenty-seven' was that they pay for everything. This put money into the pockets of Bosun's people and after our summary punishment of the three rowdies there was no further trouble about browbeating the natives.

Trelawney was jubilant at the changed manner of the ruffians, but also, as he said, "I wish we had your gang aboard with us. I'll bet we'd soon have that blasted mob straightened out."

Tiny turned a speculative eye on the young subaltern. "Your boat is big enough anway," and indeed this was no exaggeration. The huge square sterned hull of the 'twenty-seven' towered over and dwarfed our insignificant sampan, and already the comparison had brought some uneasiness into our hearts.

Trelawney caught the trend of Tiny's thought and was eager.

"Yes. Of course it is, and, oh boy!" he rhapsodised, "what couldn't we do with our party of officers and your gang combined."

"H'mm! Yes," Tiny said, "but the other two crowds wouldn't take to the idea, they might even fight about it."

"They probably would," Trelawney agreed, "and the blighters have even got a couple of Tommy guns."

"Well, I wouldn't like to see any blood shed," the skipper lied, "but surely most of them must realise that they have no hope of reaching India without organised leadership."

"They do. I'm sure most of them do realise that," Trelawney said, and Tiny cut in.

"Well, then, listen! You go back and have a go at talking them into the idea, they must want to get home safely, and after all they are soldiers and should realise that they'll have to give an accounting to authority in time."

Trelawney went off full of optimism about the future, leaving us looking at our cockleshell of a boat with relief that we would not have to face the Indian Ocean in it.

It was a horrible shock to us when we found that in a free vote amongst 'the twenty-seven' we had been turned down by a substantial majority on the grounds that their craft would not carry enough food and water for any larger party than they already possessed, and also that the boat itself could not accommodate us. One or two of the officers sided with the men, and even though the reasons given were ridiculous, we couldn't shake them. Besu and family were thoroughly disgusted at their refusal and immediately said that in the circumstances they would give no further assistance either in work or in goods to the newcomers. It was a difficult task, even for Doc, to get any help for them. We could have forced the issue, and with the whole town on our side, plus some of 'the twenty-seven' could have taken over the whole works by force, but we eventually relinquished the plan altogether and resigned ourselves to the thoughts of the *Venture* once more. Strangely enough, when we reached this stage our gallant little ship resumed its original proportions, and in a very short time we were feeling rather pleased that we still had her. Such is human nature!

It was decided to get rid of the unsavoury bunch as quickly as possible, and all work was suspended on our boat to concentrate more fully on the single task. On the second day of the stay, the large barque was ready to go. We had been on land for four days. No time was wasted by 'the twenty-seven' - on the same day they assembled and were gone.

We watched the swaggering troops strutting about the deck, each with his weapons, and wondered how long it would be before things came to a head there. Six of the natives went aboard to take the barque out of the harbour. The sail slowly unfurled without any help being given by the British, the white sheet billowed, her nose turned and she was away to destruction, as we were to see later.

CHAPTER THIRTEEN
FEAST AND FAREWELL

With the departure of 'the twenty-seven' the effort on Operation Venture was redoubled and the air rang with the sound of matchets and saws as the islanders transformed our boat.

They caulked the open seams, built a floor over the bilge, erected an attap and bamboo roof, put shelves under the eaves, strengthened the outriggers, cut spare outrigger arms, made a new boom, gave us two spare booms, stitched and reinforced the sail, gave us spare oars, supplied bamboo sweeps and when all was shipshape they stocked the boat with provisions.

Two bags of rice, a sack of peas, tins of fish, beef, pork and the Dutch Army ration 'nasi goreng' - matches, tobacco, tea, sugar, coffee and they even filled every available corner with firewood, bananas and coconuts. Finally, they lashed twelve bamboos to the side of the boat, each about fourteen feet long with a diameter of about three inches. These each held about two and a half gallons of water in addition to the fourteen four gallon tins stowed below.

Meanwhile we made our plans, had our meetings and gradually and definitely set our course. A discussion of the pros and cons saw the final relinquishing of ideas on the Australia route as being too hazardous because of the great tracts of enemy occupied territory including at least Sumatra and Java and maybe Timor. Admittedly the fifteen hundred miles of landless ocean between us and India made a formidable proposition but we reasoned that we'd done the hundred miles from Sumatra in two days and besides this we might run into Allied shipping at any time. Super optimist Tom was quite sure we'd have our feet on Allied territory in a week.

We also put Tiny's status as skipper on a democratic footing in a free vote. Tiny himself suggested it, he pointed out that he'd just sort of gathered us together in one band which did not necessarily make him leader. He mentioned me as a prospective leader and I laughed outright at him. He pointed at Lissy and Lissy guffawed but as Tiny proceeded we did realise that there certainly were other prospective leaders. Dicky was a natural, although something had happened to Dicky. He was no longer lithe and active as he had been, but instead was unnaturally lethargic and indolent. He had no physical energy at all and the Australians were a little contemptuous of him. Poor Dick, whatever it was that sapped his energy was to afflict him for a long time yet.

Doc was another natural leader but he firmly waved aside all talk of him being captain.

Lofty Eastgate, despite his youth could have led us all to safety, at least by sea. In fact, he was the only member of our gang that we couldn't do without.

Finally, of course, there was Bosun and now indeed the issue was simple, in a gang of captains, he and Tiny were way ahead of all of us. Clearly the skipper must be one of these and a vote was called for and then immediately vetoed by Bosun himself.

He stood up and held out his hand to Tiny. "You'll do me, Tiny," he said, and so it was.

Tiny was still our skipper. Lissy and I of course were already Tiny's slaves but I must admit I had grown close to Bosun since Padang days. I'd long ago passed the stage when I had been wary of his disposition, and took just as many liberties with him as I did with Tiny and Lissy. I had no qualms about pushing him, fully clothed off the pier one day and I know he enjoyed an after dinner tussle on the grass just as much as I did. Funnily enough, I could always picture him smiling, though it was his eyes really that smiled at us. It was odd, as Bosun had been such a grim personality in Padang.

We didn't spend all our time in talk of course. Lissy and I got our eyes on one of the Dyak girls who came out of the jungle every morning with her tray of bananas and mangos, and the little minx knew it. She had an expression in her eyes which was lacking in the other Dyaks but I was outclassed by Lissy for her favours. We didn't get past the ogling stage but I'm sure that we could have improved the acquaintance if we'd followed her when she returned to the jungle, as she always looked back at us.

Titch and Lofty spent their spare time in forming a choir of native children. This started quite informally but the kids got enthusiastic and the Australians taught them two songs, one of which was the unprintable army version of Barnacle Bill, and the other was worse. I hope that no visiting female tourist ever gets the full show turned on for her by the kids.

By the fifth, or maybe it was the sixth, day we were ready for sea. Tiny was not the one to dally and so he ruled "We sail on the tide in the morning."

He shocked us out of the pleasant indolence into which we had drifted on Siberoet. In the carefree serenity of the town where we had been really happy for the first time since the war had started, the struggle seemed far away. Even now some of us were almost ready to accept Besu's offer and drift through the war in the blessed peace of this haven, but as Tiny and Doc pointed out it would only be a very transient peace. The Japanese could arrive at any moment.

Meanwhile, we had been invited to a party by Besu's father and we spent our last afternoon in grooming and combing without succeeding in looking anything other than beachcombers. Except Doc, that is, who had been forced by Tiny to keep himself at all times impeccable with the aid of our combined wardrobe. He even had his major's crown up, and Tiny swore he'd strangle any one of us who didn't stand to attention when Doc spoke to him. The people of Siberoet loved this and they in turn almost bowed themselves double to Doc. He really could have been king of the island and it was because of Doc that we got so much kindness and service.

Now Doc wanted to repay this kindness and he wanted us to surrender to the villagers two of our revolvers with a good supply of ammunition. He was a little concerned about the Dyak menace when we left and felt that a display of arms would be deterrent enough until the Japanese came, if they ever did.

I don't think there could have been any other circumstances where we would have given up any of our weapons, but for Besu and his people we were all joyous about the thought. When we finally strolled to the headman's house Tiny was carrying two well wrapped parcels.

The residence was ablaze with lanterns. We were welcomed almost as royalty by Besu, his father, brothers, uncles and everyone of importance in Siberoet. All were resplendent in their finest clothes and all were beaming at us. The ladies, bless them, were like angels, flitting about, solicitous and anxious to forestall our every wish and innocently unaware of the yearnings I, at least, had for them. I think the rest of our gang were more pure in heart than I was.

The feast itself was like something out of the Arabian nights. It was incredible that the first dish I sampled was the most mouth watering I'd ever tasted and I could have gorged myself on that alone. My neighbour was my appointed guide and led me through the banquet from sweet to savoury, from curry to meat balls and each mouthful surpassed all others. Each complemented each other and when at long last my reluctant sigh of surrender ended my orgy I knew that I should have given in at least ten minutes earlier.

However, I didn't have to move from my chair, coffee, cigarettes and speeches were to come and Doc started the ball rolling. None of our friends except Besu understood him but Besu must have interpreted well or improvised to good purpose. The applause and smiles of appreciation would have been complimentary to the most gifted orator in any circle. At last he'd covered everything and mentioned everyone and he was done with talking.

Now was our moment. Doc raised his hand, Tiny walked to him with a parcel. In dead silence Doc opened the parcel and exposed his treasure, the belt and holstered revolver of an English officer. Gently raising Besu's father to his feet he fastened it about his waist.

The old boy couldn't believe it, he was speechless, he looked at the belt, he looked up at Doc, then at us and then abruptly he sat down trying to control the tears of joy flooding to his eyes. Doc's own eyes were wet and so were mine. Then somebody shouted and in a moment every voice joined in the ringing acclamation of released joy. It was incredible, contagious and almost hysterical. I think that the gathering must have realised that in one little revolver lay the salvation of Siberoet. The Dutch, of course, would not ever have allowed their coloured subjects weapons.

Doc was still standing as the noise died down and then almost dramatically he raised his hand again. Once more Tiny came forward and now Doc beckoned to Besu and under the shining eyes of the proudest father in the world he buckled round the boy the twin to the first revolver.

Besu's father really cried now. He embraced Doc, he clasped Besu to his arms and if we'd been anywhere near we would have got the same treatment. Then he straightened and clapped his hands and from the doorway at his back came his daughters, carrying his present to us. It was food, his and his family's collection of tinned foods, collected over months of peace probably, and now our eyes glistened as the pile grew on the table beside Doc.

Bully beef, milk, tongues, herrings and pork, the whole lot were handed to us in one grand gesture. Life blood for us probably just as the guns were life savers to our hosts. A good trade indeed carrying as it did sacrifice, goodwill and brotherhood from and to both sides.

We walked back to our compound for the last time with hearts as full and bursting as were our stomachs.

Brotherhood was indeed blessed.

CHAPTER FOURTEEN
INDIA HERE WE COME

Lofty lustily sang the refrain he had picked up from the Islanders, while his steady hand on the tiller kept the nose pointed away to the north.

We were retracing the course we had followed from Pig Island and intended to travel north until Siberoet Island could be rounded and sails set for the west and India, 1,500 miles away, following the route as best we could on our only navigational aids which comprised a school atlas, a Chinese map and two basic compasses.

This was the 26th day of March, only five and a half weeks since the fall of Singapore and only nine days since we left Sumatra, but both Singapore and Padang seemed to be years past and India seemed to be just around the corner.

A shore breeze kept the sails full and the *Venture* pelted along until about mid-morning when the breeze died away to leave us wallowing and wailing for the prevailing winds of the North West Monsoon.

The winds didn't fail, but in the afternoon they unaccountably swung round to the north so that all Lofty's tacking failed to gain even one sea league. It was terribly disheartening to beat away out to sea in the east until the land lost its features, turn the other tack and scoot back to the land, exactly to the point we'd left behind. Night fell and found us full of chagrin with the realisation that Siberoet and our friends were only a few hours from us.

During the night, even this northerly wind dropped. The unfailing on-shore breeze of the morning only relieved the calm for less than an hour, before dying away to leave a cloudless sky and a mirror-like sea without even the odd ripple.

The main sail hung limp, without a rustle in it. The outriggers only splashed, to set the eddies circling when one or the other of us moved and upset the balance of the boat.

The day wore on and not a breath of wind disturbed the air. Night followed day, stifling and sultry. The only change the morning of the 27th brought was to throw a great light on the eternal calm without even the on-shore breeze to break the monotony.

Tiny spent much time with pencil and paper working out the scale of rations and even ladled, from bag to bag, cupful by cupful, the whole of the rice store to obtain exact statistics. This finished, he called in Dicky, the navigator, and Doc, the counsellor, to check and re-check on the course to be followed.

We all gambolled and swum about the boat to our heart's content, except Lofty whose shrapnel wound in the side was not yet healed, and Tombola who was similarly handicapped with his facial wound.

For a time we contemplated a swim to Siberoet but later gave up playing altogether because it gave us a hunger which we had no chance of satisfying as Tiny absolutely refused to listen to our pleas for a good feed despite my (and Lissy's) arguments that the journey had not yet started.

"It's started all right," he asserted grimly, "and we're not touching land again until we hit India."

"But we haven't properly left Siberoet yet, Tiny, blast you! I could swim ashore from here," I retorted.

"I'll blast you in a minute and put you overboard to try your swim, if you don't shut up, you ... you ..." words failed Tiny and Lissy filled the gap,

"Shark, Tiny?"

"And you shut up, shrimp," I flashed, snatching at a welcome diversion as I pounced on Lissy.

I had never before in my life accepted, meekly or otherwise, the kind of abuse which Tiny was prone to dish out as a matter of course. But from the skipper I did not even resent it and certainly it was not because I feared him, in spite of his dominating and almost crushing personality. Fear begets hate and I couldn't hate my boss and certainly would not have dreamed of challenging Tiny's right to say what he did.

Some time afterwards, maps were put aside and we were called aft where Tiny made his usual opening.

"Listen, you fellows," he said with his usual pause, "about this calm. We're not in any kind of jam because of it, yet, but," - again the pause, "if we'd been out in the middle of the Indian Ocean, we could have been stuck there for days and, in fact, for all I know, weeks."

"Well," he went on, "I've worked out the rations of food and water, so that we can stay at sea for THREE MONTHS." He almost shouted the last two words and there were gasps of horror from almost every corner.

"Three months?"

"Why, we might be picked up within a week."

"All right," came the answer, "if we are picked up in a week, it won't have hurt you to have been a little hungry and if we don't get anywhere in three months, we'll still survive. Anyway," he concluded, "you made me skipper and that's that."

We groaned. "What's the ration to be?" I asked.

An ordinary-sized enamel drinking mug was held up.

"Two mugs full of raw rice per meal," I was told.

Lissy rolled his eyes. "Each?" he asked innocently.

"Fathead," said Tiny, with a grin, despite himself, "even you couldn't eat that much. No, it's two mugs between the lot of us and there will be two meals per day."

"What about water?" asked someone.

Again came the details. "We'll get some water in the cooking of the rice and over and above that, we can manage one half-pint per man per meal unless we catch extra rain water."

Lofty's tongue was already lolling as he said plaintively, "Why didn't I stay with Besu?"

Tiny had one other item to cover and again it was to do with the becalming of the *Venture*. "It appears," he said, "that we are in the doldrums and might easily be stuck again later, so, the obvious thing to do is to get out of the danger area." He looked about him, "Does anyone object to going all out to the north until we're clear?"

"I reckon that's a good idea anyway," I said, "if we get far enough north before we beat to the west, we've a better chance of hitting India."

The skipper cast a pitying glance at me, the imbecile capable of such a remark, but did not pursue the subject and the vote was carried without discussion.

We spotted and overtook the huge vessel of 'the twenty-seven' by mid-day of the 28th. Goodness only knows what she'd been doing since the crew left Siberoet, but it gave us a real kick to find we could sail rings round her and that we would certainly be in India long before them.

We overhauled them at a point just level with the bay we called Pig Island, the place at which we'd first landed and we waved as we sped past them. They did not wave back but we didn't mind.

It was Lofty who first noticed their change of course. "They're turning into Pig Island," he said, "the blasted idiots, they'll never get in."

We turned and watched them and Doc said, "We'd better warn them about the channel."

They shouldn't have needed any warning because the tide was out, and here and there we could see rocks dotted across the entrance.

"Swing her round, Lofty," Tiny called, and, "Stand-by to go about!" yelled the Australian.

We now knew our drill and Lofty swung the tiller round so that we were speeding in to the south west to intercept 'the twenty-seven'.

Even if we'd caught them I doubt if we could have turned the boat, but we were too late anyway and she went hurtling ahead of us to disaster. The coral shelf must have been just under the surface and they went into it with a crash which shook half of them into the sea. We were not too far from the reef ourselves now and once more Lofty yelled.

"Mainsail! Mainsail down!"

Tiny was nearest and with one swift jerk he pulled the hoist rope loose and we hauled in the boom, while Lofty skidded our boat in a circle, just clear of the dangerous shallows.

"And now what?" Tiny said, more to himself than to us.

Already some of the crew were wading frantically to shore while others were clambering back on board their own ship. It didn't look as if there was any danger although obviously the ship wouldn't sail again. She was almost on her side on the coral reef, and must have had a terrible hole torn in her.

Some of the men were shouting to us but as far as we could see no one really needed help. What they would all need now was a lift to India, but as Lofty said.

"We can't take them all, and if we tried to help some there'd be trouble."

"They'll all swarm aboard if we go in," Tiny mused and then, decisively, "OK Lofty, get the jib up."

At this point Lofty was on watch at the tiller and the tiller-man was supposed to relay the skipper's orders.

We cruised round for about ten minutes on the jib making sure we didn't get too close. 'The twenty-seven' got quite frantic at us, probably wondering why we didn't go to them, but when we did sail away I suppose they must have thought it was our revenge for their behaviour in Siberoet. Anyway we persuaded ourselves that they'd still manage to exist on Siberoet (this was still Siberoet Island). At the worst they'd eventually be taken off by the Japanese. If they'd been a more tractable crowd we could have at least taken some of them, but right or wrong we left the lot.

Snowy was an affable, gentle creature, always friendly. Yet he had been a fighting artilleryman and was the bosom pal of Bosun. These two had something between them which was quite beautiful, they could almost have been brothers. I don't yet know what they had in common but then Jimmy Jewell and John Freeman were opposites. Anyway Snowy who as sergeant was Bosun's senior, worshipped Corporation Bosun Rawson, and I think that each would have died for the other. But then we all loved Snowy. I think we all felt like mothering him too, yet he wasn't helpless. He'd more than pulled his weight, from Singapore right up to now.

Now, Snowy had a fever. All of us should have been down with malaria as we'd been plagued by mosquito hordes since the Japanese invaded Malaya in December. We'd had some dread of sickness but except for Lofty whose shrapnel torn side had not yet healed, and Tom who still had trouble with the shrapnel wound running like a sabre cut across his face, we were a robust gang.

Snowy went down before we got to the top of Siberoet Island and by the time we were ready to swing to the west into the Indian Ocean he had been well and truly flattened.

Most of the time he was burning and tossing in the throes of his fever. Even between bouts he was weak and helpless. We all worried about him and Bosun scarcely left his side. Doc produced quinine from his pack, which had been his personal and secret burden since Padang, but still the fever raged. Doc also produced chocolate to tempt him but it only made our mouths water. Snowy couldn't take anything.

Tiny called a conference while the sick man lay sleeping down below. There was a decision to make which the skipper felt must be made by a vote. We could scoot for India and pray for Snowy until we got him to safety, we could turn back to Siberoet, hoping the Japanese weren't there and let our friends help or we could even turn back to Sumatra and trust that in Japanese hands we could get help for Snowy.

In the end we decided that the best course lay to the west, especially as we now had a wind which was bowling us along at an estimated eight knots, in just the right direction, north-west. We wanted to get north, out of the doldrum area and we needed to go west towards India. The wind was steady and strong and could almost take us right across the Indian Ocean.

"Full sail, course northwest."

CHAPTER FIFTEEN
MAST AWAY

Northwest it was once again, and with the boat running almost full before the wind and speeding forward as she had never done before, it really did look as if the last lap had started. The outriggers were cutting the water at an estimated eight knots, fast enough to take us nearly 200 miles a day, so it was no fantasy to conjecture on the possibilities of seeing India within the week.

By midnight when Lissy and I handed the watch to Lofty and Ernie, the wind had even freshened and the might of a full mainsail was straining at the bending and creaking mast. The usual instructions were passed with the changeover as Lissy said "I should say we're doing nine knots now." When Lofty cast an expert eye at the trail of foam he whistled, "You're not kidding, cobber!"

"The wind's swinging to the east," Lissy informed us, and Lofty's eyes shot to the mainsail, he turned his back on the wind to feel the exact point of blow. "Oh, she's right enough," he decided and with Lofty as the acknowledged expert they left it at that.

There was not enough room for comfort down below so we clambered forward and stretched out under the mainsail with our heads pillowed against the mast.

I wasn't a bit happy. "I wish we'd dropped the mainsail," I grumbled but Lissy dismissed this fear.

"She'll be OK as long as they head west," he said, but I was still dubious.

"Ernie's got a set against the Doldrums and he'll try to edge north to get out of them."

"Oh, shut up, you're an old woman," my friend chided and we settled down again but sleep evaded me.

We'd all been taking chances with the ship trying to edge to the north as well as west. The few days we'd been becalmed had frightened us and we had for long stretches sailed much too close to the wind for safety, especially as the wind was veering from south to east.

As we lay in our sheltered position we saw, rather than felt, that the wind was still building up and, worst still, was becoming gusty. Every

In the uniform of the East Surrey Regiment.

I

Denis with two Chinese soldiers in Shanghai before hostilities.

The author in tropical uniform, 1939.

The author (seated) in Shanghai, 1939.

*The grave of
Major H. Kilgour,
who died on
30th August 1942,
before the
wooden cross
was replaced
by a stone memorial.*

*(below)
Major Kilgour's
permanent memorial.*

(above)
The author (third
from right) with
fellow soldiers,
photographed in
Chittagong, and
still showing the
physical effects of
captivity.

(left)
Denis Gavin in
1946, taken at the
Queen Alexandra
Military Hospital
near St. Albans,
after three months
in an Indian
hospital.

The photograph Tiny sent to the author, taken in 1946.

Lofty in 1945.

VI

The author's diagnosis on return to England.

6142886 Sgt. GAVIN, D.   Age 29

Diagnosis: Nutritional Retrebulbar Neuritis.

History: Was taken prisoner on 19th May, 1942 in Southern
Burma.   (Had been in Singapore when it fell on 15th February,
1942 - escaped to Sumatra in a rowing boat; thence to Southern
Burma in a sailing boat.)
          Captured at Mulmein, Southern Burma - was there for
one month: then moved to Rangoon where he was till the time
of his escape on 28th April, 1945.
          He reached British lines on 12th May, 1945.
          While at Mulmein (May 1942) diet comprised 2 meals
per day consisting almost wholly of rice (unpolished), with a
little bean soup.
          While at Rangoon they had plenty to eat but for the
first twelve months the food consisted largely of rice, with a
small amount of vegetables (potatoes, marrow, cucumber, pumpkin),
and small quantities of meat.   They also had a little sugar.
          Thereafter the rations were increased; they received
more meat and bran (rice sweepings), was added to the diet.
          On 14th July, 1943 (his Birthday!) while reading a
book he suddenly found that he couldn't see to read it - and he
didn't finish the book! For three months prior to this he had
been suffering from pain and numbness of legs and had experienced
some difficulty in balancing himself: his legs did not swell.
          He was in a Hospital (of sorts!) being treated for
Diarrhoea but he received no specific treatment for his other
symptoms.   The pain, numbness etc. improved slightly with the
addition of rice sweepings tothe diet but his sight did not
improve.
          He had been wearing glasses prior to capture but these
were taken from him by theJapanese.
          Was in Hospital in India June and July 1945 - thence
evacuated to U.K. by air.
          Admitted to Shenley Military Hospital on 18th July, 1945.

Examination Pupils equal circular and concentric:
react directly and consensualy to light.

          VAR < 6/60 + o   -3.25   6/60)
                              0   )
          VAL < 6/60 + o   -3.5   6/60)   J 12
          Fields:- N.A.D.   +o, S.

          Scotometry:- No Scotoma demonstrable as
                patient could not "fix".

          Fundi:- Generalized pallor of discs.

The author at work on this book, 1988.

Denis Gavin taken during an interview in New Zealand in 1988.

fresh gust set a strain on the mast and sail, which even we landsmen could see was dangerous. Sleep was out of the question as every time gusts of wind hit the ship we were startled by the creaking of the mast in our ears and sat up, certain that the others must have taken alarm.

Lofty however, was resting quietly at the tiller, singing very softly to himself without any apparent concern. Confident of Lofty's seamanship we nestled down again. Soon afterwards he did swing more to the west and the creakings and groaning of the straining mast eased to a soothing peace.

One o'clock saw us still awake and listening to Lofty handing over the tiller to his fellow-watcher, Ernie, and soon afterwards we saw the stars swing round and knew that Ernie had veered to the north again.

The gusts had noticeably increased in strength and tempo, and even Lissy took fright.

"Hey, Lofty!" he cupped his hands to carry the call to the watch men only.

"Hey! Lofty! what about the mainsail now?"

"We must be doing ten knots," chortled the Australian, and Lissy snapped back, "You're doing twelve at least and that blasted mast'll be down in a minute."

"Aw! She's all right," Ernie said confidently, "India! here we come."

"We'll get there better on the jib." I warned and was shouted down.

"Get away with you. We'd only do about four on the jib."

"Anyway," Lofty said, "we'll watch our backs and with you two up there we can get the sail down in a jiffy."

Lissy was no more happy than I now, but accepted the watchman's right of command, and lay down again.

We must have dozed, despite our foreboding, when suddenly my eyes opened to full wakefulness with that sixth sense of impending disaster. Simultaneously, at my side, Lissy bounded to his feet and at the same time Lofty's voice boomed out, "All hands on deck!" and, following this, came his frantic yell, "Mainsail down! Get the mainsail down!"

As he spoke a gust howled and whipped suddenly from the east and the sea began to boil as everyone below tried to tumble out.

There was a whip-like crack as the mainsail snapped into the strain and set the boat cleaving forward with a plunge that buried her nose in the foam.

Lissy, ever quicker than I, even within seconds of waking had the mainsail hoist in his hand as Lofty's voice boomed again, "Mainsail! Mainsail down!" and his last despairing shriek, "Mainsail down!"

Even as Lissy clawed at the rope in the dark another gust hit them, this time from further north and well behind the canvas.

With a thunderclap of noise the sail hurtled round to port, the heavy boom just missing Lofty's head, and crashed into the wire stays supporting the mast.

There was a horrible tearing, wrenching sound from the already outraged mast, and in a moment Lissy and I up forward were enveloped in a chaos of broken spars and ropes.

Crashing down like a stricken forest giant the mast took everything before it. In a moment the boat was filling with water, with the mast still clinging to its broken stays, lying on the port outrigger and pulling it down so that the starboard outrigger hung incongruously pointing to the sky.

In my panic my only coherent thought was a frantic desire to pull the mast away from the side and right the balance of the boat. Madly I clawed with torn fingers at the broken end of the mast in a hopeless endeavour to move it.

I heard Tiny's voice beside me, cool, calm and sane. "Good work, Gabby. Hold it there."

Utterly exhausted I hung on grimly with all my weight on the mast. I sensed that Bosun was at my side, chopping and hacking at the retaining wires in a mad race to free the boat from the dragging weight.

With the steerage way gone the boat swung round broadside to the squall and to the running seas. Wave after wave thumped at us, every smack pounding the hull with great hammerlike blows. The sea boiled and I closed my eyes to shut out the horror of it. The wind howled into a fury and tore at the shredded and soaked canvas, while the rain slashed down in torrents with a force I had never believed possible.

Doc was in place beside Bosun, straining to tear the wreckage clear. Tiny leaped to the top of the boat-roof, and braced against the storm which howled and plucked at him. Even in that moment I sensed that the skipper was calm. Not one of us had any other idea than to be clear of the weight that was dragging us to destruction, except for Tiny.

"Bosun!" he screamed. "Bosun!" and then, "Out there!" he yelled. "With the chopper!" pointing to the devil's cauldron about the port outrigger, awash under the weight of the mast.

No other living man but Tiny could have seen what he saw in that moment, and nobody anywhere in this world could have obeyed such an order except Bosun. I certainly could not have faced that sea. But Bosun supported Tiny and in a moment he was far out on the outrigger, water sloshing above his knees,as he chopped at the wreckage.

Just hanging on with both hands would have been a miracle, but Bosun, calm and methodical, not only hung on but chopped and pulled with cool deliberation as the skipper's voice shouted directions.

The frail-looking Doc, without orders, followed Bosun into the thresh. There they worked, visible one moment and the next buried in foam. Even now we all thought that Tiny was merely clearing the wreckage until fresh orders came bellowing out.

"Dicky! Grab that rope! Hold it! Right!"

"Ernie! Titch! Over here! Pull in!"

"That one, Bosun!"

"Tom! take that from Bosun. Right! Now altogether! Heave! Heave you bastards! Pull!"

Tiny had the whole gang at his disposal, and yet with Bosun and Doc the three of them alone would have saved the mast. But still with many hands and Tiny's screaming insistence, we all pulled and, suddenly and unbelievably, the outrigger was free, the mast was in, and the *Venture* was once more riding on an even keel.

Almost before it was aboard Tiny was off his perch and had a lashing securely about it, still yelling.

"Lofty! On the tiller!"

"Ernie! Dicky! Titch! Tom! Get the oars out!"

Not waiting to see the rush to carry out his orders he turned to the next item.

"Down below Lissy and bale her out!" and then "Gabby?"

I turned with Tiny to face the bowsprit with the jibsail flapping and tearing at its hoist, stretching, it seemed, far, far out of reach.

"Out there!" Tiny pointed now to the starboard outrigger and in a moment he was climbing to the tip of the bowsprit, his great weight bending it over.

At the third attempt his clutching hand caught the flying jib, and slowly, with all his strength pitted again the wind, he hauled it in and eased himself back to the deck.

I was waiting sitting astride the outrigger. Tiny cast a rope to me, and from there on it was easy. With the jib and bowsprit saved and secure, Tiny turned to me.

"Help Lissy, Gabby," he said. On this final task I thankfully sped below.

The sight below was almost worse than that on deck. For a moment I paused in horror. Poor old Snowy, too weak to get right out, had only just managed to keep his head clear of water until Lissy had arrived to pull him to a shelf to lie down, moaning piteously.

We started to bale out with a kerosene tin in each hand, but as fast we got it out, it seemed to fill again.

As suddenly as it had come, the wind dropped, and with it passed the rain, and we paused for breath and to look about us. The attap roof was torn and shredded, the dark racing clouds showed through the rents. The boat looked gaunt and naked without its towering mast and was indeed a wretched hulk, barely afloat. The hold was still half-full of water and every article of food and clothing was floating about in the swishing waters. Underneath, and out of sight in the dark water, all the water containers mixed their freshness with the salt sea, and the tinned foods rattled and clinked with them.

India! What price India now?

CHAPTER SIXTEEN

CRAB ISLAND CASTAWAYS

On 28 March dawn broke, dull and threatening but quiet, and found only Tiny, Lissy and me on deck. We were tired, and despite our plight could have dropped to sleep in a moment. The others slept, except Doc and Bosun who sat by Snowy's side below decks. The course was set due east, straight towards land, and three pairs of eyes were strained towards the horizon.

No sun appeared in the sullen sky, but right in the place of the sunrise, by the grace of God, was a small dark smudge. The kind of smudge that we all recognised, and with scarcely more than a glimpse of it Tiny's head turned and he bellowed, "All hands on deck!"

There was need only for one shout and every man was out ready to meet a new peril, but seeing instead Tiny's pointing finger.

"Land ahead!" And then, "Get the oars out."

The boat was cumbersome and heavy under the oars and the oarsmen were not at their heartiest. But never before was a craft pulled with such zest as was the *Venture* to that one speck in an otherwise boundless sea. Slowly, the island drew closer and closer until at last we could distinguish the ring of white breakers on craggy rocks.

We rowed almost in a circle round the small wooded rock before, we saw the break, a thirty yard strip of sand that, though it looked inviting, might be more treacherous. As we gazed, the first inkling we had of Tiny's intention was the splash as he dived overboard, and then he was away, churning with powerful strokes towards the beach.

In ten minutes, his survey completed, he was back with the good news.

"We'll be all right in there, and as we might be here for some time we'll beach the boat, so in we go."

We cut into the beach and no sooner had she grounded than Tiny was ashore with a long line with which he took a half turn on a coconut palm and we were set.

The first job was to get Snowy ashore and comfortable in blankets

89

on the sand. Then to secure the boat as each wave of the rising tide lifted her up, and with each lift, we took in slack rope until she was really high and dry.

Having done this, Tiny set most of us about the task of getting the stores ashore. He told Ernie to prepare a meal and he himself went off with Lissy on a reconnaisance of the island. He returned before the meal was ready with good news and an armful of freshly cured fish. They had found two fishermen on the island smoking their catch, and had gathered that fishermen came here regularly for that purpose if they found themselves far from home with a full catch. There were also two large wooden huts on the island, deserted and derelict, but nevertheless habitable, where we would live while on the island.

We ate the fish ravenously, despite the fact we had just eaten our other meal and then went about the task of transporting everything to our new quarters. The sun had come out and everything looked better.

Tiny made his plans that night and started us all on our tasks next morning, and we didn't let up for the next eight days. We were on the island for ten days altogether, and thoroughly enjoyed every minute of it. Tiny allowed us to have three meals per day instead of two, as he said that while our meagre ration was enough for the sedentary life on board ship, we would soon use all our reserves of strength if we tried to work on the same ration now, and would be beaten before we started again. The tasks in question should not have been difficult under normal conditions, but here we had to improvise the tools for most jobs.

First the broken stump of the mast had to be removed from its socket and the lower end of the mast had to be chopped with only a penknife and a Malayan parang, which required endless patience. Then a hoist had to be made out of felled trees to raise the mast into position again, and these trees had to be felled with the parang alone which was a monotonous job. The sail was in shreds and had to be sewn with only two ordinary sewing needles, and every stitch had to be put in with the utmost care to save the needles. Besides this mending, the sail also had to be reefed to fit the new shortened mast.

The soaked food had to be saved and, in the case of the rice, had to be spread to dry and every single grain inspected for mildew before it was passed as salvage. The unsalvageable stuff was eaten at the next meal.

Despite the irksome and monotonous tasks life in Crab Island was very pleasant, and we gew fit and healthy, if hungry, even under the increased ration. There was plenty of leisure, and the sea was ideal for swimming and frolicking. Lissy and I spent hours practising the tricky and terribly exhausting art of palm climbing, although with the profusion of coconuts always littering the ground it was never necessary to climb anything. These nuts were to be found in every stage from the freshly fallen nut to the one containing the green shoot, reaching skywards from the still unrooted nut. We soon found that the fruits showing tiny sprouts contained inside a most delicious bulb, which had fed on the milk and flesh inside so that it had the full coconut taste and yet was fibrous and soft to eat.

Doc told of an interesting theory concerning the evolution and growth of coral islands in the Pacific which we found was accurate. At sea we had seen many coconuts floating and drifting at various times, nuts which had fallen from some beach palm and rolled seawards. Some of these nuts drifted perhaps for months until they rotted, but occasionally one might be snagged on one of these shelves or reefs of coral which are found here and there just below the surface. Miles from any other land the nut would send its roots down to the coral and its trunk rearing skywards. Later we actually did see a palm growing apparently in mid-ocean.

Quite often the single tree lived and died, and all its fruit was carried away by the tides, but occasionally about the base of some lone sentinel its offspring also sprouted. A catchment was formed for any kind of debris brought by the sea so that over the ages the sea was displaced at the base of the growing family to form a foothold for grass, weed or flower seeds contained in the dottle of resting birds.

The island on which we now lived could easily have followed this pattern, only halting its expansion when the coral shelf ended in its precipitous drop into the deep water. It was certainly well-separated from any possible parent island and it was puzzling to visualise it as a populated and cultivated copra plantation. There were still piles of rotting husks close to the two huts, but most amazing was a rusted and derelict lorry. The rubber and cloth parts had long ago been eaten by crabs and the metal was encrusted with rust, but the petrol tank was still intact and Tiny spent almost two days of his spare time removing and cleaning this.

Work on the lorry caused the discovery of a bricked-in well where it stood which astonishingly contained a never diminishing source of sweet fresh water. This, so far, was almost the most delightful feature of Crab Island, although drinking water in the area of the 'Sumatra' (cyclone winds) with their torrential downpours was never likely to cause any problem.

Alongside the lorry and well, a cobbled road had once run down to the sea. It ended at the long stone pier, which was still intact and still firm although the top, like the road, was overgrown with grass, weeds, flowers and cone palms.

The edge of the water along the beach also showed a tantalising spectacle of teeming whitebait, which seemed so numerous that one ought to be able to scoop handfuls of them. But only one solitary fish of one and a half inches was ever caught and then by Doc, with luck only. He enlisted the aid of Bosun, Lissy, Lofty, Titch and myself to catch thousands of whitebait in a trap. To fix this we ripped three planks each twenty-five feet long from the base of the larger hut. The three planks were to form the three sides of a trap with the beach as the fourth side. Starting from widely separated points, three pairs of castaways gradually closed up the distance separating them by cautious advance until most satisfyingly and excitingly the trap was closed, and the swarming silvery fish were leaping about inside.

This was done several times and each time the trap was edged shorewards to drive the fish into the beach. But each time the whitebait poured back to freedom over the top, between the edges, and even under the planks where the shifting sands trickled away with the receding waves. Each time the catch dwindled and dwindled until not one solitary fish was left in the trap.

Finally, Doc in despair got his trap closed and pegged the sides in position before wading inside to attempt to scoop up the fish in his enamel plate. When the whitebait slipped and slithered out of harm's way he lost his usual serenity and patience.

"Blast the dratted things," (or something similar) he shouted, throwing down his plate in rage. The plate splashed as its flat bottom hit the water, a fish jumped, landing on the plate, and for a split second Doc goggled before he grabbed it, and triumphantly bore it ashore. He ceremoniously cooked and ate it for supper.

Not the least interesting feature was the teeming crab life on the island. In fact, we called this 'Crab Island'. These crabs were not apparent at first as they fell still at the sound of any movement. It was only when we sat on the beach on the first night watching the sea that we heard the strange rustling noise of the crabs and, at the same time, saw that the whole of the beach, which we had until now thought was covered with pebbles and dead shells, was one mass of movement, and that the shells and pebbles were hermit crabs. Fascinated, and a little horrified, we watched them, and watched the way in which every movement stopped at our least sound and commenced again when we were silent. Doc said that they should make an extra item on the menu, but we told him that he would have to try them first, which he did.

Later, when darkness had fallen and we were sitting round the blazing fire, blazing because once more we were at the mercy of the mosquitoes, Doc put his plan into operation. He had a tin of water boiling on the fire and another empty tin by his side. The crabs, as we found later, were greater scavengers than the ants and when Doc killed a few crabs and threw them down beside him, there was soon a vast movement by the crabs to the feast. Then all Doc had to do was to sit and wait for the bigger fellows and scoop them up for his tin. When he had this full he emptied the whole lot into the boiling water which brought them from the protecting shell, and, with a pin, he started his feast. This was a long and laborious process but we soon all followed Doc's example. Later we caught larger and more satisfying crabs, but, even with these, we only dared eat the flesh of the claws. When we found the ever battling crabs were not greatly inconvenienced by the loss of one claw in battle with their kin, we stopped killing them and instead pulled off one claw and let the crab go free.

We saw before we left the island that some of these had started to grow a new claw. In our moments of leisure we also tried to catch fish from the stone pier, but, although our mouths watered at the sight of some of the monsters which abounded there, we had no luck except for a leather-jacket which Bosun caught by using a stripped bamboo fibre and a bent pin with a crab for bait. He tried every way of making this edible, and was fully determined to eat it, whatever the cost, but he had to give up in the end, so that the leather-jacket, the curse of all anglers, still won the day.

The only man not working on Crab Island was Snowy, and for a time it looked as if he was not going to improve. He hadn't the strength even to sit up at first, and Bosun and Doc spent hours working on him. Bosun with his talk of home and encouraging conjecture of the short time it would take us to get to friends and Doc with his amazing bag of tricks which contained tempting bars of chocolate and goodness knows what else. Amazingly, in two days Snowy was on his feet and as soon as he reached this stage Bosun starting carrying him to the beach in the sun. Snowy took to the water, gradually at first but gaining in strength until by the eighth day he was eating all of his food and looking for jobs to do. In fact he did help with the last job of all.

This last job was to get the *Venture* afloat and really did develop into a heart and back-breaking task. She was high and dry since her first beaching on a storm tide and had not been touched by a wave since then, so we had to undermine by digging away the sand underneath and heave her towards the sea. We couldn't dig too deep or we'd have had her below the level of the beach by the time we'd made the number of shifts necessary. The first wave would probably have caved in the sides of the channel to embed the hull firmly in the sand.

Even when she did at last float, we were aghast at the sight of the water pouring into the boat where the sun-baked boards had dried and warped. Baling out was a full time job for two men at first, and it seemed as if the slowly soaking and swelling beams would never close the gaps.

When the inflow had abated somewhat, Lofty, Tiny, Lissy and I took

93

the *Venture* for a cruise round Crab Island. Lofty pronounced her 'sweet' and glided easily in to tie up at the wharf this time.

Once more, stores were loaded on board, lashings made secure, and we turned 'homeward' for our last supper and our last night ashore. Tiny had a nightmare on this night and woke up screaming, "All hands on deck!"

We sat up, wide awake and startled, and in sitting up shook off our bodies the swarms of hermit crabs which nightly invaded the hut.

Tiny was whimpering and shaking, even now not fully awake, and it really shook us to see the Skipper like this, especially as he could not be consoled for some minutes. Doc put his arm about Tiny's shoulder to comfort him, and this in itself, the tiny Doc with his arm protectingly about the giant Tiny produced a frightening incongruity.

Sleep was banished from everyone's mind and we lay for some time listening to the howling of the wind which had crept up during the night. The breakers could be heard thundering against the stone pier and I, at least, huddled under my covering very glad indeed to be ashore. But not Snowy.

"I'm going for a walk," he said, and away he went.

We were just beginning to doze again when, for the second time that night, we heard the cry.

"All hands on deck!"

Heard ashore, the cry sounded unreal but there was nothing unreal about the urgency in Snowy's voice.

My hair prickled as the wind carried the sound of Snowy running through the grass, and as we met him outside, could sense the fear in his voice.

"The boat!" he gasped, "It's broken loose! The rocks are smashing it!"

We sped to the wharf and heard the dreadful thuds as the breakers smashed the boat against the pier, and, for a moment, it looked as if we would really be castaways.

The *Venture*, fortunately, still had one rope fast, but it took nearly twenty minutes to get her secure. In this time the poor boat took crack after crack against the pier, until it seemed she must splinter at any moment.

Tiny put Lissy and me aboard as a safety watch for the balance of the night but the storm died and we spent a peaceful night, away from the mosquitoes and land crabs.

CHAPTER SEVENTEEN
CORAL WONDERLAND

Next morning we weighed anchor, and spread full sail. Crab Island dropped rapidly astern. Having now developed a horror of the sea, I watched the receding island with much misgiving. I tried hard to convince the others of the ease and desirability of living out the war on Crab Island with a few preliminary trips to the islands for supplies. But no one else had any interest in the proposal. They did at least agree that the boat was no longer seaworthy enough to tackle the 1,400 miles of open sea in the west. Tiny, Doc and Dicky plotted a new course of island hopping which would keep us within limping distance of land until we left Sumatran waters behind us to face a 500 mile stretch to the Nicobars. Then another big jump to the Andamans, and the final home stretch which would take us to the coast of Burma from where we could creep around the Bay of Bengal to India and Allies (we hoped). Anyway, we had to call in somewhere to replenish the much depleted stock of food.

Dicky, our navigator, and Doc pored over our maps and eventually pointed our estimated position, and from this calculated a course to get us back among the islands once more. Dicky's navigation was a simple matter but amazingly accurate as we were to find out when next we hit land.

He used the North Star as the infallible indication of our progress north. This was simple as he pointed out. The Pole Star was just on the horizon at the equator and exactly overhead at the North Pole which meant that there were ninety degrees to traverse from the equator to the pole. All Dicky had to do was divide the distance, 6,000 miles, by ninety. We got the answer, that each degree that the star rose in the sky meant we had travelled about sixty-six miles north. Measurement of degrees was done with our hands. Any British serviceman knows the formulae.

Longitude calculations were not quite so accurate as we were dependent on Tombola's watch, but this was a good one and we looked after it. Dicky had also acquired the sunset and sunrise times for weeks ahead before he left Sumatra. Every night and morning we all made a ritual, weather permitting, of counting the seconds as the rim slid into the sea at night or first peeped over the horizon in the morning. Dicky had worked out that a discrepancy of, say, four minutes in the observed time

95

as against the time it would set in Padang meant there was a difference of one degree latitude with that of Padang. It just about equalled seventy miles, so we could get our longitude from the north star and our latitude from sunset time.

By the evening of the second day after leaving Crab Island it was calculated that we were south east of the next island in the chain. This was Batu Island, and, according to the map, was really two islands with a very narrow strip of water between them. There was a small town straddling this gap and we thought it might be possible to get some further provisions here. Doc and Dicky set a course which they said would bring us right into the centre of Batu Island, although no one seriously thought that there would be any danger of accuracy in their estimate. When night fell and there was no land in sight, we gave our navigators a sticky time.

Lissy and I were on watch at midnight when Lofty and Ernie came to relieve us.

We gave them our course which was supposed to take us right through the channel, and left them to carry on with it. We did not feel a bit sleepy, and went for'ard to lie under the mast and talk in whispered confidences, and to listen to the everlasting murmuring of the ocean. We had just about dropped off by 2 a.m. when we suddenly heard Lofty's excited whisper. "Hey, Ernie, can you see anything?"

In an instant we were wide awake and alert, but could neither see nor hear anything amiss, although once more the sense of danger was there. We sat up and could see Lofty, upright and listening, at the helm in the stern. He had been lying down and only idly swinging the tiller to keep his star above the mast. Lying on his back thus he had not been watching where we were going, which really did not matter as we thought we were miles out to sea, and, even if we did get close to land, we would be able to hear the breakers long before we approached too close.

There was no sound yet, but we nevertheless remained alert, peering about us. It was an idle remark of mine about the sea which in the starlight looked beautiful and green that affected Lofty.

At the mention of the word green, Lofty cast a startled glance overboard, and in a moment his voice was bellowing, "All hands on deck! All hands on deck!" and out they came, tumbling and stumbling to obey this only too well-known call.

The danger was not apparent to the sleepy crew, at once, so Tom said, "What's up Lofty?"

Lofty pointed, "We're in shallows."

Even now our course of action was not clear as we did not seem to be in any immediate danger, and all we could do was watch the sea. There was still no sound of breakers ahead, but as we peered overboard there was a sudden dark shadow under the boat, and then it was gone.

"Stand by to go about!" Like clockwork, we sprang to our stations. We were racing back the other way almost before a count of ten, but even in that time the dark shadows were racing below us. Lissy and I had our station sitting astride the starboard outrigger when going about, and we sat there dangling our feet in the water, watching the black rocks. Then suddenly we looked up, startled again. There was no mistaking now the far-off noise of breakers, but the sound was ahead of us.

We looked at Tiny, and even as we waited the sound became louder and menacing. Tiny didn't hesitate. "Lower the mainsail," he bawled, and down it tumbled, but still the boat sped forward, although at a reduced speed on the jibsail and we peered anxiously overboard. The black rocks were everywhere and we shuddered to think that we must already have passed over this ground. We rapidly hauled down the jib and were soon idly drifting in the dead calm of the green water. The green became lighter, indicating yet more dangerous shallows, and everywhere we looked the black rocks on the bed of the ocean were visible.

We prodded and probed in all directions, moving slowly forward on the oars, in a desperate endeavour to be clear of those encircling rocks. But at every move we only seemed to get deeper into danger, and finally had to use long bamboo poles, punt fashion, to keep the jagged coral from tearing out the bottom of the boat. Even when we decided to anchor until morning, the boat dragged the anchor and we went drifting into danger again.

Dawn finally ended a night of terror, but even before it broke in full splendour, the half-light had allayed our fears somewhat in showing us that the bottom of the ocean, apparently so near, was so only by the illusion caused by the crystalline water. Rocks that looked as if they would scrape the boat were out of reach, even with a thirty foot bamboo pole, and those which were apparently on the surface were only just within reach.

Full light disclosed an amazing sight. We were completely shut off from the open sea by an almost unbroken circle of land, and try as we might, we couldn't see even a hidden outlet. It needed the map to solve the mystery and show us that we must have sailed dead on our estimated course and were now in the channel between the two halves of Batu Island. We must have come into the channel with the tide high, and thus cleared the perimeter which now, at low tide, was above the sea.

We were trapped until the next high tide but our prison was paradise, even breakfast was an interruption. Below us was a coral wonderland of colour and landscape more beautiful than anything that could be created by any artist. A fairyland of colour and panorama in crystal clear water which put everything almost within reach, and in this glory was life, serene, unhurried and equally glorious. Small fish, and big fish of every colour and every shape imaginable. Almost every new vision was one which brought an excited call from the viewer, who had to share his delight with the others.

We lay on our stomachs just gazing entranced, and it was Tiny who tore us away at last. We were reluctant, but the tide was up and the way ahead was clear, so we crept slowly through the blue channel of deep water, flanked by the green shallows, to the open sea.

CHAPTER EIGHTEEN
SURF! SURF! RAGING SURF!

When we were safe through the channel and in the open sea once more, a sigh of relief went round. With the wind fresh from the south, the mainsail rigged, full, straining and taut, we slid through the water at an exhilarating speed.

For two days we moved steadily to the north, past the island of Nias with its unbroken perimeter of menacing surf. No chance of landing there so on we sped to the next and last chance of landing, the final island of the chain, Simenloe. Here, Tiny decided we must land.

Snowy was sick and feverish again and was gradually giving way to a lethargy from which even the bullying of Bosun and the cajolery of Doc couldn't rouse him. It was decided that he simply must have a few days ashore with good food and possibly medicine.

Besides this the food had dwindled alarmingly. Simenloe, with its main town of Siramboe would be the last island before the Nicobars which would probably be occupied by the Japanese, as might the Andamans. But we had to put in somehow.

And all of us longed for the feel of firm ground under foot, we wanted to be able to stand up without holding on to something and walk about without feeling our way from one hand-hold to another. This, we could never do in the *Venture*. She was such a cockleshell of a boat, so light and buoyant that even in the calmest of seas she bobbed, rolled and tilted, tossed freely by every swell.

The smokers passionately desired tobacco, and more than anything else we all wanted, and needed, a good satisfying meal. It was almost a month since we'd left Padang and, except for the few days of plenty in Siberoet, we'd been rationed for the whole of that period. Since leaving Crab Island we'd switched to the original meagre ration of rice and tinned food washed down by half a cup of tea (no rain had fallen since Crab Island) and this left a gnawing hunger with us during all waking moments.

Tiny still allowed one coconut to be opened each mid-day and this nutting procedure became a ritual with eyes constantly on the sun, hungrily waiting for the time to start.

99

The milk went to each of us in turn. The husks were fashioned into drinking mugs and the flesh was meticulously divided into ten equal parts with the skipper even scraping shreds off one piece to add to another before he was satisfied.

Coconut shreds however could not give us what we needed. Food, lots of food was the only thing that would satisfy us. It took three of us at this stage to raise the mainsail, Tiny, Bosun or myself could do it alone when we left Sumatra, when it was a bigger sail than we had now.

Lofty was not in good shape, the shrapnel wound in his side was still troublesome. Dicky scarcely had enough energy to raise his head. Lissy was getting fevers, and all of us except Tom and Bosun were at our lowest.

So, Siremboe, here we come.

When we did find the town we landed on a mystery which we never did solve and we escaped from it by the skin of our teeth. Whatever it was, we were lucky.

We sighted the town in late afternoon, spread along a sandy beach but protected from the sea by the most gigantic racing surf any of us had seen. Even the Australians swore that nothing could come in, or out of, that beach. But it was dotted with boats and they hadn't flown there.

We anchored in the lee of a small island in the bay for the night and Doc, Tiny and Bosun went ashore in the canoe next morning, not through the surf. They took weapons with them but it looked as if everything would be all right as Tiny sent two fishermen out to bring us in. They had a note from the skipper and we lost no time in going to raise the anchor. The anchor is probably still there as we never did get it up. We tried everything to jerk it free, even sailing the boat over it but rope and anchor held and we only jarred every beam and bond in the *Venture*.

I went overboard to try to get down to it, hauling myself hand over hand down the rope but I nearly drowned in the process. In the end we had to cut loose. The fishermen headed us straight towards the surf, which at close quarters was frightening. We hurtled to the beach and they set us down, light as a feather, almost at water's edge and we jumped ashore to where the others were waiting.

Something was wrong there. The village was obviously hostile and suspicious or at least wary. The shops were shut and the village headman swore that there was scarcely any food to spare. He very grudgingly agreed that we might buy a meal from one of the eating shops but it was ages before the proprietor would open his door to our knocking. Tiny and Doc deputised me to get food for them and went off after the headman again.

This was the beginning of the mystery. They heard a telephone ringing in his house. He denied such a happening though Tiny heard him answer it. The skipper got tough at this point, drew his revolver and scared the wits out of the man. Then the man said it was an English master who had telephoned so Tiny said he'd shoot the headman if he didn't get him back on the phone.

Doc took the phone and introduced himself when the call was made but could get nothing out of the man at the other end except a promise of supplies. Tomorrow that was.

This wasn't so bad until we were waylaid surreptitiously by an old native who hissed at us from the shadow of a hut to attract our attention. "German! German coming," he said, then shuffled off.

"German!" said the startled Tiny.

"He must mean Japanese," and then he realised, "The telephone." He sped back to the headman's hut, caught him in the middle of a voluble conversation and unceremoniously pulled him back and took over.

It was the mystery voice again but Tiny got the assurance that everything was all right. Supplies would come from the headman, he was sorry he couldn't come to the village himself, but he was at the other end of the island.

Tiny let him go, then pulled the telephone out of the wall and once more we saw our skipper in action.

"We're going out on the tide," he said and he drove those of us who were not sick into feverish action. He made Bosun and me change all our fresh water. We were the strongest two available and the task needed strength and stamina as we had to carry the water in four-gallon tins from the village well.

Tiny and Doc went scrounging for food, and in the process Tiny broke into a village store and took its whole stock of tinned food; eighty-two tins of herrings mainly. He also got a small sack of rice, and meanwhile Titch and Ernie had stocked the boat with fresh fruit, mainly bananas and mangoes, plus coconuts.

Titch and Ernie acquired an anchor which Tiny buried in the sand at the edge of low tide. He tied the other end of the anchor rope to the capstan on the poop deck, planning to use the anchor as a winch to give us a pull through the surf when the tide came.

The final jobs were for Lissy and me to salvage our canoe from the point a mile away where Tiny had left it and then to get the invalids aboard. Snowy was feeling better but Lofty still had his fever. We kept our eyes on the only road which could lead the enemy to the village. We had decided there must be a Japanese force marching from the other end

101

of the island, and it would be touch and go whether the tide or a hail of bullets would reach our boat first. The villagers were out of sight except for the headman and two armed police.

The tide was close to the boat when Lissy and I got back with the canoe, so we carried Snowy aboard once more. Lofty walked aboard himself and took his place at the tiller. He knew, as we were all to know soon, that in the approaching battle we were going to need every possible helping hand.

When the first waves started to swish around us, Tiny put everyone except Dicky and Lofty on duty by the outrigger arms, and there we waited. Dicky stood by the anchor rope ready to take in every inch as we gained ground, and at Tiny's shout a few moments later, when he felt the boat lift to the waves, we all strained to the task. There was a movement forward and for a few moments we got her riding free, only to settle down again as the receding water left us. In this moment Dicky won a few inches, and with the next wave we were surging forward and were almost riding free. Again and again we strove and heaved, and again and again we gained only inches at a time, but nevertheless, always forward, until at last she was riding steady and we had to get aboard as each wave now lifted us off our feet and left us hanging on the outrigger arms.

The beach had gradually filled with natives watching our efforts, but they were silent and we missed the cheers we'd had at Siberoet.

Tiny got us at the rope now, but the cable was braced and taut against the waves and we could win nothing from the sea. Then an incoming wave turned us and we were left with our beam facing the battering sea.

The waves were bigger now and left us with no chance of getting her nose round to face their onslaught. Backwards and forwards we were swung, like a huge pendulum, from one wave to another, and each wave hit us harder than the last.

"Oars," Tiny roared, and we sprang to obey. We got the nose facing the waves squarely and rode them better, and as we slid into the trough, Dicky gained inches on the rope before the next wave pulled it taut and firm again. We pulled ourselves to the spot where the anchor was buried but still the worst of the surf was before us. No manpower could take us through that, and we knew that as soon as our anchor was raised we would be flung right back to the beach.

Still Tiny shouted, "Row! Row!"

We couldn't get the anchor free anyway, and then suddenly the capstan broke, and like a cork we were picked up and tossed back onto the unfriendly beach.

We picked ourselves up from the various corners where we had been thrown, but even then Tiny had gone into action and was battling with the sea in a mad effort to get our anchor rope back. Bosun followed him and he reached the boat first with the end of the cable in his hand. The whole job had now to be done over again, but a miracle had happened. The swarm of silent villagers had taken over, and with scores lifting where there had only been twos, the task was lighter. Whether the villagers had opened their hearts to what they considered to be a gallant fight we didn't know. Maybe they were still anxious to get rid of us, and were afraid that we would not make it alone but this was belied by their smiling faces.

We still took a pounding, but got to the anchor again in half our previous time, but again were faced with the task of getting it free. Tiny made a decision with his usual speed, and with us all pulling our hearts out at the oars, he chopped the rope free and again started his screams.

"Row! row!" and again "Row! row! Row you bastards, row!" We were all right for a few moments and held our own against the lashing surf with the oars pulling deeply into the water. Then suddenly we were on the crest of a wave and the oars were thrashing the air, and in that helpless moment the next wave hit us and broke over us, and once more we were flying bruised and battered in the scuppers, and the boat was lying again on the beach.

Still there was no respite from Tiny as he screamed again, and once more the awful power of his voice drove us to our posts. The natives were now a cheering, helping mob, and yet again we were riding the waves and pulling desperately to move forward. Again we made it.

Tiny shrieked. "Get the jib out, Bosun," and in the same tone he yelled at me, "Come on, Gabby - pull. Pull!"

The jib sail was stuck and frantically Tiny called, "Get the bloody thing loose, you stupid bastards!" and once more Bosun hacked and tore, and then in a moment we were away as a puff of wind from the shore filled the sail and sent us riding forward up and down, up and down, but riding now like a bird - and FREE!

We paused for breath only when we were clear enough of the menacing surf to look back at it as at something far away. Doc went scuttling down to Snowy who was moaning and helpless in a boat half full of water, and we looked at our skipper.

"You're a bastard, Tiny," I said coldly and dispassionately, and Bosun added to this with, "Captain Bligh would learn from you, Tiny." But Tiny only grinned. He knew that we had seen him prove once more that he was the skipper, and he also knew that we were a worthy crew, so that when I said to him later, "I'll follow you anywhere, Tiny," he knew that I meant it, and the words set a seal on our friendship that was never to be forgotten.

CHAPTER NINETEEN
RATIONS AND RAGINGS

Astonishingly, despite the terrific battering we received at Siremboe, Snowy had a restful night and appeared on deck next morning, ready, as he said, for duty. Indeed his eyes were bright and the flush of fever was completely gone from his cheeks although he was terribly emaciated and his wasted pinched face looked ghostly with the teeth showing in a dead man's grin. Nevertheless he ate his food to the last mouthful and chattered unusually as he sat on deck all afternoon talking to Tiny who was checking stores again, carefully measuring the rice purchased on Siremboe. Tiny finished his count, put the food away and made his calculation with every eye watching him and every tongue longing to ask the question finally voiced by Titch.

"More grub Tiny?" and the skipper grinned as he answered, "More grub Titch!"

He'd worked it out that we could use 3 half mugs of rice each meal instead of 2 halves, almost enough to switch to three meals a day had it not been for the firewood situation.

Even on two meals a day we'd be using deck boards as fuel if the trip lasted the two months that Tiny still calculated on.

As he said, despite the fact that we had covered 1,000 miles in a month since we left Padang we had only knocked off 200 of our original 1,500 mile trip. In fact if we stuck to our island hopping plans we'd still have 1,500 miles to go. We'd be no better off than we'd been four weeks previously or rather much worse as an inventory of the boat's condition showed.

We were sorely tempted to take a chance and strike out to the west. There was the tantalising possibility of just one good blow of two or three days carrying the boat almost half way across the Indian Ocean into the Allied half, with possible warship patrols. But, restraining us was the badly looking boat, cracked outriggers, on which we relied for balance and a loose and rattling bowsprit. And Snowy might relapse again and need medical attention which was possibly only a week away to the west but probably weeks away to the north where the enemy lay. There was another factor in that we were not clear of the Doldrums, and could easily

104

be becalmed for weeks unless we cut to the north, out of danger of calms.

Tiny eventually decided on compromise in his proposal to go north past the top of Sumatra to a solitary island near Nias, above the mainland and then in a narrowing Bay of Bengal head straight for the east coast of India.

We had a huge and exciting 'Leggi' (extra) that night to celebrate finalising everything. It was particularly exciting because Tiny said nothing until we'd finished our meal and only then said to Ernie.

"Same again Ernie!" and handed the open-mouthed cook rations for another meal, one of the enlarged meals at that. The second meal almost satisfied some of us, but gave us all a feeling of well-being and a sensation of new life and energy seeping through our bodies.

We crept up the coast of Nias at night and had the most frightening experience of the trip when we were actually caught in a running tide. With the roar of breakers in our ears we just couldn't locate the direction of the sound. When we did spot the surf we were appalled by the closeness of waves such as we'd never dreamed of. Even the surf at Siremboe was puny by comparison but worst still, the waves were crashing on huge black rocks, jagged and hard. Not a man or a plank would have survived the first impact and the moments it took us to jib and go about were enough almost to set us screaming. Never again after those few moments of terror would anyone of us hear or see an angry surf without the nightmarish recollection of this last glimpse of Nias. However this was the rounding of our last island and with our nose to the west we faced the ocean with nothing before us now except the sea.

We had no choice actually about going west as the wind came down from the north and even when we tried we couldn't get a point above the west.

The sun was strong and the wind still fair next morning as we put the leagues behind us. With the certainty that the wind would freshen it almost began to look as if we were going to India, after all.

On we sped through that first day with the wind ever freshening and exhilarating every man except me. I was fearful and made no bones about it, the creaking of the boat and the straining of the sail filled me with foreboding. I pleaded, almost tearfully, that the mainsail be lowered. Lissy jeered at me and Lofty sang ecstatically as the outriggers cleaved through the water, and still the wind rose. We must have been doing twelve knots and every hour of this wind was eating up the leagues separating us from India. But to my mind every hour was merely sending us deeper into the clutches of a sea that was indifferent, ruthless and cruel.

The rains came and temporarily I forgot my fear as Lissy and I raced to fill water containers from the stream pouring down the sail. Soon every container was full but even the thought of 'Leggi' didn't keep my spirits up for long.

The sun didn't come out after the rains had passed, and by evening the whole sky was grey and threatening with dark clouds racing overhead. The pace increased and still no one would hear of the mainsail coming down. I began to wonder if they'd taken leave of their senses.

Night fell and morning came to find me hollow-eyed and worn from lack of sleep. The howling wind terrified me and one glance at the now turbulent waters sent my lips moving in silent prayer. The sea had built up that persisting wind before and the ship was now racing forward on mountainous waves or sliding forward in deep troughs. And still Lofty, sang at the tiller which he would not relinquish.

I sulked and brooded, inwardly raging at the jeers of the others who picked on my fears with the cruelty of children. All, that is, except Doc, who looked at me through wise old eyes and saw what was coming.

I was breaking, my nerve was going. Doc could see it and tried to offer me sympathy and understanding but I sneered at him where I daren't sneer at Lofty, Tiny or Bosun. I wanted to hit all of these three but I hadn't the guts to do so and showered my viciousness on Doc until he left me sulking and alone down below, with the others, all joyful, on deck.

I ignored Tiny's yell of "All hands on deck" and listened in fear and trembling as they finally lowered the mainsail. I sulked as they battled before a minor squall which went as quickly as it came, and without delay up went the mainsail again.

My cowardice was obvious now. I was an outcast, a shirker, and even my friend Lissy didn't have anything to say to me. Still I lay alone with my rancorous thoughts.

Surreptitiously and cunningly I rummaged in Doc's bag and shamefully I wolfed a bar of his precious life-saving chocolate. I went on deck again to accuse Tiny of eating extra rations and of giving extra food to the others to make me weakest. Again I sank in my brooding while unknown to me Doc chided the others on my behalf.

"Gabby's had more to take than any of us," he told them. Indeed I was actually the only soldier in the gang in the sense recognised by the infantryman with his contempt for the 'Service Corps'. Lofty tried to make amends to me by a new playfulness. My brooding broke in a storm of maniacal fury as I went for him when he playfully swung the boat broadside to a wave which sent me reeling against the bulwarks. Beserk and raging I hurtled at him with intent only to kill.

Tiny brought me down in a flying tackle but I was almost away from him when Bosun lent a hand and even then Lissy had to help them before my paroxysm suddenly subsided in shuddering sobs.

Lofty had been shocked to silence but he was the first to come to me with his "I'm sorry Gabby!" but I ignored him and crawled below where Doc followed me.

We were scarcely below when the world exploded in a thundering crash and jagged holes appeared in the aft roof. Canvas flapped and tore and the huge mast had crashed on the roof, rolling drunkenly and gratingly with every lurch.

My fear gave way to gloating as I yelled curses at the rest. They battled for survival again, still without any help from me but they kept silent even when all was lashed and safe. The boat was battered and bruised by the hammering seas for almost twenty minutes before they finally got the mast lashed on the roof and the jib rigged to give us steerage way to get the stern facing those battering waves.

But it was done at last without my help and all I could say was "I told you so," and "now what about your blasted mainsail?"

I was still supposed to be Lissy's partner on watches but unobtrusively Tiny had slipped into my place and left me free of all duties. For two days I was allowed to keep my madness. For two days I was mad. Then suddenly in the stillness of the night Lissy and Tiny kicked me to my feet and motioned me to go on deck where we three were alone. And Lissy lashed me with all the fluency of his able tongue. He called me every name imagineable and his words sank into my brain. I took his tongue-lashing. He told me I was mad, he said that I could only cure myself and in breaking me he shocked me back to sanity.

"The only regular soldier aboard!" he said, "The only East Surrey!" (I was boastful of my regiment). "Blubbering and bawling like an old woman and trying to blame the war." His words scared me.

Tiny put his arm about my shoulders and hugged me when Lissy had finished and gently the rough and tough giant skipper consoled me. "Don't heed him, Gabby," he said, "he couldn't face half of what you have," but this didn't console me much. I had been the first to break, the weakest member of our gang. It hurt like hell but I could do nothing about it now except get hold of myself. This I determined to do although for one wild moment of shame I wanted to fling myself overboard.

I didn't have much to say during that night. But grimly determined the next morning I climbed up to Lofty on the tiller and cast an appreciative eye over the storm wracked water, smiled and said, "Hi, Lofty, nice stormy morning."

Lofty's mouth dropped open before he grinned at me and said, "You'll do, Gabby!"

My madness was over and for this I will be eternally grateful to my two cobbers, each is 'the Thousandth Man'.

CHAPTER TWENTY
MAN OVERBOARD

By the 4th day from Nias, Dicky and Doc calculated that the storm had blown us almost 300 miles out to sea. After that screaming hell of noise and darkness, every man aboard wished with heart and soul that we had stayed in Siberoet, Padang or even Singapore. No prison camp could be worse than the fury we now faced, in fact no battle or war could be more terrifying.

Every man aboard except Tom Bowler and Bosun were seasick and miserable, weak from struggling, long past the stage where we wanted to bother and thankfully we left everything to these two. They did nearly all watches, cooked meals, chopped wood, did the never-ending baling and, in fact, ran the boat.

It hadn't been so bad for the first two days until the wind dropped and then veered round to the east. Within hours it had howled itself to a fresh crescendo right across the seas built up by days of northerlies and we had the horror of cross seas.

Now we had a fresh nightmare with waves pounding us from the north unless we faced them. But once we got our nose into them, we had wind and seas from the east pounding our beam.

All ideas of sailing on a set course was gone by this time and the only thought in our minds was to ride the storm out somehow and pray for strength to limp safely ashore anywhere. Snowy was the only one who was without fear, but he was too far gone to fear anything. Doc was almost constantly by his side, even sleeping there with Bosun at the other side. But it was Bosun to whom Snowy turned in his conscious moments, for consolation, and Bosun talked to him for hours, always telling his friend of the things we would do when we got ashore and were safe among our allies.

He told him of the reception we would have and of how Snowy would be taken to a warm and dry bed, and, besides this luxury, would have nothing but the most tempting of foods to eat. He always added an injunction on the necessity of holding on just a little longer, and on the further necessity of eating some food now, no matter how repugnant the idea, just a little to keep his strength for another day or two. But when food was brought to Snowy and his stomach revolted at the attempt, Bosun would change his tactics and start bullying him.

Snowy was really too low. Only proper facilities and care could help him. Maybe he sensed that it was all useless and got a smile out of the treatment. At any rate, he used to close his eyes with a half smile on his mouth and sink quietly into his coma, while Bosun would clamber back on deck to work.

There wasn't a break until the fifth day of storm. Then in the afternoon for the first time came a lull. For the first time for days it looked possible to get forward along the roof and catwalk to our stocks of reserve firewood.

I was sitting on the starboard side of the aft deck as Bosun pulled himself to the catwalk and stood up. No one ever stood without a hand hold even in calm weather, but Bosun edged forward, his body leaning inwards as he progressed. There was a sudden lurch and a splash and there was Bosun in the water by the side of us and there came a cry from one of the others who saw it.

"Man overboard!"

Tiny leaned over the side and stretched an arm to Bosun bobbing alongside and then in a moment it happened.

A huge wave swept in and the *Venture* surged forward, at once twenty feet away from Bosun and as the boat lifted to the crest of the wave the wind whipped into the sea and hurled her on.

Tiny and I were on our feet in a flash as the skipper yelled "Stand by to go about!"

But even in the moment it took our galvanised crew to scramble frantically to our posts we were swept relentlessly forward so that Bosun was now 100 yards astern.

"Bring her round Lofty!" Tiny yelled, and the *Venture* heeled to the turn, but even as we cleaved over, the boat slipped back into the trough, wallowed there helplessly, and the following wave smashed over us as we lay, broadside to the seas.

The boat heeled over, almost dipping the jib sail in the water. Then she struggled upright to be sent reeling again by the next thundering smash and almost immediately afterwards the sail billowed and again we surged forward. I heard Tiny's screamed command. "Jib! Get the jib down!"

"Oars! Get the oars out," he shrieked and every man except dying Snowy sprang to obey.

We saw Bosun again when the straining oars had turned the boat and it seemed that he was nearer until another crashing wave smashed us backwards with oars flashing helplessly in the air. We lost our direction, and Bosun, and then we saw him once more on top of a wave. We saw his upraised arm and we lost him altogether.

The sea increased its raging and turned us broadside again, placing us gently in position, almost playfully and then setting us reeling with another thundering blow.

Lofty put all his strength against the tiller but steerage way was gone. Even the oars could not turn the *Venture* again and as we strained, another hammer blow set every timber shaking.

The outriggers cracked and we could hear them splintering as we battled. Tiny stood there in indecision for the first time in his leadership, knowing his boat faced destruction if she didn't dodge those blows and get her stern to the waves. Only the sail would give us steerage way and the wind in our sail would send us swinging forward away from Bosun.

He turned and looked and there, almost out of sight, Bosun waved again and as Tiny waved back he turned slowly about.

Another blow made every man cringe and Tiny spoke quietly. "Jib up boys!" he said and sat down heavily on the deck heedless as to who obeyed his order.

We shipped the oars and still hesitated until Doc spoke. "Bosun's gone now," he said gently, "Tiny's right," and slowly the jib unfurled. Lofty turned the nose and we were riding the waves smoothly and easily.

We turned round and could not see Bosun, and then suddenly, far, far away, he was there on the crest of a wave. Then, with a last wave of his hand, he was gone!

It didn't seem possible that Bosun, who had been with us only a few minutes before, would never again be seen by men. That even now he might have given up the fight and was perhaps floating and no longer struggling. Bosun, who had been so active in everything, was out there somewhere and we couldn't even tell where he was. He might still be swimming.

He was a strong swimmer with a stout heart and would not give up easily. When evening fell we wondered if he was still swimming in the darkness or whether he had realised the futility of it and had let himself go under. Again, if he was still swimming, would he be thinking of us and of his other friends and family at home? And we realised that we didn't even know if he had any family. Only Snowy had been his intimate friend, from Singapore days, although everyone on the trail knew all about his exploits since then. Titch had been with him on this trip and had a store of anecdotes about him.

Ernie, veteran of two wars whose first contact with Bosun had been when Bosun knocked him down in the food queue at Padang, sobbed his heart out over him, and Lofty cried without shame. Those of us who were dry eyed wished that the tears would come to give relief from the pain of our loss, and I, who had no tears, was more stricken than any of them. It was I who had been cross with him only two days before and had deliberately picked on him. I wished that my tongue had been torn out before I had said some of those harsh things to him, and I could still picture him looking at me out of his cool, grey eyes without comment. He had seemed to know the reasons then, and I wondered if he still did.

Did he know that we had to leave him, or did he think, even now, that we had turned our backs on him?

Ernie had no thoughts of preparing the evening meal that day and none of us wanted food. We were still sitting with our thoughts when darkness fell. All, that is, except Doc who was down below with Snowy who was calling for Bosun. We were still sitting there when Doc called to Tiny to come below and we heard their voices for a moment before Tiny came up and said: "Snowy's going. We want a prayer book."

I had the only prayer book on board, one of those soldier's prayer books, issued to me long ago in Shanghai, and it was produced by one of the others who had borrowed it from me. It was terribly delapidated from its travels, but still readable. Doc was able to find what he wanted and to read softly in the light of one of our candles. Doc didn't really need a prayer book as he, in his natural goodness and sincerity, was fittest to plead for help for Snowy. His voice would be heard by the guardians for souls. Snowy could not take part in his own defence, but he could not have had a better advocate than Doc.

We sat listening to Doc until the candle went out, and Snowy's soul went out with its dying flame.

We brought him on deck and looked at his poor dead face, and again, as with Bosun, we felt guilty. There were so many things that we might have done and had failed to do, and now it was too late. We might have stayed at Siremboe, and even if we had been captured, he would have had rest and might have lived. We also knew that if we had stayed submissively in Padang he might not now be dead, and as we expressed our thoughts, Doc pointed out that we were hardly to blame for any of these things.

We made as little splash as possible as we cast him into the sea, and we could still see him for a short time, as like a ghost, we crept on. Once more we had a vision of Bosun who might perhaps be waiting for his pal, or who might still be fighting his unequal battle, and still refusing to surrender.

Bosun swimming and Snowy still and silent, or Bosun and Snowy both still and silent, or, perhaps, Snowy swimming with Bosun.

ANGRY SEA

As if content with the toll paid by us, the storm died down after the loss of our pals. Dawn broke next day on a clear sky and on a sea which was already subsiding. As the sun rose in the heavens its rays shone strong and warming.

We had been wet and cold for six days and were glad of a chance to strip off our wet clothes and let the warmth sink into our bodies. The wind was scarcely perceptible and we wished now for the mainsail which was gone, as the jib was useless in any but a fresh or more than fresh breeze. The outriggers no longer cleaved through the water, but flapped idly up and down.

Dicky's calculations showed that the nearest land to us was to the north-east and consisted of a chain of islands, the Nicobars. When a breeze came up in the afternoon from just the right direction, our hopes began to rise again.

We heard the breakers during the night and found ourselves with land, it seemed, in every direction when dawn broke. We could not take our eyes from this feast of delight and immediately wanted to get our feet on the blessed soil once more. Even when close contact showed us that every island was ringed with a protecting line of rocks and surf we might still have pressed on and smashed ourselves through the surf if we could have been certain that the islands were still occupied by our allies and not by the Japanese.

We passed island after island and each one was just as inaccessible as the last, until finally we were up to the last one and could see nothing but unbroken water before us. Now we had to make a decision.

We knew that we should not go any further without a mainsail which would at least double our speed and yet we obviously could not get ashore to do that job. The thought of making an attempt without firm ground under our feet had not yet entered our heads.

On this last morning in the Nicobars the sun was shining and there was one of those unusual flat calms which made the sea like a sheet of glass. It was this that made Tiny decide that we could, and would, do the necessary repair without going in. We had lost our anchor at Siremboe, but Lofty said that he would make a sea anchor which would hold us and got busy on this task. Titch became his assistant, and Ernie was detailed to shave the jagged end of the mast and shape it to fit into the socket. Lissy and Doc started on the sail to make a temporary reef, and the rest of us set about making lifts for the mast.

On Crab Island we had been able to use trees and had planted them firmly in the ground. It was a fairly simple matter to haul up the heavy mast, but here we could not do that and we would have to lift it from underneath.

We lashed two long bamboo poles together to form a cross so that the mast could rest on the cross and we could push it up from the deck. We got the mast up to an angle of forty-five degrees easily enough, but this was not sufficient to make it slide forward into its socket and the bamboo rest had to be moved forward. Tiny, Dicky and myself got our shoulders under the mast to take the weight so as to be able to remove the poles and take them forward. It was when we took this terrific weight that Tiny's feet suddenly broke through the attap roof where we were standing and in a moment he was down and the whole weight was on Dicky and myself. It felt as if a sack of coal had been dumped on to an already overloaded back, and it was only instinctive bracing of our legs that saved us from being flattened down with Tiny and the mast on top of us. Since we left Padang Dicky had always been a sick man and now he just managed to gasp out, "I can't hold it!" and then he was down, weak and trembling.

Even before he went down, Tiny, still trapped, had yelled out: "Hold it Gabby," and even my legs had braced at the skipper's command, so that when Dicky fell I still had it. My breath immediately started to come in gasps and I could feel my heart pounding with the feeling of an encircling band of steel around my chest, while my knees were already beginning to bend again. I was going down when Tiny's voice came again with "Hold it Gabby!" and once more I straightened my bending knees, then the others had the rest in position and the weight was gone.

Waves of blackness were shooting through my head and I folded up and rolled over on the deck, but that didn't matter now. Tiny was saved, and even in my weakness I exulted in the knowledge that I had done well and no other man on the boat could have done what I had, except Tiny himself.

The remainder of the job was done without Dicky and myself who could not have stood upright without shaking, then Tiny swam out and lashed the broken outrigger safely and we were ready to sail once more. It was fortunate that we did the work at this time, as we later passed through the Andaman Islands without being able to find a suitable spot to land, and we never again had the flat calm necessary for the job.

We had no way of knowing in whose hands the Andaman Islands were now, but felt that by now the Japanese must have occupied most of the important islands within reach of their other occupied territory. But in passing these we felt that at least we were approaching allied waters, if we were not already in them, and we could see the end of our wanderings. Any day now we might see an allied warship or aircraft, and we really began to feel that we had, after all, achieved something. We did hear an aeroplane passing on the last day in the Andamans and again on the next day, but Dicky and Tom, our airmen, both said that it was a Japanese Zero.

CHAPTER TWENTY-ONE

DIARY OF TWENTY-TWO DAYS

It was the 22nd April when we left the Andamans behind us. We were full of satisfaction at the thought that the next time we touched land it would be allied territory - and all our troubles would end with the end of our travels. Our destination now was the north-east coast of India in the Bay of Bengal. We were sure that, even if the Japanese had run through Burma, they would have been stopped at the borders of India, so our only task was to reach this coast in one piece.

Things looked better now than they had at any time. Although neither we nor the boat were as good as we had been thirty-five days before when we left Sumatra, we had faith in our ability and in that of the boat to weather any storm that came along. Any future trials could not, we felt, be more severe than those we had already undergone.

We tried to get Tiny to increase our rations when we started on this last stretch. We could no longer see any reason for existing on our present meagre rations, but Tiny was adamant and refused to give us a grain more.

We had enough for another forty days at this rate, and expected to be in India within a week, or perhaps even to be picked up before then, but, as Tiny pointed out, if this was going to be the case, then we could easily hold out for this short period and make up for lost time when we got to safety. If, on the other hand, we were not picked up, then we still had our rations left to see us through.

I have reconstructed the type of diary I might have kept on that voyage.

<u>First Day</u>

The wind was steady, the sun was shining and we forged ahead as if the ship also knew it was heading for home. Although we were all desperately keen on the idea of friends and home, we again felt, as on other occasions, that there was no real hurry now that the end was in sight. Already we had covered more than a thousand miles since leaving Padang under conditions as adverse as could be expected anywhere, and we had faith in our own and the boat's ability to go through anything that came along in the future. We had weathered storms that would have tried a large liner, and we couldn't visualise any storm that would beat us. At least it would only leave us a little more battered, but still afloat.

Second Day

The wind and the sun were still smiling on us.

Third Day

Our good luck still held, but the wind had eased slightly and although progress was still steady, we were not going quite as fast as before.

Fourth Day

Tiny began to show signs of optimism and still with a calculating eye on the stocks he said that as long as the weather held favourable we could increase the ration by one pot of rice per day. This was to be with the morning meal, as we felt the pangs of hunger more keenly during our waking hours. The effect of this first extra ration was felt almost immediately, and we could feel new energy pulsing through our bodies.

Fifth Day

We began to start guessing how many days ahead of us lay our destination and someone suggested a lottery on the landing. The idea must have come from one of the Australians, Titch or Ernie, who would have gambled their rations away if they could have found any takers, but the suggestion caught the imagination of the rest of us.

There were nine of us, and as nobody dreamed that we would be more than nine days in reaching safety, it was decided that each of us should take a day and the one who had the day on which we sighted land would be the winner. Doc produced two bars of chocolate from his bag and said that the winner would get one and whoever first sighted the land would get the other. No one wanted to take any of the next four days, but Ernie, always the super optimist, took the fifth which would mean we had been nine days out of the Andamans and Tombola jumped at the next. Lofty, Titch and myself followed on, with Dicky, Lissy, Doc and Tiny taking the later options.

Tiny was considered to be well out of the running.

Sixth Day

This day brought us our first close up view of a whale. We saw it on the surface of the water in the distance and thought at first that it was an upturned boat and even when Lofty, who had the binoculars said that it was a whale we discounted the idea. We though that whales were cold blooded mammals which only lived in polar waters, but as we drew closer we saw plainly that it was indeed a whale sleeping on the surface of the sea.

We almost ran into it and just managed to shove ourselves clear in time. The near view fascinated us, especially when we saw that the huge mass visible on the surface was really only a small portion of the monster. It didn't move at all or attempt to dive and was still rocking gently in sleep when we left it.

Seventh Day

The breeze had died down to a very light whisper and we began to fret about our lack of progress. It was realised that our twice broken mast with the mainsail reefed on each occasion had made a terrific difference to us. Tiny decided to get more sail by lengthening the mast and unfurling part of the reef in the mainsail. It was easy enough to lengthen the sail, but the mast was more of a problem as we dare not take it down again. Even if we'd had the strength to do so, we had no confidence in our ability to get it up again afterwards. Eventually, with planks and bamboo lashings we built a stand on the top of the attap roof. Dicky came out of his unnatural lethargy to splice a spare gaff onto the end of the mast. It was really spliced halfway down the mast, but there was still about nine feet added to the length. Before it went on, Tiny let out an eye in the gaff and lined this with a smooth tin surface, using empty bully beef tins. This was to take the rope of the mainsail.

Eighth Day

The increased sail had given us much greater speed. We were again buoyed up with the progress, although on this day the wind dropped and left us becalmed for several hours at midday. During this period the time was filled in quite pleasantly by swimming in the vicinity of the boat. This swimming didn't tire us and left us feeling quite refreshed.

Ninth Day

As this was his 'chocolate' day in the Lottery, Ernie jokingly raised cries of "Land ahead". But as the day wore on he reluctantly had to admit that he was out of the chocolate race. Again we had our midday swim, although there had been some talk of sharks. The Australians had told us some very lurid tales about the sharks in their home waters. In the afternoon it was blowing a bit harder than usual and the whitecaps were dancing high in every direction. There seemed to be more flying fish than usual and they were a constant source of interest to us. Some of them really seemed to take wing, they skimmed over the water until they were out of sight, but they were, apparently, still 'flying'. These fish fled from their enemies under the water and we always hoped that their hurried and unpremeditated flight would send them floundering onto our deck, but, so far, they had always managed to avoid us.

Tenth Day

We heard a thud and the threshing of one of the flying fish during the night, but could not see anything so we thought it had floundered back into the water, but Titch was there first in the morning and he salvaged the dead fish from the bottom of the roof. It wasn't large enough to share with every man, so we started another roster for future occasions, and Ernie and Titch ate this one between them. A surprising thing came to light when the fish was cooked on the hot coals. It was found that the wings, or fins, and even the bones, were soft and edible. I've never found out if this is a peculiarity of flying fish, or whether we were simply in the condition to appreciate even bones.

Eleventh Day - and the Chop

We got another flying fish this morning and Lissy and I followed the Australians example and ate every scale on it. We also had a funny experience with what we called 'the Chop' for about two hours at midday.

The sea was calm and almost unruffled until about noon and then Ernie, who spent most of his time in the prow still searching for land, suddenly spotted a dark line on the sea which looked like a wide reef stretching under the surface of the sea. When we got closer we could see it wasn't that, but couldn't even hazard a guess what it was. When we got into 'the Chop' we were rocked and slapped about, although not with any real force, just as we would be in any choppy sea. For two hours we were in this, and then, just as suddenly as we had sailed into it, we were out again and could see the dark ruffled waters dropping astern. Lissy guessed that we must have passed the point where the mighty River Ganges, sweeping into the Indian Ocean, met a cross current from some other stream, and 'the Chop' was the resulting upheaval. This explanation, being generally accepted, made us hopeful that we might now run into sight of land. This day also put Lofty out of the chocolate stakes.

Twelfth Day

This was Titch's day, and he ousted Ernie from his place in the prow so that he could be the first to see the end of the journey. We were growing distinctly weaker again and most of us didn't even come on deck except to stand watch and eat. The task of bailing out from the boat, which went with the watch duty, was a real ordeal, and we were all everlastingly grateful to Tombola, who had assumed the energy of Bosun, and willingly did most of our chores. The rest of us, apart from the lack of desire to do anything, were afraid to exert ourselves too much, as any effort or exertion left us exhausted for hours afterwards. Our ribs were all showing and our cheeks had the same sunken look we had seen in Snowy before he died. This, together with a collection of beards and long hair, plus the fact that we did not wear any clothes, must have given us a strange appearance had there been eyes to see us. We were also blackened by the sun and it would have been no easy matter to have guessed our nationalities. 'The Chop' materialised again at mid-day and discounted Lissy's theory about the

Ganges, unless, of course, it could be accepted that we had drifted back during the night, and even then we would have passed again through the tossing waters.

We just couldn't understand it as we passed out of this turmoil again after about two hours, and saw it still tossing behind.

Thirteenth Day

This was MY chocolate day, and it was generally agreed that my chance was a very good one. I had not been in the water for a swim recently, but went in for what was to be my last venture in the Indian Ocean. So far I had been too scared at the idea of sharks to venture in the sea, but we saw several small sharks in the clear waters on this morning, and they seemed so small that I felt I would welcome the chance to take a bite at one of them rather than fear being bitten. Lofty said they were Gummy sharks, and told us that, not only were they completely harmless, but they never grew to any appreciable size. After the swim I lay resting on deck, and turned over to watch these small sharks in the water. I turned my eyes to the water and was immediately petrified by what I saw. Just two feet from my head was what seemed to be the father and mother of all sharks. I had never seen any but the smaller breed before, but there was no mitaking this brand. He was a killer without doubt! Then he rolled over on his back to take a good look at me with his baleful eye, and as if to complete the display, he opened his mouth to show the frightening row of razor-like teeth. I gazed fascinated for a moment and then called excitedly to the others who crowded to the edge to look closer at the monster who, not a bit disturbed, slid smoothly along with the boat.

Dicky was below deck and Tiny called to him: "Get a revolver Dicky." As Dicky was unwrapping the guns from their protective coverings, we watched the shark, still unhurried and seemingly unmindful of us, gliding along. Lofty grabbed the gun when it came up and hastily shoved some rounds in, then, leaning over the side he held the gun against the head of the unsuspecting shark and pulled the trigger.

The unaccustomed sound was deafening and the effect was instantaneous. The lazily moving shark was galvanised and the mirror of the water disappeared in a swirl of movement. The water cleared in a few minutes, but although we gazed searchingly in every direction, there was no sign of the shark, and we never saw him again.

Darkness fell on a still unbroken horizon and with the end of the day my chances of chocolate also ended.

Fourteenth Day and Acrobatics

We couldn't believe that another day would pass without bringing us in sight of land. We assumed that we must be almost at the top of the Bay of Bengal and that whether we sailed north, east or west now, we would come to a friendly land. With this in mind it was decided that we could run dead before the wind in future, in any direction above east or west, and then get the maximum speed possible all the time.

The wind was fresh on this day and we were flying before it when we had another accident with our sail. This time it was the rope through the mast that parted, and although no damage was done, it was no less a calamity than when we had lost the mast, as we had no means of getting the rope threaded again. Titch and Lissy, who were the only lightweights on board, tried to climb the mast, but their strength and skill was unequal to the task.

Tiny, Dicky and Lofty were not to be counted on as they were much too heavy for the thin top of the mast. As we were discussing the situation I could see Tiny's eyes on me, and sure enough it came. "Can you do it Gabby?" he said, and I had no choice but to try.

I had always been adept at this sort of climbing and, in normal times, would have been up and down rapidly, but things were far from normal, and I dreaded the attempt. I gathered my strength for the ordeal and was surprised to find that it was no real task at all to shin up the thick part of the mast to the point where the thin and pliant gaff was lashed to it, but as I felt it sway my nerve failed me. The deck already seemed to be to be miles below and I knew that if I fell and broke any bones they wouldn't easily mend. I knew too I would have to wait in pain for days before we landed and I could be got to a hospital. Besides this, the sea was as much under me with the rolling of the boat as was the deck, and it was swelling more as the time went by. I could not forget about sharks. I knew that the thin gaff wouldn't hold my weight and appealed to the others for support.

Tiny turned to Ernie who had been a joiner and was supposed to know all about wood and asked him, "What about it, Ernie?" Ernie looked calculatingly at the gaff and said, "She's sweet. She'll take more than his weight," and my last avenue of escape was gone. None of the others could climb even to where I was, so I was the only hope of getting the sail functioning again. I rested where I was for a few minutes to regain my strength and then, with all the misgivings in the world, I gripped the frail-looking pole with knees and hands and started pulling myself up. It seemed to my distorted imagination that the gaff was bending like a bow about to release an arrow, and halfway up I looked down once more for a reprieve from someone. Their upturned faces were silent, and I spoke to Ernie, "Now what, Ernie?" Without a pause he replied, "Go on, she's OK." and with final resignation I shot up until my arms were resting on the very top and I was perched like a monkey on a flag pole.

The gaff bent right over and I expected every moment that it would

120

snap and that I would go crashing down to the deck. Then in the next second the boat had lurched over, leaving me high above the sea. Tiny saw the danger now and I could see him getting some of the others at the oars ready to pull round to get me out of the water if I fell.

During this time I was fumbling with almost unfeeling hands at my waist to get the thin bamboo strip to thread through the eye, and my strength was so far spent that I had to close my eyes three times and let my hand drop lifeless to my side, just hanging on with legs and an arm for a minute or so. It was undone and through at last. I passed the end down to the others while they hauled the rope to follow the thin thread, and I was free to come down.

The descent itself was endless and the temptation to let go and take a chance of broken bones was almost overwhelming. But with the knowledge that I had only a moment or two to go, I held on and slid down the last few feet into the waiting arms of Tiny and Doc. They eased me to the boards and I closed my eyes and lay there to let the strength gradually seep back into my body. Doc never said a word, but went to his bag and brought me a bar of chocolate which he gave me without a word. I couldn't help grinning at the thought that small boys get pieces of chocolate for being good.

The incident brought home more than ever that we were getting dangerously low in energy. Tiny got a few cracks about our rations, and, in fact, for the first time in his leadership he found himself subject to criticism.

Fifteenth Day and Conflict

The muttering against Tiny was becoming strong. Doc did all he could to smooth things, but feelings were rising high. Tiny felt it badly and sat alone with his face set and broody, but wouldn't give way. Ernie was the one who set the spark of Tiny's wrath, and he might easily have been strangled. He never had been particularly friendly towards Tiny and this had prevented Lissy and me becoming intimate with him. We knew enough of him to realise that he was one of those souls who would rebel at discipline in any shape or form, and perhaps this was why he didn't like Tiny. He had often snapped and sworn at Tiny, but Tiny had always taken everything until this day when everyone's hand was against him. He suddenly let out a roar of rage and went for Ernie. He hit him and knocked him flying head over heels, and was diving for him again when Doc and I grabbed him.

We tumbled over together, and suddenly, by an old and almost forgotten instinct, I had a full nelson on Tiny, and, combined with this, had my bare legs gripped tightly round his waist. He struggled like a fury, but was helpless, and I was able to sit there and hold him until he calmed down. It wasn't until he promised to let things go that I untwined my legs and took my arms away.

Ernie was very subdued after this and we could see he was a little frightened at what had happened. He apologised to Tiny for whatever it was he had said, and they shook hands.

Sixteenth Day and Reconciliation

Lissy and I talked things over during the night and, although we felt resentment against Tiny, we were a little ashamed of ourselves and went out of our way to show that we were 'all for one and one for all'. This cheered him up a lot and opened his mouth a lot more, so that he talked all day of his wife in India with the baby who had been born there while Tiny was in action in Malaya. Doc joined in, and Tombola, who was too placid and good-natured to hold any ill feelings for long, also chatted to Tiny, but not to the others.

'The Chop' came as usual at midday, but this time we saw some packing cases in the water and a large empty oil drum, which excited us, as we thought we couldn't be too far from land as the drum would have filled and sunk.

If it really was a river current, were we being swept all the time towards the east, and were we after all not so near to the Indian side of the Bay of Bengal as the Burmese side?

Seventeenth Day - and end of the Chop

Tiny stayed with Lissy and me on deck all night and we spent all the hours of darkness in peace and reminiscence.

We went on watch at 10 p.m. and didn't wake any of the others at all. The night was starry with a light breeze, and I lay on my back beside the tiller holding it loosely with one hand, with my eyes straying to and from the Pole Star which was lying just to starboard of the mast. It was distinctly higher in the sky nowadays and gave us hope that we couldn't possibly go much further before we sighted the northern coast of the bay.

On this day we set adrift the canoe which Besu had given us in Siberoet. It had been very much in the way for weeks now as it lay along the bottom of the roof, and we had to clamber over it to go for'ard every time. Lissy and I had been sleeping in it as it gave us the freshness of the night with a protection from the chilly night breezes, but it had no other value and we could not, in our worst moments, visualise not sighting land today or tomorrow, so finally, with perhaps just a little reluctance, we cast it away. We also cast away the fourteen bamboo poles which had held water, and this left the boat looking much clearer.

There was no Chop today, and if our theory was right, this meant that we were well north of the Ganges.

Eighteenth Day - and end of the Chocolate Race

This was Tiny's 'Chocolate' day and was the last day of the lottery. We also began to feel that this land was a myth, and wondered if we would ever get there, especially when night fell and Tiny had not won his chocolate.

Nineteenth Day

We were becoming so weak and listless that Tiny said the ration must be increased. We still had about three weeks of food on board, and if we were going to be adrift that time we'd go under through starvation anyway. Someone spoke longingly of the time when we could eat as much as we liked, and, on impulse, Tiny told Ernie to cook double rations of rice for today, and he then sorted out the fish and gave a large tin between three all round. It was wonderful to eat our first plateful of rice and then, like Oliver Twist, ask for more and to deliberately and methodically enjoy every single mouthful. Not only did we feel a renewal of energy, but our spirits rose wonderfully, and once more we were optimistic of the future.

We saw some debris in the sea and thought again that land must be close.

Twentieth Day

The chocolate lottery was over with no winners. It was unbelievable, and yet it had happened. We were, on our twentieth day, out of sight of land and could not understand it at all. During this time our course had been north or north-west and, according to our estimate, we had in this time covered about 1,500 miles, but as this would have brought us to land, our estimate must be wrong. The horrible thought came that perhaps there was a current running against us which, against the outriggers, would create a wash and give the illusion of speed. From this idea came the thought that perhaps we had not even got very far from the Andamans. However, this could not be, as the North Star was much higher in the sky than at the Andamans. Tiny and Doc did a lot of peering over the maps and finally decided that if a northerly course did not bring us anywhere in the next two days, we would sail right over to the east and reach land somewhere, even if the land was in Japanese hands.

Twenty-first Day - and Ship Ahead

Lofty came on deck in the morning and swore that he could smell land ahead of us, but the day wore on and the horizon was still unbroken, so we lost faith in Lofty's nose.

The wind had been blowing hard all night from the north-east, and the sea was beginning to build up into a heavy swell, so that we lurched and rolled in the old familiar, but nevertheless, alarming manner. A cry of "Ship ahead!" galvanised us in the afternoon, and, sure enough, even I could see a large steamer ploughing across our path on the starboard bow. It was coming from the west to the east, and this seemed a good sign so we waved and shouted ourselves hoarse, but the ship passed unheeding and left us still shouting, to disappear as quickly as it had come. The only good thing which came out of this was the conviction that we were in allied waters. India was to the west whence the boat had come, clearly indicating that it was one of ours. It didn't enter our heads that India was anything but allied territory still, and as the boat was going east, there must also be an allied port to the east, so, without hesitation, Tiny ordered us to turn eastward before the wind which had now backed to the west. Also the current which we now took for granted was flowing in that direction.

Twenty-Second Day

It was now the 13th May and we all came on deck in the morning full of expectancy. Actually there was no reason for this as the sea and sky still showed the same unbroken contour, but somehow we did expect something. We kept our eyes glued ahead searching for the haze which would denote our journey's end. In the afternoon Ernie had everyone peering at what he said was land ahead, but it disappeared as cloud shortly afterwards. Then again Ernie had us at it, and again the haze disappeared. Ernie still peered and peered, and again and again he pointed here and there at points which he said were land. His false alarms stopped as he tired of producing no response. Then suddenly Lofty yelled, "He's right fellows, she's there!" and this time he was indeed right.

By evening they could all, except me, see points here and there where the haze was beginning to solidify, and before nightfall I could see the mountains with the binoculars. We had won and were home!

Three months of wandering were ended - we were safe! Tomorrow would see us with our friends and allies, and, who knows, in a few days we could be flown to England.

CHAPTER TWENTY-TWO

INTO THE WEB

The instinct which was also an intense yearning in everyone's heart was to cram on full sail and fly headlong to the nearest point of land, even if to land we had to pile ourselves on the rocks. Ernie and Titch particularly were ready to swim ashore if necessary for the sake of tobacco, and even though tobacco and its evils had been out of my mind for nearly two months, I had a sudden yearning for a smoke.

Lissy and Dicky were after food, and even if the coast did turn out to be barren were all for cooking a really bumper feed from our sadly depleted stocks.

Tiny was the only dissenter and even suggested going about to the west and across to Calcutta - but even he was shouted down. I believe that if he had persisted Ernie, at least, would have dived overboard to swim for it.

We assumed at this stage that the land in sight was the Eastern border of the Bay of Bengal, but, as Tiny pointed out, we had no way of knowing whether it was the coast of Burma or whether we were near Chittagong in the north.

We did not consider it as a serious possibility that the Japanese were here. The steamer we had seen was now completely accepted as being British. Sailing from an eastern allied port to its goal in the west, in all probability.

Anyway, nothing could be settled from here, so in we went until we were close enough to see the jungle sweeping down to the sea. Then, as we crept in shore we had our first jolt. It was the sight of a number of pagodas in the distance, and to all of us, it was obvious that at least Burmese people lived here.

We still thought we were well north and a hurried discussion resulted in the swinging of our prow northwards from the shore. If this was Burma, with the Burmese people an unknown quantity, we wanted to land as unobtrusively as possible, and it was two hours later before we edged close to the mouth of a small river far removed from any large village.

The smell of the land and the sight of the vegetation had an uncontrollable thrill after the trials of the last three weeks. Progress seemed dreadfully slow. In our minds our voyaging was over and even

125

if not actually home, we were convinced that a short trip by land would get us to sanctuary. We would quite cheerfully have driven full speed to the shore and ditched the boat.

The complete indifference of a pair of native fishermen at the entrance of the river encouraged us. This indifference, however, evaporated when, in sweeping further inshore we fouled their nets strung across the river mouth. We had no need of Lissy's linguistic ability to know that it was real, heartfelt abuse that came from them.

As soon as we were well into the mouth Lissy, at the tiller, ran the boat into a mud-bank, and our voyage was over. I leaped ashore with the others and was amazed at my inability to stand still. As soon as I started to walk the whole earth gathered itself to smite me and I sat down hurriedly. Then, feeling sick and muzzy, I clambered aboard again.

This was an awful state of affairs - to find that having reached sanctuary we had to flee to the haven of our old prison. However, a second attempt was better - and we were soon able to start exploration. This disclosed first a path, then a well beaten bullock track, and from here, away went Lissy and Tiny.

They were back in an hour carrying a squealing pig plus a huge basket packed with vegetables and fruit. Even before they had time to recount their adventures Ernie had most of the pig in the pot which he had ready for just such an opportunity. The attempt to clean and singe the pig was discarded as a waste of time.

The main vegetable looked like English carrot, so into the pot went as many as was practical. These carrots turned out to be ginger roots and besides turning our brew a faint green gave me an awful shock when I bit one, but they only seemed to improve the pig. Goodness only knows how the stew would have tasted to ordinary palates, but we waded in with delight. With huge helpings of rice steamed with pork fat we tore on and on until even the bones could not have made an honest contribution to soup.

By the time we had eaten most of the fruit in sight we had a number of native visitors and they succumbed to Tiny's old charms and had soon parted with most of their cheroots.

Lissy and Tiny had not procured the pig easily. In fact they had walked into an openly hostile village a short distance down the bullock tracks. Their requests by signs for food had been met with noncommittal gestures of 'no savvy', until Lissy had produced some Malayan coins. The sight of the king's head brought a startled query "Inglis?" from the villagers. The vehement affirmative had worked wonders and if the language had been understood Lissy said he was quite sure that one of them called "Hey, you chaps, these fellows are English."

126

Anyway the moroseness disappeared in fluency and despite the language barrier things began to flow. It appeared that a large Japanese raiding party had been here a week ago and had cleaned out the village of its livestock and they had thought we were just a second party. This was not too complimentary to our appearance but we let it pass.

We left the village little wiser than when we had arrived. Our friends answered with a decided "yes" to all our questions, thus eliciting the fact that there were Japanese to the north, south, east and west, there were also British and that they were all present in large and small numbers at once.

We left our refuge next morning taking with us a live goat and two ducks as a snack to last us until we reached dry land. Once again as at Pig Island we were faced with the problem of butchering the goat and once again Titch nominated Doc. He was used to this by now, and did a good job. We ate it on the first day with as much rice as we could manage and lay down to sleep in peace and security that night.

For the first time since December 8 of the previous year, almost six months before, we felt completely secure. We were out of the war, out of Japanese territory with 2,000 meandering miles behind us. We had not really been conscious of the kind of tension which had held us all the time we were in enemy territory and waters until we were free of it. Now we wanted to find civilisation and occupying forces instead of avoiding them.

We found our civilisation the next day and a great cheer went up when we saw the thriving port we were heading towards. We could see in our mind's eye the welcome we'd get within the next hour or so when once more we made ourselves the responsibility of the British Army. No more striving, no more dodging, no more hardship and danger, nothing ahead of us except luxury, security, friends and home. Our journey was over.

Then Dick spotted a Japanese flag fluttering down a large steamer in the port and consternation and chaos reigned.

We were sailing into a Japanese-occupied port not an allied base! Then we found we couldn't stop and couldn't even turn off our course. We were being swirled helplessly along in the grip of one of these infernal rip tides, common to southern Burma.

We managed to turn her nose towards the shore but couldn't get closer than a hundred yards and so, broadside to our course which was parallel to the coastline, we swept on to and through the port of Moulmein, which had been the first major conquest the Japanese had made when they invaded Burma in January. If we'd been a marauding force of commandoes we'd never have got near. As we were just helpless fools nobody molested us, not even the Japanese sailors gazing curiously from their ships.

Our battered *Venture* was as much out of place as a Chinese junk on the river Thames. Lofty's golden hair should have attracted attention. Tiny's gigantic stature would have turned heads in any street and added to this we'd all dressed in bedraggled uniforms for our grand entry.

So it was we went through this crowded enemy port.

Then we hit an area of shallows and sand banks and bang - our rudder was bumped right out of its socket and sank like a log, out of sight for ever.

We swished round a headland and were in calm water and Tiny got us at the oars. He and I wielded two of them as sweeps to replace the rudder and with these we crept to the shore.

There was a river mouth there and into it we scurried to be swallowed almost at once by the enveloping trees. A quarter of a mile upstream the river started to narrow and in a quiet backwater we beached the *Venture*. Her sailing days were over and we were stranded, goodness only knows where, but certainly in enemy territory.

The panic of our narrow escape still held us and we hustled to get our belongings packed and ashore, ready to take to the jungle, ready to race away from the danger around us. Then a native prahu sailed majestically down river and somehow things looked so peaceful that we paused for breath.

No one seemed to be after us, no one seemed to have bothered about our mad race. Tiny hailed the next prahu. This one was going upstream and they told him they were on their way home to a village not far away.

"Come on Lissy," the skipper said, "we'll see if we can find someone you can understand."

Lissy spoke several Indian languages fluently, including Urdu, Tamil and Bengali. Off they went in the prahu (pronounced Prow) leaving behind seven very nervous adventurers.

Lissy found a Burmese who spoke Bengali in the village and got all the information he wanted. More than he wanted in fact.

We were not even in the Bay of Bengal but were well south of it in the Gulf of Martaban. That wretched current must have been edging us to the East ever since we'd left the Andaman Islands. We were still a thousand miles from India, by land that is, and would be in enemy territory until we got to India. Burma was completely occupied by the Japanese, so they told us, but of course we didn't believe them. The fiasco of Malaya hadn't taught us anything, the debacle of Singapore hadn't shaken our belief that the British would soon swarm back. And now, without a single victory behind us, we still didn't believe that we were losing.

ANGRY SEA

Mad dogs and Englishmen!

"If we can get another boat," Tiny mused, "we can edge round the coast until we get to the British forces."

Most of us planned and schemed over the next two days about our proposed future progress by boat. Lissy made some very satisfying plans with his village friends who promised cooperation in everything we asked. They fed us well, supplied us with tobacco, offered to take us by night to a village further up on the coast and set us safely on a route which would take us to India.

Tiny was more in favour of putting out to sea again to sail to the west of Calcutta. Direct and easy, he said. I said nothing, took no part in their discussions, I knew what I was going to do and when they'd made their plans, I dropped my bombshell.

"I'm not coming with you, Tiny," I said and they all turned to me, startled.

"No more boats for me," I told them, "I'm going through the jungle."

They said I was mad at first but I pointed out that I was at home in the jungle, could forage there, could sleep in safety and certainty, count on help from the Burmese villagers en route. "I'll get through," I boasted and my faith did something to them.

"I think I'll go with Gabby," Lissy said.

Ernie deserted Tiny's party. Lofty left the skipper. Titch came over to us. Doc wavered.

I looked at Tiny's stricken face and if I could have faced the sea again I would have gone over to his side. The thought of splitting our gang was saddening and Doc said, "I think we should stick together."

Tiny gave in. "We'd better have a new vote on a leader," he said, "I'm out now."

We'd deserted him after all he'd pulled us through and it had really knocked him. "Tiny," I pleaded, "don't leave us now. You take us through the jungle. We still need you."

"Come on skip," Lissy coaxed, "how about it?"

In a moment they were all clamouring for Tiny and his face lit up.

"All right," he conceded, "but we'll still have a vote for leader."

"Me for Tiny," I said putting both hands up for two votes and unhesitatingly every pair of hands followed.

Tiny was still skipper.

Negotiations with the Burmese were now for guides through the jungle to another friendly village. No trouble about this they assured us, we could start tonight. But all this time they had been negotiating with the Japanese in Moulmein. Even now the Japanese were closing in on us, hundreds of them in a wide semicircle to hem us in with the river at our backs.

On this river they brought their patrol boats and when all was ready the Burmese gave the signal and the villagers around us started to disperse. I don't think all the villagers were in the betrayal but they got the muttered alarm from those who were and so did we.

Titch stood up and looked around. "Cripes Almighty!" he said, "Cop that lot!"

They were closing in, an endless line of armed men and we looked about us desperately.

"The river," Ernie said, "Come on!" and at that moment the motor boats roared into life.

The last of the Burmese were still slinking away and Ernie threw off his clothes. "I'm off," he said, "who's coming?"

I think we all estimated chances in one brief moment while Ernie hesitated, then he turned to me. "Come on Gabby," he pleaded, "you and me."

I wish I'd known Ernie better, I wished I'd gone earlier and again Ernie beseeched me. "Come on Gabby," but I shook my head and then he was gone, strolling off with the Burmese, tanned almost to their colour and dressed not very differently to them.

"Put your hands up," called the leading Japanese officer running forward towards us. "Walk out here with your hands up."

Now we were eight.

Bosun gone.

Snowy dead.

Ernie gone - and it looked as if we might be gone too.

CHAPTER TWENTY-THREE
THE SPIDERS

"Put your hands up!" the enemy shouted again. "Walk forward."

Sullenly, as we slouched towards him I shoved my hands in my pockets. It was obvious we'd had it and nothing any of us did could worsen our plight. Besides that, although I'm the most placid creature possible, just once in a while I get stubborn and I don't like being humiliated and even an empty gesture helps - like the small boy who puts his tongue out at the big bully.

Anyway I got myself tied up for my gesture, along with Tiny and Dicky. It was understandable tying Tiny up, if I was a half pint Japanese who had just captured a 6' 4½" ruffian I'd tie him up too. Goodness only knows why they picked on Dicky though.

With us three fastened, arms behind our backs and the rest seated in a circle facing inwards, he stopped his strutting and stood before Tiny.

"Where is other man?" His English was certainly good except for that odd hiss.

Tiny looked round in surprise and counted. Sure enough there was a man missing and he shrugged his massive shoulders in negation.

The man turned, and barked an order and a horde of the captors took off. We sat and waited, then Tiny thought of the food we'd been about to eat and he pointed it out to the enemy. The enemy, now in high good humour laughed and had it brought to our circle.

"Eat," he commanded grandly, and despite the stupidity of it we were suddenly hungry.

Tom fed Dicky, Lissy and Lofty took it in turns to feed Tiny and me, and Doc started on our captor.

"What will happen to us?" he asked and a reassuring hand was waved. "It's all right," he said "you will not be killed with kindness." I think he really did mean to comfort us and perhaps after all his English did have limitations.

Some of us felt easier anyway, because Lissy started smearing fried chicken over my face when I opened my mouth for a bite.

Everybody roared with laughter and all we needed for a real party was a case of beer. Anyway we ate our fill and sat in the tropical sun for an hour before the roar of a motor boat from the river was heard. Not the little river where our wrecked boat was hidden but the main river to the south.

This was what we'd been waiting for and we were hustled to our feet and forward across the fields. This trek was a forerunner of many discomforts in bare feet. Try walking in bare feet across a sun-baked field that has just been harvested to leave an inch or so of sharp stiff stubble and you'll see what I mean. But we got to the waiting motor boat and roared across the harbour we'd already seen. In fact the steamer we'd sailed past was still there. Still nobody took any notice of us.

It wasn't until we got to Moulmein that we excited some interest when we disembarked and set out on our march through the streets. Have you ever tried walking on a hot road in bare feet? The Burmese of Moulmein followed us chattering and suddenly we were electrified by the words. "Have good heart masters, your friends are near."

It took some of us years to learn that Burmese are eternally reluctant to pass on bad tidings and will say the most outrageous things to cheer you up. Like the news that continually came into jail, about rescuing British armies close at hand. The phrase "They're coming down" became a mockery to all except the super optimists who continued to hope. This particular Burmese got a real beating for his pains and we got a nasty jolt at our first illustration of Japanese discipline.

Two guards pounded after him as he tried to flee, caught him and dragged him back so that they could all have a go at him, even the one we'd begun to think was a good natured-civilised human being. They kicked and beat him savagely, working themselves into a screaming rage and when they'd finished they dragged him to a roadside tree and chained him there. I wondered if the chains were new or whether the British in Burma had used them for something else. Anyway he was chained there and slapped and dragged to his tottering feet.

Then he was forced to raise his hands and on those hands was placed a table and the guards, now jovial again, stood back in laughing glee. The glee evaporated into screamed imprecations as the legs and arms of the poor wretch started to sag and they pushed the table on high again.

Thus we left him with one guard to see that he didn't sag.

I wondered what would happen when eventually he collapsed and could not be kicked into consciousness.

CHAPTER TWENTY-FOUR

PREVIEW OF JAIL

We didn't know it then but we were to be in the bag for the next three years - almost three years that is, Lofty and I escaped to the jungle on Anzac Day 1945.

The others were later released by the invading 14th army, except for one whose bones were left wrapped in old sacking, in a shallow grave in Rangoon. Eleven of us had left Padang, seven of us lived to see the end of the Japanese dream and each of the seven who survived will carry the mental and physical scars for the rest of his life.

But it wasn't all scars, some of us came out of it with a treasure chest of memories.

And oft' when on my couch I lie

In thoughtful and in pensive mood

They flash upon that inward eye

Which is the bliss of solitude.

Lissy, Tiny and I who started the gang will forever see in the others 'The Thousandth Man'.

"One man in a thousand," Solomon says,

"Will stick more close than a brother."

In fact I have before me a snap of Tiny taken with a leopard he'd just shot (this was after the war) and inscribed on the back is the message,

To Gabby

The Thousandth Man

From

Skipper

I'd face ten years in a prison camp for that tribute from such a man.

I only wish that Bosun, Snowy, Ernie and that other one in Rangoon had come through also.

I did a pilgrimage after the war to the families of those who'd died. I visited and stayed with Bosun's mother and father and his sisters in Kent and I visited a sweet gentle mother in Edinburgh who was just like her son.

Then I went wandering again and I visited my friends in Australia and New Zealand. I dropped in on Lofty's wife in Lembourne while he was at work and I was lurking behind the door to pounce on him as he came home from work. I stayed the night and slept with Lofty, he turned out his beautiful young wife to the spare room and we talked and talked.

There was another instance in Wellington, New Zealand when I dropped in on Chuck Ferguson, a bosom pal of Rangoon days. He was in bed with malaria and my appearance shocked the fever out of him. I'd brought a toothbrush with me and I borrowed Chuck's pyjamas for that night.

I must drop in on Lissy and Tiny one of these days.

However, I was talking about our three years 'in the bag' and I find it most difficult to start on the story and continue with any hope of continuity or accurate chronology. The initial phase in Moulmein jail is clear and so are the last few days just before Lofty and I took off to the jungle and freedom, but the story between is confused. Anecdotes and events stand out but I couldn't for the life of me remember which year it was that a Japanese sentry pinched a water buffalo for us, or when I set the candle factory on fire, this was pure accident incidentally although it couldn't have been bettered as a carefully planned sabotage. I can't even say when the American bombers came and plastered our prison.

I suppose a journey of a thousand miles would be just as difficult to describe mile by mile from memory, but, there's much to tell, and it deserves to be told and listened to, especially by those who visualised every Japanese camp as all hell, misery and degradation. Nobody who saw The King and Prince of Thieves in action could fail to see the funny side of it. Lofty was kind and he once stole an iron cooking vat from a Japanese barracks. Titch the Prince once stole some porthole curtains from a Jap ship to make loin cloths.

And nobody who heard Lissy arguing in fluent Japanese with various sentries could visualise them as intolerant monsters.

A lot should be said about the Australians, 'the loud-mouthed uncouth Botany Bay Bastards'. I love every one of them.

ANGRY SEA

The Americans too, that race which none of us really understands even now. And the Japanese themselves - some of us began to think that we were learning to understand them towards the end, and certainly I gladly swapped addresses with two of them with a view to future friendship.

Strangely enough we found disease to be very interesting, academically that is, and I do believe that even now some of us know more about beri-beri, malaria, dysentery, hookworm and cholera than the majority of western doctors. We even brought captured pigeons very low with beri-beri - then we cured them. We certainly learned a lot about attitudes to illness, the attitude which caused men to die unnecessarily and the attitudes which kept men alive who should have died.

Food is another subject which needs discussing, some misconceptions need clarifying.

My final chapter of course will be our escape which nearly didn't come off because I hadn't the heart to kill a Japanese guard I'd learned to like.

CHAPTER TWENTY-FIVE
MOULMEIN JAIL AND THE MOULMEIN CROWD

Moulmein jail, grim and forbidding as prisons tend to be, loomed before us. It had been built by the British as a civilian prison, with massive iron gates and behind them was a canyon-like courtyard. The doors clanged behind us and the frightening silence and loneliness of claustrophobia descended on each of us. Now we'd definitely had it, we couldn't make a run anywhere. We were really caged.

In fact we were literally caged half an hour later after we'd been searched. Some of our possessions, including maps and compasses were returned to us, while other items like the binoculars were already in the hands of our two Burmese friends to add to their coins from the grateful Japanese.

It wasn't difficult to see who had betrayed us and we noted the two scowling Judases for a promised re-union in the future. We really made that promise at the time, but somehow I don't suppose any of us ever will go back there. They passed out of our lives and we passed to our new home, the cage.

It was part of a gaunt isolation block, totally cut off from the rest of the jail. The cell itself had only one proper wall, the other three being just bars from the ceiling to the concrete floor on which we were supposed to sleep without any covering. So far we'd had no indication that we were to be shot, beheaded or tortured and when later a Burmese trusty, accompanied by a Japanese guard, brought us an enormous ration of rice and beans, we really began to hope.

We could not imagine any stomach holding as much rice as we got in our ration, so we guessed this must be a once a day meal and we saved half of it for breakfast. We still lay down gorged and almost content.

When the monsoon broke that night and we heard the torrents of water, I at least wouldn't have swapped my dry sheltered cage for the best boat in Burma. At sea in this lot we'd have been fighting with every nerve and sinew to stay afloat, and alive. Most of us would have known fear and I, at least, would have been in terror.

Morning brought an end to the storm but didn't bring us any breakfast so it looked as if we'd guessed correctly about the daily ration and we cleaned up what we'd saved then waited. We did a lot of waiting that day but we did get two more meals and this time we ate most of the ration. Our stomachs which had shrunk to adapt to the microscopic ration of the last two months were beginning to stretch.

By the following day when we were taken out for interrogation. Most of us were going batty with boredom and most of us, including me, would have taken any chance to get back to sea.

There was apparently no proper interpreter from English to Japanese so someone had jacked up a chain of communication from us to a Burmese who spoke English but not Japanese, and to a Japanese who spoke Burmese but no English.

Some of us, with me as the leading tongue, had decided that when question time came the Japanese were not to be played about with. That silly Geneva convention rule of nothing but number, rank and name should go overboard. The Japanese had never ratified the convention and weren't likely, on the basis of what we'd seen so far, suddenly to start observing the niceties of international agreements on the humanitarian treatment of people in conquered territories. In fact I persuaded myself, and some of the others, that if we answered every question they asked we'd still give nothing away as we'd been out of circulation for three months and just didn't have any vital information. Really, I just wasn't feeling heroic and that was that, so, we told all we knew.

Fifteen battleships in the Indian Ocean was the answer to one question despite the fact that few of us even knew exactly what a battleship was, and certainly we'd never seen one.

Dicky thought there were also seven aircraft carriers and an outrageous number of submarines. The climax came with a demand as to how many motor cycle squadrons there were in India.

All the ridiculous answers went down and there were never any repercussions though surely someone somewhere must have realised we were talking off the tops of our heads.

The end of interrogation ended the necessity of keeping us together and next day we were marshalled again outside the guardroom with our meagre belongings. Doc, Dicky, Tiny and Lissy were classified officers and marched away. The rest of us were marched to our permanent home.

Home was now a huge, two storey block with a wide verandah encircling each floor. The ground floor was occupied by a crowd of Indians still distinguishable as soldiers. We went to the top floor, which consisted of one room, not unlike a barrack room except that it had bars instead of walls. Upstairs we trudged, clang went the door and we looked in shocked horror on the creatures already there.

There were eighty-three of them, men who had once been soldiers but who could now scarcely be classified at all. Bearded, pallid and emaciated, those who were on their feet moved round us. They were beastly, bleached and unwholesome beside the bronzed health of our bodies and we almost felt like brushing them clear of us.

Decay and rot was everywhere in the room and the stench of urine and excreta was sickening. More revolting than anything were the flies, the men lying down were covered and those who were on their feet had their own swarm.

Some of them had been in that room before we left Singapore, three months ago. They'd had nothing in their lives since then except two meals a day and their degradation. They couldn't stop asking us questions until one of them gave a yell of "Mishi!" and at once we were deserted while they fought and scrambled for position at the cell door.

We heard the rattling of tin plates on the ground floor verandah, the rattling passed to the next block and then later, much later, we heard the booted feet of a sentry coming up the stairs. He laughed and joked at the still scrambling, pushing men, made one or two mock gestures of opening the door and then suddenly he did open it and flung himself out of the way of the stampeding mob.

Some of them, fleet footed and agile as deer leapt into the front and then in a few moments they started to return, each with his plate of rice and beans jealously guarded and shielded.

We went downstairs to our rations, what was left of them. They'd been trodden, spilled and depleted by thieving hands and the flies which for a short time had been ousted were back on them.

We were hungry, but not that hungry, yet, still, we took our plates back to the room. Even if we couldn't eat them, we thought somebody could, eighty-three somebodies, and if we'd had a dozen rations the flies would have been crushed aside and the food would have gone.

CHAPTER TWENTY-SIX
MUTINY

I'd not realised before that Lofty could be so angry and so forceful, perhaps he'd felt eclipsed previously against a background of men like Tiny, Lissy and Doc. Anyway he got stuck into the mob that evening. It should have been me, I suppose, as I was senior to Lofty and we were the only two sergeants. Still, I was quite content to just stand beside him with my hands on my hips and he said all that was necessary.

Australians can be devastating with their tongues, they don't mince matters and Lofty really read the riot act. Dignity and decency, prestige and pride, hygiene and health, he covered the lot and he made it very clear that in future if any man made a rush for 'mishi' he'd personally flatten him. They'd file downstairs quietly behind him and each man would take the food in turn, big share or little share.

I'd be the tail of the queue just to keep things cosy and Lofty pointed out that I was an instructor in unarmed combat. He also added for good measure that I was a battalion welterweight. The only part of this that was true was my weight, a nice steady ten and a half stone.

We couldn't do anything about the flies on the food while we waited for the sentry to let us out, but by the end of the first week we'd stopped noticing them anyway. In fact if Lofty hadn't organised things when he did we'd probably have been in the front of the scramble ourselves. Then the nagging knowing hunger obsessed us and started Lofty on his next project. We wanted more food and he asked the sentry if he could see the commandant. Naturally nothing happened so Lofty demanded to see the commandant.

What incredible naive innocents we were!

The sentry, whom we called Goggles for obvious reasons, very much approved the era which Lofty had brought and the demand was repeated in Lofty's inimitable style.

"Commandant... more mishi-ka." The sentry thought that the big Australian was hungry and he personally saw to it Lofty's plate was filled and overflowing.

I don't think that Australians are noted for patience in times like these and he decided that drastic measures were needed to attract the commandant's attention. He got his inspiration, a food strike, 'that was it' and would really put the wind up the sentry. Even if we missed some meals we'd be better off in the long run.

Was there ever such a bunch of nincompoops as we were? We all agreed to this hair-brained scheme.

At the appointed hour Goggles came to open the cell door for mishi. Every man sat at his place and Goggles gaped.

"Mishi!" he yelled and then questioningly, "MISHIKA?"

Lofty stood up and made a lordly gesture. "Mishi - nay!" he stated.

Goggles goggled and his eyes swept the room while he tried to assimilate the situation. "Mishi!" he almost screamed and as there was still no movement he turned and stamped off. He left the cell door open and we breathed a sigh of relief.

This had been the test and we'd won. He hadn't done anything because he daren't and he left the door open, hoping we'd relent and take our rice. We hadn't relented when Goggles returned after doing the rest of his rounds.

Quite mildly he asked again "Mishika?" and when Lofty shook his head he unhurriedly locked the door and departed. He was back very soon accompanied this time by a sentry with a rifle. Goggles had a big thick stick and with this he started to lay about him as soon as he got inside.

"Mishi! Mishi!" he screamed with each blow and there would have been a scramble downstairs if Lofty's stentorian voice hadn't bellowed out. "Hold it! Hold it you chaps! Don't give in!"

Goggles stopped screaming and looked at him. "Anchow - ka?" he asked and Lofty nodded. We knew by now that 'anchow' was 'leader'.

Goggles beckoned and Lofty followed him out of the cell. He locked the door and turned to the 'anchow'.

"Kiotsiki!" he screamed but Lofty just stood there, we didn't know yet this was the command 'attention'.

Then they started on him, Goggles with his stick and the other sentry with his boots and rifle butt and in a moment Lofty was reeling and staggering. I couldn't stand it and jumped to the bars. "Hoy! Hoy!" I yelled, "Leave him alone, I'm anchow. Leave him alone I'm boss."

Shades of mad dogs and Englishmen.

In a moment I was lined up beside Lofty and we were both catching it although after the first appalled shock I felt nothing.

Inside the room Tom couldn't stand it and yelled out, "Stop it! Stop it! We'll have your flaming rice!"

"Mishi okay - ka?" enquired Goggles and Tom nodded.

The beating ended and the mutiny was over and everybody except Lofty and I slunk down to rescue the food from the flies. We weren't allowed food now but we didn't feel like it anyway.

Goggles came into our cage, all grinning and jovial next morning, he thought it was a helluva joke. He had a look at our bruises and gabbled a lot of unintelligible advice. More to the point he brought some ointment. Lofty grinned back at him in camaraderie.

Goggles brought Lofty some extra beans and rice that night. Perhaps he wasn't so bad after all. When all was said and done I suppose he had to do something about the situation. He'd made his point anyway, we were not allowed to complain.

So we pined in the foulness of Moulmein jail. No sunshine, no exercise except the appalling monotonous and wearisome up and down pacing in our few square yards of cage. Our hunger became so bad that we awakened in the morning with our minds on food. We counted the hours and the minutes to Mishi time and we wolfed it down when we got it. Then we started counting down to the next meal.

We had no washing water, just one drum of drinking water, outside the cage but within reach of our arms. Mugs of every degree of filth were dipped into it.

The benjo (latrine tin) was the ultimate in degradation however, one drum inside the cell for eighty odd dysentry-ridden prisoners. It filled and overflowed every day and there was no way of cleaning the mess. It was loathsome, and yet there was always a rush of volunteers to empty it. This job gave a few minutes in the blessedness of fresh air and sun even if it meant wading through filth to get it.

Sleep should have been a refuge. It wasn't because as soon as darkness came, so did the bugs. They converged in hordes on every warm body in the room and five minutes after lying down, their biting drove all hope of sleep away. Until one was thoroughly exhausted that is, then he'd probably wake up with the vile stench peculiar to squashed bugs in his nostrils, sickening enough to turn the strongest stomach.

There we languished for five weeks, some of the other poor devils were there for six months. No one died there but they died off in the years to come. The brand 'One of the Moulmein Crowd' became a phrase embodying the ultimate in misfortune.

Then on 23 June we were marshalled and shepherded to a bath house

141

outside the prison walls. There were showers and there was soap and under the eyes of the grinning guards we were allowed to cavort and scrub in the pure bliss of cleanliness. It seems that the blessings in life only become known when they are taken away.

We were marshalled again next day in the courtyard. So were Lissy, Tiny and Dicky looking fit, fat and clean. We were allowed to fraternise with some of the old hands from whom we learned just how badly the Burma campaign had gone for the British. By the time of our arrival in Moulmein, our troops had given Burma up as lost and were beating a desperate retreat into India. The general gloom was worsened by the news that the patrol sent after Ernie had got him.

Bosun, Snowy and Ernie. Three gone, eight to go.

Then we left Moulmein forever. Perhaps not forever. I'm going back there some day on a pilgrimage just as I'm going back to Siberoet.

The Japanese crammed us in the hold of a dirty tramp steamer, way down in the bowels of the ship. It wasn't nice to be at the bottom of a deep hole, although a compensating factor lay in the remnants of cargo with us, particularly the 'jaggaree' or Burmese sugar.

No-one had any idea where we were going but when we were disgorged to a thriving, humming city some of the crowd recognised the Golden Pagoda. We were in Rangoon.

Rangoon jail looked something like Moulmein, they both recalled British days. The most startling thing was the sight of white prisoners walking about in the compound towards which we were herded. Perhaps they were trusties; perhaps they were traitors; they must be traitors because one yelled out an unfamiliar command and everybody stood to attention. The one who'd yelled bowed to our guard, he bowed back ceremoniously in return. Again came a command and everybody relaxed.

The officers went on their way while we were handed over to the care of an Irish sergeant major of the Iniskillin Fusiliers.

This was 'Tim', Sergeant Major Finnerty, and he was the compound's greatest blessing in those early days. He was a disciplinarian of the British regular army with many years of command behind him. He roared at and shepherded his command as if he still had a row of guard rooms and the whole British army to back him up and somehow he got away with it. He had fatigue parties cleaning the compound, cleaning the barrack rooms and cleaning themselves, he had a barber functioning, a hospital of sorts. He had everyone jumping at his bid severely unconscious of the fact that his badge of rank (which he polished daily) meant no more here than the power of his good right arm.

Tiny Dainty could have got away with it with his massive physical presence, Tim got away with it by never doubting for a moment the power of his sergeant major's crown. Anyway, in a twinkling Tim had us washed, shaved and shorn and had allocated us to our respective quarters.

He gave me command of the Duke of Wellington's. They had no sergeant at that time and I had no regiment and under his approving eyes I once more assumed the status of Sergeant. He would have formed a sergeant's mess, given half a chance.

CHAPTER TWENTY-SEVEN
DEATH OF THE BEST ONE

Moulmein had just been a place in which to keep us - Rangoon jail was a real prisoner of war camp. Not that the Japanese recognised POW status, neither did they recognise the Geneva convention rules about prisoners. In fact they didn't recognise anything except 'The New Order for Greater East Asia', the Japanese Empire that is. Goodness only knows what impelled them to house and feed us at all. Certainly the rank and file of the Japanese army disapproved. To them a man who stopped fighting before he was dead had failed. Any Japanese who became a prisoner no longer had a country, a home or a family. He was worse than dead. This was their belief and so we really were contemptible creatures.

As such we had to recognise our masters. A British colonel who was captured was inferior to the lowest one star Japanese private and, as such, he must salute his superior. This was the law, hence the screamed 'Kiotsiki!" we'd heard on our first day. So also the bow which was the salute of the Japanese soldier. They did bow, most politely, back at us.

This bowing to the Japanese sentries who patrolled the prison was a hateful thing, but the consequences of disobedience were also hateful. Corporal punishment was also the rule in the Japanese army. They didn't spend time, energy and manpower on what they considered wasteful procedure. If a man, or officer for that matter, had done wrong, correction took place then and there. A Japanese sergeant would beat a Japanese corporal and and a two star private was allowed to thrash, in correction, a one star private. We of course didn't even have the dignity of one star.

We were slow to learn and the lessons were painful, often repeated as we didn't understand what was wrong. Dumb animals in training must go through a lot of terrified anxiety.

I started to acquire a Japanese vocabulary early in Rangoon days. I had to because Tim wouldn't. He could count in Japanese, this was necessary for roll-calls every night and morning. He could also 'Kiotsiki' and 'Yatsumei' (stand easy) but that was about the limit of his concession. So when one day we heard Goggles, who'd come from Moulmein with us, yelling for the 'anchow', Tim collected me on the way and we went to see what he wanted.

ANGRY SEA

Goggles wanted two men. He didn't say why so I gave him two fairly fit fellows. Most of the really fit ones went out daily on a work party. Everyone wanted to go on work parties but so far only Lofty and Titch of the Moulmein crowd had made the grade. Tim kept me in the compound, as Permanent Orderly Sergeant.

Anyway the two men came back with a sad tale. One of the officers, still in solitary after two months, had been ill for some time and was rumoured to be suffering from severe dysentery but the Burmese trusty who looked after the solitary block had not bothered to report it. Goggles had seen this officer lying on his bed unable to rise even for 'benjo' and he'd beaten the Burmese and then brought two British prisoners to clean the sick man.

He'd stood over them while they washed the man and had threatened to beat them if they spoke so no one knew who it was as there were many officers in solitary. Goggles took two men every day for the next few days. Then he took four men and they carried the sick man, bed and everything to our compound. I was standing beside Lofty when the bearers came in and we got a glimpse of the poor wasted face below us.

He opened his eyes and the light came to his face. "Hello" he said and closed his eyes again. He still kept that smile.

It was Doc. This was the 'Best one', the most loved of our gang. Greater than Tiny, gentler than Lissy, stauncher even than Bosun, loved by all, those who were still alive and those who had died. Now he was dying. Unless we could save him, and for our comforter we gave of our best. We washed and fed him, and stole for him, Lofty and Titch came back every evening with the food they had stolen. Eggs, bananas and fruit and it was spooned into Doc by Tombola who scarcely left his side.

He rallied too and we were able to sit by his bed and talk to him. Then he failed again. His dysentery was of the worst kind and as soon as he was cleaned he'd need cleaning again.

He strove and fought hard to live but it was no good. He'd been neglected too long by our Burmese friends and the fight was hopeless. In the midst of his friends and cared for as only loving friends can care, he died, on 31 August, 1942.

We wrapped him in a Union Jack, loaned by the Japs for these occasions, and we buried him in the shallow grave in the cemetery in Rangoon. Lofty, Titch, Tom and I said goodbye to our friend and counsellor with a prayer for Doc who'd said a prayer for Snowy and Bosun and Ernie.

Four gone, seven to go.

CHAPTER TWENTY-EIGHT
THE YANKS ARE COMING! HOORAH!

I had watched friends and acquaintances sicken, die and go out on their last trip to Rangoon without any great emotion and I was beginning to think I was becoming callous. Until Doc died that is and then in the wave of desolation which came over me I grieved and sorrowed as I had done over Gerry Hawkins and Henry Hall in Malaya.

I worried too, worried about Tiny, Lissy and Dicky, still in solitary and possibly sick and neglected as Doc had been. Lissy had never appeared to be robust, he had been down with malaria when I first picked him up on Ration Island, and though Tiny was the old indestructible I knew by now how dysentery and malaria could level even the mightiest.

I missed them too when Doc died. I was very much alone at that time. Lofty and Titch were on work parties and were drifting their own carefree way and I wasn't even seeing much of Tom.

I was friendly with Tim to a certain degree but there were one or two things about me which earned his disapproval. Nobody addressed me as 'Sergeant' for example and on one occasion I hit one of the privates who abused me.

Then one day the Japanese emptied solitary of all officers and into our compound strolled those indomitable three I longed for, Tiny, Lissy, and Dicky, dirty, weak from lack of exercise but otherwise unharmed.

I fell on them and unashamedly hugged big Tiny and my good friend Lissy. I wrung Dicky's hand, and had a good speculative look at him. He still wasn't fit, but he had a grin for us and that was good enough to start with. We set about feeding and fattening them and they started their duties as senior warrant officers in the compound. They were both senior to Tim and gently took over the reins from his hands.

They took it in turns to be compound sergeant major and of course ran the place smoothly and easily. Tiny was the biggest, roughest and toughest in the compound and no one ever dreamed of arguing with him, though there were other very tough and rough men. Lissy had no trouble either; he had a way of spitting out an order that I couldn't easily imagine anyone defying.

ANGRY SEA

From then onwards new prisoners were not kept in the solitary block for very long and the advent of the first Americans was like a refreshing breath of heaven. Four of them breezed into our compound after their interrogation and we looked and listened in open mouthed awe. Nothing like this had ever been seen before, not off the movie screen at any rate. They spoke like the Americans we'd seen on the screen, they looked like them and that's what they were. The Yanks had arrived!

No they hadn't, four Americans including three Yanks had arrived and we soon found that all Americans were not Yanks although all Yanks were Americans. I'm afraid we'd been most frightfully ignorant until now but then of course none of us had ever talked with a real live Yank, American that is, before.

They were glorious creatures with all their arrogant pride in the unconquerable might of their country, despite their good-natured toleration of anyone who wasn't American. They talked, how they talked, it was fascinating and there was never a time when they talked without an audience of delighted listeners.

They told us how the fighting on the ground had almost reached stalemate and that there seemed little immediate prospect of the British re-taking Burma from the Japanese. But from what they said and from what we'd seen with our own eyes since shortly before Christmas 1942, it was clear that the Allies were determined not to let the Japanese have it all their own way and were flying bombing missions deep into occupied Burma.

They were the remains of a crew from a Flying Fortress which had made a raid on Rangoon and had taken on the whole available mass of Japanese Zeros in the process.

Flight Sergeant Malek was senior and maybe because of this he was taciturn by comparison. But he was no shrinking violet; I saw this same quiet man in a stand-up fistfight with a compound tough called Piggy Martin who just liked fighting and he and Malek slugged at each other for almost an hour until Martin collapsed, just before Malek himself dropped exhausted.

Both these fighters were killed later in a bombing raid on the jail. They shared the same trench and collected the same bomb.

Sergeant Hal Cummings the second member of the crew was the greatest joy we had. Quick-firing, descriptive, never ceasing, he bubbled over with good cheer. He was even more American than the American films, it was like seeing a cartoon come to life.

Ely Gonzales was also a sergeant with a little pointed black beard and although his name sounded Spanish or Italian or something he was as much a Yank as any of them. I liked Ely.

Corporal Radcliffe was the boy of the party, a big southern farm boy who drawled his way through the story of their final sortie.

We'd never met anyone with the story telling ability of these Yanks before. Their powers of description, their ability to illustrate, and their facility for changing tone and expression was entertainment in itself, quite apart from the story they had to tell.

"Thar we were boys! Lamming it for home, wit' de whole goddam nip force on our tail! I got de foist one coming up in on my tail and I chalked dat bastard up. De bastards didn't know we had a sting in de tail. I missed one dat shot past me but de belly gunner got him."

On and on went the tale, round and round went the battle and down and down went the Zeros. We listened and we loved it and we didn't believe a word of it. Still we never tired of it and then, months later one of our own captured pilots brought us the truth of the story. The truth was the story was true.

Still we couldn't be blamed. They were just too good to be true.

Hal Cummings and Ely Gonzales were also killed by the bomb which got Al Malek and Piggy Martin and it was this bomb which broke up one of our escape plans. Ely, Hal and young Radcliffe were part of our escape gang and their loss upset it.

While these four were our only Americans in the compound they were our blood brothers, and then when the Yanks came drifting in in larger numbers they were collected as a unit and segregation seemed to do something. They became a faction, not part of our unit, which was a great pity in many ways as we lost touch and with that we lost understanding.

We started disapproving and there was no doubt that they held a very disparaging view of us. We started sneering, we called them bomb-happy, workshy and gutless and the gulf widened. We also thought they were stupid.

I think they were bomb-happy as a matter of fact and later on when air raids became monotonously frequent and we lost track of alerts somebody noticed that the presence or absence of Yanks in the open compound served as a perfect alertometer. If there were no Yanks about the inference was that they were in the trenches. A Yank anywhere in the open meant that the all clear must have gone.

We were, of course, unjust to them because they were a solidly welded unit within themselves.

Somebody, Len White probably, (I've got a lot to say about Len later) noticed something else about the Yanks. Len made the astonishing statement that it was possible to pick out nationalities by their physical condition. It was strange and inexplicable but it was undoubtedly true. In a compound where the usual dress was a loin cloth there were no distinguishing national marks and we mentally separated everybody by physical condition.

On one side we put the cadaverous bony, disease ridden specimens. They usually turned out to be the dirty ones also, the scabrous and the lice ridden, covered with sores and wasting away. The dirt of course was a natural consequence of sick men. This group were largely Yanks.

On the other end of the scale we put the fit, clean and the healthy-skinned specimens. Clean clothing, clean skins and free of sores they almost seemed to thrive in jail. Almost 100 per cent of this group were the Australians, I should say Anzac because we had one Kiwi with the Diggers. This was Chuck Ferguson of Wellington and I have a lot to say about Chuck later.

I don't know what it was but the separation was definite.

In the middle group, not exactly thriving but not exactly wilting, just struggling through, were the other British. It almost seemed as if the British had the will but not the sheer physical power to win completely.

A funny thing about some of the Americans I saw after the war was that almost within days of release they increased in stature. They put on their superfine uniforms, ate their ice cream and hamburgers and were strong and virile at once. Almost like hot house plants, a glory to behold until they are left outside to wilt and die. Bring them back and the glory is there again at once.

The Australians were probably like the hardy bush weeds that simply cannot be destroyed, while the British, as I said had the guts but had centuries of undernourishment to fail them.

Of course not all Americans were despised. One young officer set to and established a workshop which produced plates, mugs and cutlery for every man in the compound. Another had guts to match any nationality, and with the guts he had a radiant sunny nature and I was proud indeed to call him my friend. He was one of a crew whose plane had gone down in flames and by the time we got him his burns and wounds were swarming with maggots. Our orderlies worked for hours picking off the maggots as they appeared out of his ears, nose and mouth. A lesser man would have given up and died.

Anyway that was the Yanks, Americans I mean, and I think it was a pity that segregation came to Rangoon jail. We were doing all right when we were all together.

CHAPTER TWENTY-NINE

THE AUSSIES

The Aussies started rolling in soon after the officers were released and at once I was one of them. I had been with an Australian machine gun battalion in Malaya but had never really got to know them. In fact they had severely shocked my military sense of what was and was not proper.

I had to report to the Regimental Sergeant Major of this battalion in Malaya and as my picture of an RSM came from the East Surrey prototype I knew what kind of a man to look for. An RSM was the last word in military dignity and power, even captains could quake before the blast of one of these godlike creatures and mere sergeants scuttled for cover when one was about. So I arrived and asked a bareheaded, bare torsoed character where I could find the Regimental Sergeant Major.

"Over there cobber," he said, jerking his thumb towards a group of mixed, and very disreputable hobos grouped in a circle.

I marched over and scanned the group who were watching one bull of a man who had two pennies balanced on a piece of wood.

"Up they go, Bluey" someone yelled and so up they went!

This went on several times and this character seemed to be collecting money from everybody in the circle while I looked for the RSM.

So I asked again, "Can anyone tell me where to find the Regimental Sergeant Major?"

Somebody helped me out. "Hey Bluey!" he called and Bluey turned. "Pommy here to see you Blue."

I ignored the 'Pommy' and I didn't believe my ears but it was true. Bluey was the RSM.

Anyway I hadn't known many Australians. Lofty, Titch and Ernie of course were in a class of their own and we only had one other Australian in camp so far. This was Buck Bryson, a captured commando. Buck was already a very special friend of mine.

Now they were rolling in and I knew these boys at once, they were everything and they had everything I admired or envied. Quizzical, quiet eyes yet with nothing quiet about their tongues. Big, bronzed and absolutely fearless of man or devil, they had a quiet, serious humour which could become raucous with barrack room coarseness. They were outspoken and brutally frank but could be gentle when gentleness was called for. It was hard to say which was the best.

I think John Reid of Brisbane, Peter Wilson of Bricalous and Buck Bryson of Melbourne might have been my favourites, outside of our own gang, that is. They were all real 'beauts' though – Mal Woods, Ron Haddon, Harvey Beasley, Jim Coppin, there wasn't a dud amongst them. I could fill my book with tales of the Aussies.

Take the cook-house story for example: there had always been rackets in the cook-house right from the early days when there had been only a few prisoners and cooked food had been issued in bulk from the Japanese cook-house. Then as the compound numbers swelled, a ramshackle cook-house was built, uncooked rations were issued and the cooks took over.

Rice and unknown etceteras disappeared daily into the cook-house and boiled rice and an unsalted watery stew reappeared; once a day. Boiled rice without the stew was dished out for the other two meals. The dishing out was done by cooks and the ingratiating smiles they received were sickening.

The cooks ate their food in the cook-house.

The cooks were fat and strong.

The cooks began to accumulate friends who would willingly carry water and chop wood for them.

The cooks' friends became fat and strong.

This went on even when the Japanese released the officers and organisation came to the compound. In fact some of the officers became hewers of wood and carriers of water.

Then Brigadier Hobson was released from solitary and as soon as he took over he put his foot down on this last business. He had very definite ideas about discipline and dignity. He was an associate of mine from Shanghai days when I had been a soldier and he had been a civilian. He really got his teeth into this ration business and decided that proper supervision was necessary. So, we got a cook sergeant who gradually filled out to healthy proportions.

Now the brig' put a food officer on the job and we got a fattening food officer.

This hadn't worked so a new order came to restrict each cook sergeant's and food officer's tour of duty to one month.

Then we got a succession of well-fed sergeants and food officers and it looked as if nothing could be done.

Then it came to Pete Wilson's turn as sergeant and Chuck Ferguson's turn as food officer.

Pete Wilson was one of an air crew of three in camp, John Reid was his pilot and Len White made up the third. One Englishman and two Australians. Chuck Ferguson was our only Kiwi, a fighter pilot who was supposed to be dead, which wasn't surprising as he had been shot down in flames and had hit the ground at an estimated 300 mph. He had recovered consciousness in the field next to that where his plane burned, still strapped to his seat and with a very badly broken arm. The bone had knitted with his hand at right angles to his wrist, but years later when I looked him up in New Zealand I found he'd had it straightened.

Pete was cook sergeant, and his first bright idea was to supply each room with its own quota of cooked food and let the sergeant in charge dish it out. This was a big step forward especially for the rooms which contained a few sick men who didn't want any food. Everybody in the room got a bit extra.

But the stew that went to the rooms didn't come from the same pot as the cooks' meals. Pete didn't see the sense of this, so he decreed that all food should be cooked together and each cook would go to his room for his ration. They howled at this and went en masse to complain to the food officer - Chuck Ferguson.

Chuck dealt with them and became the first food officer who had ever dared to risk putting himself offside with the Lords of the compound. They threatened to quit.

"That's all right," Chuck said, "You can go out on work parties."

Work parties at that particular time were 'on the nose'. Gardening in the hot sun miles from any kind of loot or other pickings. The job consisted mainly of carrying tins of human excreta and digging it into the furrows between rows of cabbages, silverbeet and spinach.

They wouldn't rather go on work parties.

The stews got better because the cooks' rations had to be used somehow - in our stew. The richness of the stews was unbelievable, they even had meat in them. And salt.

Then by the end of the first week Chuck Ferguson found that the stock of cooking oil was accumulating and incredibly, on one morning, every man in the compound, fat-starved and oil-hungry, had fried rice fritters for breakfast.

By the time that Pete's month was up the new era had been established and would never be allowed to slip again, especially as Chuck was still food officer and he went on to bigger and better things in food.

ANGRY SEA

Pete finished his cook-house tour just as skinny as when he started, but every man in camp was fed more richly than ever before. We had rice and dahl (an Indian split-pea dish) every morning, rice and a kind of vegetable water and beef tea for lunch and an ample meal of rice and thick stew for tea.

I'm proud of the fact that Pete Wilson, the most honest man I've ever met and Chuck Ferguson the incorruptible Kiwi, were friends of mine. Peter asked me to come to Australia after the war. Never mind the address he said, just remember our brand, somebody in Australia will tell you where we are. "You can have a horse," Pete said "and a hut, and a welcome."

Just the same I memorised his address - Pete Wilson, Bricalous, Barabee, AUSTRALIA.

Chuck was another prized friend and I did drop in on him after the war - to his great surprise! I really must go and see Pete some day.

STILL AUSSIES

I don't know whether the Japanese had a naive honesty which made them easy to fool, or whether the Australians were natural thieves who'd fool the devil himself. Either way, the Japanese we met, apart from the prison guards, were putty in their hands.

Once we had to go down to unload a food ship when Burmese coolies were scarce, there had been one or two small bombing raids. Soon after we started work I managed to slip away and do a little snooping, but not before Lofty and Titch had disappeared of course. I peeped through a porthole into a cabin and there already settled was Titch, in a comfortable chair, smoking a Burmese cigar, and with a cup of coffee beside him. He was surrounded by Japanese sailors and as I drew back hurriedly, I heard a terrific roar of laughter from the cabin.

The funny part about it was that at this time Titch knew no Japanese and none of the crew spoke English.

Meanwhile Lofty was prowling about looking for someone to catch with his stock confidence trick. Lofty didn't bother about rank and file, he was just as liable to tackle the skipper as not. His Japanese was better than Titch's so he could ask where he could get a drink of water. Then he'd put his hands to his stomach and conjure up a picture of troubles and if he got any sympathy the rest was easy.

He'd bring the conversation round to the wife and babies, and every Japanese he ever met would fall for it and produce his photographs of the Japanese wife and happy smiling children. Lofty would gaze at them in rapt admiration and then produce his trump card. This was his wife and children. He wasn't even married, but he had a photograph of a really ravishingly beautiful girl in summer shorts and jacket, sitting on a bungalow verandah with two delightful blonde children beside her. I think he's stolen the snap - God knows who from.

This girl in the picture would turn the heart of any good man who saw her and it put Lofty in good every time. The victim would give cheroots, food and clothing for the sake of Lofty's wife alone. Years later, when I was still wandering, I dropped in on Lofty in Melbourne (I was supposed to be in England) and was greeted with open arms by the girl that Lofty really did marry. She was beautiful too.

Lofty kept his friends in cigarettes, soap and some clothing, but I went in more for direct thieving and I used to get my best hauls during air raids when the Japanese dived for very quick cover.

Lissy didn't have to do any thieving or trickery at all. Within months he could gabble Japanese in a smooth conversational flow. The Japanese camp interpreter used to use him, because Lissy's Japanese was better than his English. The sentries in the prison during their lonely duties used to yell for Lissy and talk to him by the hour and not one of them would ever lay a hand on him. He even used to argue with them and we'd hold our breath sometimes when it looked as if an argument was getting really heated. Most of these sentries used to bring 'presents' for Lissy.

But I was a thief.

Then the time came when unorganised thieving became dangerous. A whole work party was liable to disintegrate in search of loot and very naturally, even the friendliest of the Japanese would become irate. Beatings were dished out. This could ruin a perfectly good relationship.

So Tiny Dainty devised a scheme which the Australian rogues developed. It was simply to keep everybody working except two or three, according to the size of the party. With most of the party working diligently two or three wouldn't be missed and would have a free hand to acquire loot for all. So, everybody was happy.

Then Lofty had a brainwave and the jail guard was puzzled one day to see two men staggering out for the day's work burdened with a bucket of cooked rice, slung on a bamboo pole. Lissy was standing by to explain that a work party was not always fed by the Japanese, (this was an outrageous lie). It was 'necessary' to take lunch from the camp.

Sometimes two buckets were taken and sometimes one or both were brought back to camp unused.

"Good food," Lissy explained. "We were fed by kind Japanese today but we do not want to waste anything."

154

"Velly good," approved the guard commander and let it go.

In the compound we would immediately dump the 'good food' (all two inches sitting on a concealed shelf) and then we'd share the loot crammed in the bucket. Then Lofty and Titch who were always appointed 'cooks for the day' meaning 'thieves for the day' decided that they didn't like their carrying pole.

This was a nice, springy, fairly thin bamboo pole, ideal for carrying. They produced a fifteen feet long massive bamboo, the weight of which was enough to stagger a man, and off they went, with the bucket of rice looking very small, in the middle. For days the same pantomime was enacted at the guard room as we worked our way through different guards.

The guard commander would yell out at the two Aussies. "Curra!" which meant 'Hey you!' 'English Pig!' 'Stupid Bastard!' or whatever you like.

He'd come to the pole, and patiently as one would to half-wits he'd try to explain how stupid it was to use a pole like that. He of course knew all about bamboo poles, all coolies did. Some guard commanders would even bring a pole to illustrate the point but Lofty and Titch would stubbornly insist that a thin pole hurt their shoulders.

When we'd worked our way through all guard commanders they gave up. We were too stupid to be shown anything. Then Lofty switched his pole to one that looked the same but wasn't really. It was hollow down the centre and would hold an amazing amount of loot. Shirts, shorts, soap, shoes, salt, anything at all would go in that pole and not one of the guards in the jail would ever find it.

When Lofty was really loaded with loot he usually carried one item openly in his hand and even if no one asked him about it he'd go out of his way to tell the sentry that it was. "Presento! nippon presento!" and even if it was confiscated it wasn't often that he was thoroughly searched.

I wonder how many of us retained or developed our cunning habits after the war. There was also the cunning of the two Australians who pinched a cooking vat from a Japanese barracks.

One of our cast iron cooking vats, a huge thing about five feet in diameter somehow got cracked and started to leak so that rice cooked in it always got burnt. We tried to get a replacement from the quartermaster of the jail, but had no luck, so we had to use one of the cooking vats twice which meant that the first boiling was not very hot when it was finally dished out.

We put up with it until Lofty and Titch found themselves on a work party in a large Japanese barracks and staring us in the face at the cook-house was a row of ten iron vats, just like ours. The two boys were of course 'official cooks' (thieves) and they set about making friends with the cook. This was easy; nobody could hold out against those two when they turned on the charm. Besides this they were so very helpful chopping wood for the cook, keeping fires going and carrying water.

In a week they'd got this bloke into the happy state when he'd buzz off after the midday meal and leave everything to Lofty and Titch. Then Lofty had the bright idea of taking freshly cooked rice for our work party and believe it or not, he and Titch staggered out one day carrying an iron cooking vat slung on two poles.

The Japanese sentries knew that all Australians were mad but this was the limit and they had to know why. All they could get out of Lofty was, "Experimento! Mishi experimento".

A lot of us used to tag on an 'o' to ordinary English words to make them more understandable to Japanese, and were often quite surprised at the enemy stupidity in not understanding.

Lofty was particularly good at this when he wanted to be dense and eventually a weary and still puzzled sentry waved him on. When he got to the place of work he set about mounting the vat in a stone fireplace just exactly like the other ten vats.

It was a very primitive brick and clay fireplace and was easy to copy. He left it there for two days and then decided that his 'experimento' was no good and took the vat back to the jail.

No one in the Japanese camp realised that in the two hours in the afternoon when the boys had the cookhouse to themselves, they had switched vats and left the puzzled cook with one cracked vat among his nine good ones. He'd have no trouble getting a replacement anyway, especially as he'd be doing his own cooking in future.

Lofty and Titch would be on other and more profitable work parties.

CHAPTER THIRTY
JAP BUDDIES

Work parties varied from gardening to unloading ships and gave us a chance to get away from the prison and pick up loot. These parties were invariably supervised by Japanese unconnected with the jail who, in most cases, were very different in disposition from the guards. It was fairly easy to cajole food out of them, good food that is, well prepared and cooked in their own cook-houses. As many work parties were engaged in building earthwork air-raid shelters in Japanese barracks we did well.

We always came in for cook-house leavings and quite often we'd be distributed among different squads to dine with them in their barrack rooms. They talked to us and gradually it began to look as if there might be some nice Japanese after all.

The memory of one is particularly pleasant. I attracted his attention first by the way I worked. In those early days I was fit and hard and was determined to stay that way, besides which I revelled with arrogant pride in my stamina. Pete Wilson, our Australian sheep farmer, was one of the very few who was more than a match for me and we were slugging away one roasting day, stripped to the waist with our brown bodies glistening with sweat.

The Japanese corporal in charge came along and watched us and then he realised in shocked surprise that the 'anchow' (myself) was working. "Curra!" he shouted.

This 'Curra' business seemed to cover everything from 'English Pig' to 'Hey you!' He was waving goodbye as the Japanese do when they mean 'Come here' so I went over to him.

"Anchow?" he asked.

"Hai!" I said, which was yes.

"Yatsumei" he ordered, meaning rest, so I yelled out for "Smoko!"

He only meant me to rest but he let it go and sat down beside me producing his cigarettes. The inevitable questions came.

"English - ka?" (Ka tagged on to the end of a sentence makes it a question) and I was soon telling him about my escape from Singapore and Sumatra. This was always a good line. We were getting along famously when he came out with the usual crack.

"Churchill no good!" and since I'd all ready weighed him up I flexed the muscles of my right arm in the universal illustration of strength and said staunchly, "Churchill - strong!"

He laughed and put his elbows in the ground with the palms clasped. Churchill, he explained, was the left hand and Tojo was the right hand. There was a momentary clash of forces and then Churchill was on the ground and all the Japanese were laughing at Tojo's victory.

"Yeah maybe!" I said, "But wait!" then I repeated the pantomime as he had with Tojo on top of Churchill who was down and out. I looked at the faces about me, waited a moment then let Churchill stir and feebly struggle. The struggles became stronger and Tojo had his hands full and then suddenly Churchill was upright and Tojo and he were fighting for supremacy. I thought I'd better not go any further than that so I shrugged my shoulders and we went back to work even though the corporal wanted me to rest until I explained to him that I wanted to work.

He went off but came back in the early afternoon and when he waved me goodbye again I followed him to the barrack lines. He took me to the bath house, which had real baths but no taps, and told me to get the fire going under the tank of water from which it was to be ladled into the bath. While it was heating he brought out his clean clothes, towel and soap and left them on a stool beside the bath. I sat down to wait for the water to heat. I filled his bath with beautiful hot water when it was ready.

When he did come back he was flabbergasted to see me still sitting there but not so flabbergasted as I was when I realised that the bath was for me, so were the white shirt and PT shorts and the towel and soap. I was even able to wash my own trousers when I finally dragged myself out of the luxurious depths of hot soapy water. I don't think I was ever so clean in my whole life as I was that day. He even gave me a note, at my request, to show the prison guards in case they thought I'd pinched the outfit.

We really got on well after this and quite apart from diplomacy I began to look forward to seeing him. He in his turn asked the prison authorities if he could have me on his party every day.

Then there was the man who gave us a prison library, almost the greatest blessing in our lives. We'd had no books up to this time and so when he asked me one day to tell him how he could help us, I thought hard and then asked if he could find any books. He said he would try and must have done some searching that night because next morning he said he had found many books and would take us to get them that afternoon if we finished our quota of digging early.

We always had plenty of reserve up our sleeves because a lot of us didn't do as much work as it seemed and by three o'clock we'd packed up and were on the truck. We were driven to a suburb of Rangoon, to a deserted building which had been an English high school. It had been looted and looted until not a thing was left except books and they were strewn in their hundreds on the floor. We fell upon them gleefully and would have taken the lot except that we knew we'd be beaten up when we got back. But we got as many as we could secrete about our bodies.

Next day and for many more days my working party was well prepared, everybody was fully dressed in shirts and trousers or voluminous sarongs and each day we returned laden with loot.

The Japanese corporal and I inspected the party before we went back to the prison and where we saw a bulge which looked suspicious we made the man with the bulge either adjust it or dump part of his load.

We knew we wouldn't have a detailed search from the guards because our corporal was giving wonderful reports about our work and behaviour and so all we had to watch was the eagle eye of the sentry as we walked past him.

The lowest forms of human life in the east are the street sweepers, who are the coolies in China and the untouchables of India. The most degrading locality for a street sweeper is the humming thriving bazaar. Humming with its myriads of flies and thriving with every tropical disease imaginable.

Some remote member of the Japanese hierarchy decided that nothing could be funnier than a working party of Europeans sweeping the bazaar. So on a certain day, a dozen grinning Japanese marshalled twenty British and American sahibs and set off for the bazaar. Large wicker baskets slung on poles were produced for refuse, shovels and bamboo brushes were shoved into unwilling hands and the sweep was on. Of course it was a farce, we could scarcely move in that throng let alone collect rubbish but that didn't really matter. The important point was that the lowest form of life was on display in its proper environment.

The Burmese loved it and laughed and jeered as did the Japanese. It was a roaring success for a while, even though the sentries couldn't keep track of us in that mob. They didn't care and soon went off to enjoy coffee and cakes so we were left to our sweeping.

When the Japanese had gone the jeers died away and in fact there were audible clicks of sympathy. Then the sympathy took on a material form and a bundle of cheroots was pushed into my hand. I was wearing a loin cloth only and there was no place to hide my gift, except in the basket, so in it went. The Burmese roared with laughter and a box of matches came sailing through the air to land beside the cigars.

The news spread as only bazaar news can. By the time our sentries returned they were staggered to see the humble sahibs happily tottering back and forward with loaded baskets to the dumping ground which was behind a house at one end of the bazaar.

Some of the sahibs were wearing shorts, shirts appeared later, bare feet gradually became shod, topees or straw hats appeared and stomachs gradually stretched almost to bursting point. We dined at various coffee shops lounging in elegant comfort and some of us even got a bit tipsy before the day ended.

A bunch of ragged scarecrows had left the compound in the morning and twenty well dressed and groomed sahibs returned that night.

Of course we were stripped of our regalia where it was obviously new, but some of us had managed to camouflage it. I got away with a pair of corduroy riding breeches although I lost my shoes, shirt and hat and gained a beating also, as did most of the others. But I still had my full and satisfied stomach.

The Japanese didn't give in easily and demanded fifty sweepers next morning. They had fifty guards to match the sweepers but they didn't have the show. The Burmese came into the game and although they couldn't pass much into our hands, there were still the baskets and all that was needed was to distract the sentries' attention for a moment and the missiles came lobbing into them. They never caught onto the basket situation and wouldn't come anywhere near the dumping ground.

Besides this we had a new idea - money! And we also had a place to hide it. At least Lofty and I had, tucked behind our sergeants stripes which we both wore today for a change. We returned to camp, less blatantly satisfied than we had been yesterday but the Japanese knew they weren't winning.

But they had another go with even more guards this time. They never noticed that almost every man in the work party had suddenly sprouted sergeants' stripes and apart from the hundreds of rupees which many of us got, all of us managed to slip away time and again during the day. All anybody had to do in the thronged bazaar to disappear was to crouch down and he'd be invisible from a few feet away.

That night the Brigadier asked if more sweepers were wanted and got a vicious slap for his question.

Except for one occasion I never saw anyone, English, American or Australian openly defy the Japanese, but there were many equally dangerous ways of defying them under cover.

The one man I saw in active defiance was a young English soldier called Haines and nicknamed Tosser. He was a headache and a nuisance to officers and NCOs in our compound; a born rebel and a mutinous troublemaker. Piggy Martin was another and naturally they were bosom pals whose main joy was in fist fighting each other. After Piggy, who was a Lance Corporal and had been a commando, was killed by a bomb, Haines was left to defy authority alone.

The most dreaded Japanese authority in the jail was the quartermaster who was a born sadist and full of inflated ideas about the importance of the sons of Nippon. Often he was charming, courteous and smiling but even Lissy was wary of his violently changing moods. Roll call under 'The Terror' could be a frightful ordeal if he was in one of his mad rages as he'd not leave the compound until he'd thoroughly beaten up a number of men. He'd find an excuse somehow even if it was only an imaginary flutter of an eyelid on parade, and he'd work himself into a fury of slappings and kickings. Sometimes he'd line up two of our squads facing each other and make them start slapping each other. Woe betide the man and his partner, who didn't slap with gusto.

He'd had a real orgy of rampaging one night and as he was strolling away he suddenly shrieked, "Move! someone move!" (his English was understandable).

Now no one had moved but he drew his huge sword and went galloping down our lines again to finish up in full view of everyone still shrieking and waving his sword. Not many people would have gone any nearer to him than a mad bull but the Brigadier did. He tried to placate him but the madman swore he'd chop some heads off.

Neither before or after that day was any prisoner threatened but, suddenly, in the midst of the petrified silence everyone was aware of movement in the ranks as a man put his head out. "Brigadier!" he called. "Tell the silly bastard I moved!"

It was Tosser and even the Japanese was stilled. Then he turned slowly and waggled his hand at Tosser.

Tosser strolled casually towards him and slouched before the madman. The Japanese held his sword in two hands and we waited horrified for Tosser's head to fall.

Tosser spat contemptuously at his feet and the sword was lowered.

"You velly brave" the quartermaster said in a voice that was now sane, and Tosser shrugged his shoulders not deigning to answer. The sword was sheathed, the play was over, and six hundred breaths were let out.

This same Jap insisted that the whole compound should drill and march like Japanese soldiers with goose step and words of command included, and it was in this that the more subtle defiance was possible.

Pete Wilson was the most audacious, closely followed by Lofty

Eastgate. Pete was a fairly tough Australian sergeant and had developed a readiness to knock down a man if necessary.

Even in an English regiment the screamed commands are usually unrecognisable as actual words and it was not different in Japanese. Consequently, it was not easy to substitute insulting words and phrases which would be intelligible to us but difficult to pick up for any Japanese bystanders.

Pete and Lofty used to take it too far however. They could have got us all shot or beheaded or something, especially in the innovation they used when goose-stepping past the guard-room. The words of command to start us goose-stepping and then 'eyes right' were quite a mouthful, but were certainly nothing like the machine gun rattle of

"Look at the silly..."

This was the cautionary formula and then would come the screamed finale, "BASTARDS"

It sounded absolutely clear and distinct and we'd hold our breaths as our heads and eyes flashed to the right, just as the guard which turned out for us came smartly down to 'present arms' and the guard commander bowed humbly in salute.

CHAPTER THIRTY-ONE
DYSENTERY

Dysentery was something prisoners learned to live with after a while but in its worst form it could, and often did, slowly kill a man. I'd seen men suffer agonising deaths from it as it grew from a relatively mild irritation to a disease that sapped all one's strength and willpower, although I also witnessed some remarkable cases where, *in extremis*, victims had apparently decided they just weren't going to die. I don't mean they decided they didn't <u>want</u> to die; not many people did want to die, even when on the face of things death could be a merciful release from the utter misery of their lives as prisoners. Sometimes the will to live was the ultimate deciding factor between life and death for those at death's door.

Not many people have this kind of will or the knowledge that will is the answer. It needs knowledge to beget faith and this knowledge of the power of will and the faith in the will is all we need.

How else did people like Len White survive with his dysentery, malaria, beri-beri and finally his broken bones? How did Percy Hall, with one of the most advanced cases of the fatal type of beri-beri, still drag his indomitable way about the compound and finally reach the stage when he held his own on work parties? Why did others with only one of the maladies wilt and die before our eyes? We could pick those who would die and those who would recover and we were very rarely wrong. We could even pick the day as often as not.

The Moulmein crowd started to die off soon after we arrived in Rangoon and the eventual toll of the original eighty-three was appalling. The percentage of deaths was even greater than that of the Americans, and that was very high.

Dysentery was already rife in Moulmein and even in Rangoon was probably the most devastating of all complaints. A man with a real attack of dysentery could be down to skin and bones in a week, which wasn't surprising when you consider that he had reason to be pleased with himself if he could reduce his daily excursions to the benjo to less than thirty.

The real trouble with dysentery was that a week of it could start a habit, almost impossible to break. It might have been habit that was formed or control that was lost, but certainly, the fact was that once you had 'the runs' for a while then everything you ate or drank seemed to go

163

straight through the bowels, liberally mixed with blood and mucus.

It really was a problem trying to decide whether to eat or drink and aggravate the dysentery or whether to use the starvation cure and risk becoming so weak that you'd die anyway. Particularly as there was no medicine of any kind in the early days and no dysentery medicine at any time, except some home-made stuff.

The home-made cure consisted of fine charcoal, ground from the charred embers of the cooking fires and washed down by the spoonful. Beastly stuff!

Our little gang all had dysentery mildly, mild that is by current standards. In normal army life one of our mild attacks would have put a man in hospital and on convalescence for a month. Here it was not a valid excuse to miss Tenko (roll-call) or work parties.

Lissy and Lofty copped it more than the rest of us who were well, but even so we all used the benjo at least six times a day.

The benjo itself had been built for non-European prisoners and consisted of a building with a roof, but no walls and filled with long rows of stalls. Each stall had in it two bricks and between the bricks was a metal tin. The bricks were for the feet and the user squatted. This position may also have helped to keep bowels open, in fact with the three factors, diet, dysentery and squat it is perhaps not surprising that no benjo tin ever contained any solid matter during the first year at least. Not a single man had constipation or anything but loose bowels in Rangoon jail.

The final paragraph about 'Benjo' before laying it aside is on disposal. None of the contents were wasted, all went into vegetable gardens, particularly the cabbage and spinach gardens and any that was not immediately needed was saved for a rainy day. The savings bank consisted of a huge crater-like hole at the back of the prison, about fifty feet across and of unknown depth, although it was at least deep enough to drown a bullock which once slipped into it. We felt great sorrow for this bullock as it happened to be prisoners' rations.

The emptying of the benjo was done by men who had been sick but were strong enough to carry the thirty-gallon drums into which the tins were emptied. Two men carried each drum slung on a bamboo pole.

I never went near the benjo without running into Len White, either coming out, going in or squatting there to meet incomers with his fat chuckle and his stock joke. "Is your journey really necessary?"

He seemed to live in the place and when I had my run of dysentery, on and off for eighteen months, the benjo became almost our social centre.

CHAPTER THIRTY-TWO
MALARIA

Malaria took a fair toll of victims which was not surprising as none of us had taken anti-malarial precaution since December 1941. Up to that time it was a military offence not to have your mosquito bed-net down after sunset, it was an offence to wear shorts or short sleeved shirts after sunset, mosquito cream had to be used liberally and anti-malaria squads sprayed all stagnant water at least once a week.

The malaria carrying female mosquito should not have stood a chance and indeed I'd only once had malaria in peace time. This was in Hong Kong in 1939 and I was in hospital and convalescing for a month. The army certainly cherished its personnel in those days, because the kind of attack I'd had then would not have excused me a work party or tenko parade. People didn't seem to die from malaria directly in jail, but a few bad attacks could leave a man so weak and helpless that he'd be a pushover for anything else that came along.

Once again Lissy and Lofty were the first of our gang to come down, and Lofty particularly was reduced to the skin and bones stage. Lissy, in Rangoon days, was never anything but skinny but he had an amazing virility and stamina for such a wretched-looking creature.

Lofty used to joke about being able to count his ribs but they stuck out like those of a cadaverous skinned rabbit, and his condition alarmed us, especially when he went off his food. Previously he would eat anything and everything, even (almost) the bullock that fell in the cesspit.

These two were over their malaria and beginning to thrive again when I got my first attack and realised what they and Len White had been through. I believe there are different types of malaria but the prison camp brand always seemed to follow the same pattern. To begin with it used to come on alternate days so a man would have an 'off day' and an 'on day'. Even the on day was not for a full twenty-four hours, and anybody who was smart could stoke up with food, even an hour before he went down, usually in mid-afternoon so that nourishment, and strength, could be stored against the demands on reserves.

Even to the most determined, eating was impossible during an attack, and as every meal missed was a serious matter it really was a good idea to stock up whenever possible.

Len White even used to scrounge an early meal if he estimated that he would be out of action at meal time. He persuaded me to adopt this habit and I think we both gained a lot of really valuable calories in this manner.

The fever would start like other fevers, with a muzzy headache and slight nausea, gradually building up to a fire that was hot and cold, that made the whole body hot to the touch yet carried with it an uncontrollable shuddering and a shivering and a demand for blankets, blankets and more blankets. Some of the blankets were really old sacks.

With the raging fever came an intolerable and unquenchable thirst and we used to drink gallons of water. This was cold in the early days but as we gained experience we found ways of getting hot water, and the mugs and mugs of hot water were like pure nectar. The drinking, shuddering and raging thirst could go on for an hour or two before the relief of sweating started, and every drop of water a man had drunk would start to come out of him to soak through the blankets and run to the floor.

Another hour of this and the friends of the patient could start removing blankets one at a time until he lay, uncovered and normal. Normal, that is, except that he would not have enough strength to raise his head, yet might have to be on tenko within the hour. In fact tenko could and sometimes did come inconveniently in the middle of the sweat. In those cases some of us used to turn off the attack for long enough to get outside, then return and resume the interrupted session. Such is the power of the will.

Exemption from tenko was out of the question for malaria only, or for dysentery only. A man had to be in hospital to be excused, and he had to be really sick to get there. Nobody wanted hospital anyway because all anyone got out of it was exemption from roll-call. There were orderlies to bring food to the patients but who wanted food and malaria at the same time? Besides this hospital was a beastly-smelling place of death and decay. When a paroxysm was over there would be about thirty-six hours in which to build up enough strength for the next attack, and as strength came from food, Len White's system wasn't so bad.

But stoking up with food wasn't easy. Food and the thought of food was nauseating during the ten days (on and off) of a bout of malaria. Chicken soup, jelly and beef tea would have been an ordeal, boiled rice was loathsome. It was worse than trying to eat sawdust and it was impossible to swallow it. Len and I used to masticate each sickening mouthful and then wash it down into our stomachs with water as one would swallow a pill.

Even then the gorge would rise and we had to fight the impulse to vomit. Vomiting was loss and we couldn't afford any loss. Besides this, Len said it was 'letting yourself go' and this was shameful.

ANGRY SEA

Len would taunt anyone who vomited, especially me and jibe with his eternal, "Ha, you're losing Gab, you're letting yourself go! We'll carry you out yet!"

But I had a few digs at him, he had more malaria than I did but even so I had at least one attack each month over the last two years. My attacks didn't always last ten days and weren't all bad, but they were bad enough.

CHAPTER THIRTY-THREE

BERI-BERI

Of all the maladies we suffered, beri-beri was, I think, the most dreaded: once it started its insidious progress in the body, it was difficult to stop. Wet beri-beri, if it got a real hold, was almost 100 per cent fatal and dry beri-beri was crippling in its effects. Blindness and deafness were the extremes and if either faculty was lost it was forever. A halt in the march of progressing dry beri-beri was possible but there was no retraction.

In the early days we knew nothing of this disease and those who went through the first stage of suffering agonising pains in the legs and arms put it down to rheumatism or arthritis. We tried all kinds of methods to relieve the pain, the most obvious one being to bask in the hot sun. It didn't occur to anyone that our trouble was caused by a vitamin deficiency due to a diet of too much polished rice.

The second stage of beri-beri was relieving in some ways but was more frightening when we knew what was happening. The frightful pains subsided or rather were replaced by a numbness like that of 'pins and needles' when an arm or leg has 'gone to sleep'. When this numbness attacked the legs the soles of the feet became terribly tender, in a paradoxical way. Walking on a gravel path felt like walking on sharp tacks. Few of us had footwear of any kind, but the feet of fit men became quite tough.

Some of us tried to counteract the numbness by systematic exercising of toes, fingers, feet, ankles, arms and legs and even to this day, whenever I sit still or lie still, I find myself twitching and revolving my toes and feet.

The next stage following numbness was the one which showed whether it was wet beri-beri or dry beri-beri. The feet would start to swell and became rubbery and a prodding finger would leave a dent which would stay there for an hour or so if it was wet beri-beri.

Some men got as far as this and then after a watchful and anxious week would see the feet reduce to normal, but in most cases the swelling continued up the legs, in the face and arms and gradually a man would blow up like a huge Michelin man. He was finished and there was nothing he could do about it. It was just a matter of time before we sewed him up in a sack, borrowed our Union Jack from the Japanese guardroom and carried him to the cemetery in Rangoon.

ANGRY SEA

The Japanese guard turned out and gave the full present arms as the dead man passed and on this occasion, for the first and last time he was not expected to bow or salute as he passed.

Percy Hall was the only one I remember who recovered from the final stage of wet beri-beri. He tried everything from exercise and sunbathing to refraining from drinking water. He was a serious, intellectual RAF sergeant who wouldn't give in even when Len White and I bet him we would see him carried out. We lost because unaccountably Percy started to sweat one day, he sweated and stank like a urinal, and he gradually went down until in a week he was skin and bones and then he started to build up and even got to the stage where he went out regularly on work parties.

He certainly had it over us because we only had the first twelve months outside. For the last two years we were on the sick list, until just near the end.

With dry beri-beri sense of balance was lost in the third stage, to the extent that a man could not stand except with legs wide apart to give a firm base. Even then if he closed his eyes he swayed and toppled. Fingers went completely numb, nose and ears got cold and finally, the world became a blur and voices a jumble of indistinguishable sounds.

I'd been up and down with dysentery and malaria for months until I just had to go into hospital with the other no-hopers. I think it was touch and go with me for a while but I made it and reached the stage when I was discharged from hospital. I simply had to get well with Len White chuckling at me every time he asked me if I was letting myself go. I almost was actually, and if it hadn't been for Lofty and Len I probably would have done. I slipped to the bottom one day and gave up and it just happened that Pete Wilson came in to see me and I told him I'd had enough and was going to let myself go after all. In fact I said goodbye to Pete who got thoroughly alarmed and sent Lofty and Len to see me.

Len stopped joking and begged me to get a grip on myself. I think he was a bit scared at the sight of a stage which he might reach.

Then Lofty came along and I couldn't believe that the young boy who'd joined us in Sumatra had suddenly grown a wise and gentle strength.

Lissy and Tiny also came and although they left me still very weak, life and hope gradually crept back and I decided to live after all. So I left hospital with my malaria, dysentery and now advancing beri-beri and joined Len again.

He would have been ludicrous if he hadn't been so incredible with his beri-beri waddle, his dysentery run, his fever blankets, his old corncob pipe (home made), his black patch on one eye and above all, his chuckle. He peered with his good eye (which wasn't very good) at anything which moved in his limited range of vision and yet he chuckled at himself as much as at everybody else.

Until my eyes got as bad as his I was his watchdog for Japanese sentries who had to have their bow regardless. I used to say to Len, "Look out Len, sentry at 10 o'clock to your front' and Len would turn and bow ceremoniously in the specified direction.

I had him bowing to the benjo, to the cook-house or to anybody who drifted past and his good nature never deserted him. Len and I had everything that was going except hookworm and sores and then I got thoroughly doused with hookworm and beat him in this.

The hookworm is picked up in the tropics usually through the soles of bare feet and in this stage is small enough to enter the veins and travel through the bloodstream to find its way eventually to the stomach and intestines where it grows to maturity. In maturity it hooks itself to the sides of intestines and stomach and feeds on blood. Once stuck with hookworm nothing, except drastic hospital treatment to evict the parasite, will serve.

Those of us who collected hookworms were stuck with them. I suppose in the end we must all have had them because few of us had footwear and the benjo must have been alive with the creatures deposited there.

Jungle sores were a nightmare to many men but strangely enough Len never got any. I only had one and that not for long. There were two kinds, male and female although I don't know if these names were meant literally. The male sore burrowed in and could go right to the bone. The female spread out to make a big wide hole. Both types putrefied the flesh, which could be scraped away painlessly as I found when I took my sore to our compound doctor, Colonel Mackenzie. He scraped away the dead flesh with a piece of bamboo which didn't hurt but he continued scraping the living bleeding flesh which did hurt. Then he poured a liberal dose of some burning blue ointment which set me dancing and almost yelping. I had no more trouble but probably wouldn't have gone back if I had, as the cure was worse than the sore.

Lofty had sores which clung to him for a couple of years but most of the other Australians were free of them, although most Americans were covered. I think scratching was the cause of most sores, a scratch could start a sore and further scratching was fatal. You could be stuck with it for a year, never quite losing the battle against complete poison but never quite getting the upper hand.

Probably one of the reasons I only had one sore was because by the

170

time I became thoroughly lousy with crabs we'd come under the control of Brigadier Hobson and he had started wheedling medical supplies out of the Japs. Amongst these supplies was the blue ointment which burned like acid but was sure death to the crabs which burrowed in the skin to multiply and irritate. I'd clung to my beard, despite bugs which we could beat and against lice which we could hunt out and destroy, but when I got crabs I gave up and parted with every hair on my body. There was no other way with crabs.

Ants incidentally turned out to be good friends against lice and crabs, we used to put our bedding and clothing amongst the ants and they'd clean out everything even the eggs. But not even ants would touch the nauseating bugs.

CHAPTER THIRTY-FOUR
CHOLERA

By the middle of 1943 I'd said goodbye to working parties. I had dysentery and malaria fairly regularly. I was well advanced in dry beri-beri in that all feeling had gone from my legs. Then the keenness of my vision and hearing left me forever and each month saw my world becoming more of a blur.

Len White, of course, was still chuckling and said that after the war he'd get a white stick, a tin mug and a beat next to mine in Piccadilly. I'd been beaten up twice in fights before I was forced to recognise that I was no longer anything but a pushover for anybody from teenage onwards. This was a very humbling situation which quickly tones down a man's arrogance.

Tiny, despite dysentery and malaria, could still whip the three best men in the compound and in fact put on a display once against three men. If the three had been six they might have had a chance.

Lofty had filled out and insisted on playing big brother to me and I didn't mind a bit. Anyway we all had a share of what was going and still it looked as if we'd come through eventually. Then in April 1944 the terror struck the whole jail community.

CHOLERA!

The scourge of the east, the plague which could knock out a whole town and devastate a province.

Cholera could break out in a bazaar in the morning and kill hundreds by next morning, and thousands by next week despite serums, doctors and unremitting toil. What could we do in Rangoon jail without medicine or in fact any means of fighting the plague?

Cholera even scared the Japanese and we heard that Rangoon itself started to empty. The first two men died and were buried without anyone suspecting the truth but when the vomiting and deaths spread it was obvious. The Japanese were really alarmed when told and within hours had contacted Tokyo with requests for serum. Then the Brigadier and our Chief Medical Officer, Colonel MacKenzie put their heads together with a Canadian doctor, Major McCleod.

The fight was on.

Food and water were forbidden to us. Cholera germs can only start in the stomach. The Japanese supplied unlimited firewood and vats for boiling water. Now food was allowed, but only on plates which had been taken from a vat of boiling water. One man had to keep the flies away while his mate ate the food, then they changed places.

The Japanese sent doctors to make tests of every man in the compound to find and separate those who carried the germ. Carriers were moved to an isolation compound. The deaths continued but now the dead were not buried, a funeral pyre was kept burning in the jail.

The battle was switched to the real carriers of the plague, the flies. Every man of our six hundred had to produce fifty dead flies each day. This only needed about six swipes with a swat in the benjo area. Fifty times six hundred is thirty thousand and most men killed hundreds, some with foresight, saved their dead flies.

Thirty thousand flies every day didn't seem to make any difference. The cess-pit at the back of the prison where the bullock drowned, which had been a hole nearly forty feet in diameter, was still a black mass.

By the end of a week the new cases in our compound were decreasing and flies were becoming more difficult to find. A few more days and the thrifty ones were selling dead flies to those who had been threatened with a beating for not producing enough.

We went for five days without any new cases. Ten days was the incubation period so we had to start again. Several new cases broke out and of course recovery from cholera was rare. Then we had seven days clear, then two more cases. We crossed our fingers when we cleared nine days. Nearly cleared nine days because we had another case in the evening. And, at last we past ten days but we did twelve for luck.

We'd beaten the plague.

CHAPTER THIRTY-FIVE

BUFFALO

As we became more organised and got deeper into the rut of camp routine, it was inevitable that an Entertainment Committee would materialise. At one period we had some form of entertainment for almost every day of the week.

The Japanese began to give us Sundays free from work, and we even had sports meetings. Lissy cleaned up almost every event on the bill, with Tiny bagging the remainder. Our diet was improving by the second year, partly because of more variation in rations. We were receiving pay for working, and half of the officers' ordinary pay doled out by the Japanese after the first year went to the general fund, while larger working parties were scrounging food outside, leaving bigger rations for the others. This improvement in diet worked wonders in those who had not deteriorated too far, and in many cases an abundance of surplus energy was produced for which an outlet had to be found.

Tiny launched a series of talks with a full account of our adventures from Singapore. He spoke well, and though he started with a handful of people in his audience this increased as the tale continued each night, until the whole compound was listening. Our gang became heroes of the moment, and many listeners realised for the first time that we had not just been picked up in Burma like the rest.

Other talks followed, and after them a series of debates which became terrifically popular. A visiting Japanese entertainment troup put on a show for us. Quizzes and dumb charades followed, bringing forth an astounding store of knowledge from various individuals.

Finally the concerts came and they stayed. A fighter pilot, Warrant Officer Richardson took the lead here. He produced an enthusiasm in our entertainment-starved lives which could not have been found in any western first night. Singers of real talent, mimics, comedians and play actors of all kinds filled the bill, in a never-ending cavalcade of pleasure.

Concert night always had an early supper as a prelude, and this in itself became a cherished innovation, when the cooks also got the party spirit and devised varied menus. Once we nearly had steaks but this turned out to be soup a day late. It happened like this.

One of the Japanese sentries had got himself a bit tipsy one night in Rangoon and when he saw a water buffalo grazing outside a cottage, nostalgia overtook and he was unable to resist the impulse to drive the

174

beast merrily through the highways and by-ways of the city.

He brought the animal right to the prison by which time he'd sobered somewhat and suddenly visualised the consequences of his folly when his superiors found out. The thing to do was hide the evidence, which isn't easy when the evidence is a half ton buffalo.

He drove it to our compound and yelled out loud and long. "Sojo!" (sergeant) "Anchow!" (boss) "Sweji!" (cook)

The boss and the cook sergeant arrived and the Japanese pointed to the animal and made an eloquent gesture across his throat. "Ugh!" he pointed, "Ugh!" he gestured and "Ugh!" he pointed again, this time to the cooking pot.

It didn't need Lissy to translate this as "Get rid of the damn thing."

We gathered round with mouth-watering anticipation. Harvey Bensley, a big Aussie sheep farmer who was as hairy as a gorilla said he'd stun it and cut its throat. He swung our hammer and struck. The buffalo shook its head and looked at him.

Harvey was indignant and swung with ALL his might. The beast didn't even get angry. Lissy called the Jap who'd brought it. "You'll have to shoot it!" he said and the poor little man yelped. He daren't fire a shot.

"Okay," Lissy said ruthlessly, "you better take it away."

The Japanese appealed to his cobber who was on sentry duty at that moment but his cobber would have none of it. "You fire your own rifle," was what he obviously said.

There was no choice so he got his rifle and we led the buffalo to an air raid trench while men stood by with shovels.

They made sure they got the right spot before the trigger was pressed and the half ton of meat thudded nicely into the trench.

By the time the investigation came the trench was filled in, the Jap was safely back to his quarters and an innocent Lissy was saying "Shot? We heard something but I think it was outside."

When the hue and cry died down the cooks set about cutting up the carcass and blunted every instrument in the compound before they penetrated the skin. The meat simmered all next day in a huge vat, and was dished out in huge lumps for the evening meal.

Half an hour later the Brigadier decided to recall the steaks and try again so everybody came to the cook-house and tossed his unchewable portion back into the pot. By next evening it had been reduced to shreds but these were still as unchewable as string so we settled for a magnificent broth.

CHAPTER THIRTY-SIX
BOMBS AND BENJO

It was in our first year that the air raids from allied bombers started and this gave us the biggest thrill we'd had so far. For the first time in our experience the Japanese were on the wrong end of the bombs. It was wonderful to see them run and to hear the crump, crump of the bombs in the distance. It was the first tangible proof we'd had that the war was still being actively waged against the rising sun.

The raids at first were very small, and sometimes weeks went by without any signs of an alert, and our hopes receded - then suddenly they would rise again. We always hoped and dreamed of a mass attack by day with parachutists pouring out of the sky to liberate us, and every time an alert was heard we prayed that this was the day.

Then we heard a raid at night and all kinds of conjectures and rumours were rampant. But still the raids went on and nothing more happened.

The camp became more hysterical with excitement one day when more than a hundred bombers came over and thoroughly pasted Rangoon. Never before had we seen the mighty Nippon so roughly treated, and with apparent immunity. The immunity wasn't real, however, as bomber and fighter crews were filtering into the prison, but they brought news, even though we didn't normally see them for weeks after capture. The airmen were clear-eyed and intelligent, and it was refreshing to have new insight on the progress of the war, which had been planned and wonderfully won a hundred times over by us debaters.

The thrill of novelty wore off the night raids, and they became an absolute nuisance after a time, as the Brigadier insisted that we clear out of our rooms into the trenches. To a man who wasn't tired there were wonderful firework displays from the flares and tracer and the thrill of the whistles of falling bombs which never seemed to be far away.

At the time when the night raids became intense in late 1944, Buck Bryson and I had little sleep. As we had tasks during the day, we acquired the habit of lying doggo in our room leaving the visiting Brigadier with the impression that the room was empty. When he had passed on his rounds we could settle, and amazingly with the bombs crashing around us we slept.

We were together there on one night when a crash louder than usual started us out of sleep, and louder than ever we heard the terrifying whistle

176

of bombs. Three exploded in quick succession, and we realised that the next one was for us. There was a double thunderous crash, one on either side of our block, followed by a terrific splattering of shrapnel and bricks on the roof. The whole sky through the bars was blotted out, and the room was filled with a suffocating dense smoke.

"You alright, Buck?" I called, and quietly came the "Yeah!" then, "We'd better see what's happened, Gabby." There was silence everywhere. The horrifying thought came that everyone else had been killed. We crept to the window overlooking the compound.

The air was clearing now, and suddenly Buck gave a startled gasp, "The benjo's gone, Gabby," and sure enough where the towering bulk used to fill the skyline, there was a clear and unrestricted view. The others were active now, and we went out to view the destruction.

One bomb had landed on our trench, blown the benjo to smithereens and buried the whole platoon. Men were scratching furiously at earth and stones to uncover something living. By the time the Japanese had arrived with tools the bodies were coming out. Ken White, Bert Flower, Sgt. Jackson, Jim Manser, Piggy Martin, Hal Cummings our Yank with his two countrymen, Gonzales and Malek, Bobby Duftan. It seemed as if the dead would never stop coming, and then at last moaning and unconscious but alive came Len White. Poor old Len, as if his dysentery and beri-beri had not been enough he had this. Still he lived, still hanging on and still refusing to 'let himself go' and in a week's time he was joking about his pals walking over him in his grave, before they dug him out.

This was our worst raid for casualties so far, and left our platoon of Aussies, Yanks and British Air Force NCOs sadly depleted. We were nine short and for days the room was full of ghosts.

After this the prison got a good many bashings. Time and time again we were called out to build up a breach in the prison wall, while our own walls began to look as if they'd been used by a firing squad.

For many nights after this big raid we made no more complaints about going to the trenches, but at this period the display by the RAF and Americans was worth turning out to see. The Japanese ack-ack and searchlight batteries were worth seeing also. We never ceased to marvel at their unerring ability to send a finger of light up in the sky to the east, a terrific barrage of gunfire to the north, and to completely ignore the planes in the south or west.

The Japanese fighters also had an instinct which enabled them to go scooting over the horizon before our planes arrived, and to start chasing about the sky in full view when the raid was over. We used to look on this as a particularly good omen, feeling that the Japanese dare not risk many of their few remaining fighters.

CHAPTER THIRTY-SEVEN
SPOOKS AND SPIRITS

Buck Bryson was the central figure in our spiritualism. Buck and I spent many sleepless nights together, and became really close friends. We not only knew all about each other's lives but also had a fair knowledge of the workings of each other's minds. Buck had had a long illness with brain fever, and had been transferred to the sick compound, leaving me in the other.

We had daily administration liaison with the other compound and after a while began to hear of a run of seances which were being held in the other block. We grinned when we heard that Buck was the medium, as he was the greatest practical joker in the camp. Then a spirit told Buck that the brother of a certain man had died in Singapore, and another man's mother had died of a broken heart in America and we realised that this was no joke.

Buck acquired a large following by correctly forecasting a number of major events, and we began to have real forebodings. Lissy, Tiny and John Reid were all friends of Buck's and were all Roman Catholics with a Catholic's view of spiritualism. Buck also was a Catholic, and they could not for the life of them understand how a Catholic could allow himself to set such an example, and to do so much harm to the Catholic Church.

When my transfer to the sick compound could be delayed no longer, I was detailed to hold myself in readiness to move next day. That night was sorrowful for me at the prospect of leaving my friends, but amongst other things John Reid gave me a definite job to get to the bottom of the spirits. Several others, apparently level-headed, had gone as sceptics, and returned as believers and even we were beginning to wonder.

Buck received me with some distrust, and I could read his thoughts as he avoided all discussions of his seances. However, I brought it up eventually. My professions of curiosity and interest in the subject persuaded him to talk about his obsession. He even agreed to include me in a seance. Buck, myself, Titch Hudson and another Englishman gathered on the scheduled night in the spacious cook-house of the sick compound after lights out, and even then I started seeing ghosts.

A rickety card table was produced with four petrol drums for seats, then the system was explained to me. We were to sit with our hands on the table and wait for a request from a spirit to come in. This request would take the form of an agitation of the table. The messages would be taken by Buck in table rappings, each rap spelling out a letter of the alphabet, and stopping at the required letter. For example, the word 'Don' would be spelled out by four raps, five raps and fifteen raps. The process might be shortened if a word was guessed by the medium, or a question asked and an affirmative, or negative, signalled by one or two raps respectively.

This seemed a long-winded process for spirits to use, and I began to wonder how the others had been deceived.

An hour spent in absolute and eerie silence put a different complexion on the situation, and even I as a non-believer was affected. In the starlight I could see the absence of any stage props, the hands of everyone were visible on the table, with legs and knees well clear, so that when suddenly the table jerked violently up and down on the floor my scalp prickled, and I could feel the hair rising on my head. Panic mounted in my heart as I realised horrifyingly that I'd got more than I bargained for, and I all but fled there and then. My lips moved in prayer for help, and as they did so my mind raced - I knew that I would always be sorry if I didn't see it through.

I prayed again to my God to protect me from all others, and waited. Buck had started speaking and my scalp prickled again at the sound of his voice. It didn't sound like Buck, and indeed it was not he. He was possessed, and then suddenly I could have grinned in sheer delight as the spirit came through - it was an old flame of our medium, and her first communication was an expression of her desire to be with Buck tonight and every night. This saved me for the moment, as I thought it was a bit worldly for a departed spirit, and I began to wonder how it was done.

I began to tentatively explore the under edge of the table with my thumbs, when suddenly I was petrified again as the table began to gyrate and chop angrily on the floor. I felt my temerity in butting in. I had the horrifying feeling that something was behind me, and was about to smite me and again I made my silent appeal to God.

The rappings continued serenely, and I tried to decide on my course of action. My every inclination was to leave well alone and be thankful if I came out alive, but again I knew that I couldn't fail Lissy and Tiny, not to mention devout and sincere John Reid, who had tackled me on the subject that morning.

Once more I prayed for a guardian for the next few minutes and once more I put downward pressure on the table. The strain of force against me seemed terrific, but I hung on determinedly and, wonder of wonders

I held the table down.

I was all right now, in the full realisation that even if I was pitted against the supernatural I was winning. Then suddenly the thing took a new turn - the edge of the table opposite me tilted, and banged with frantic entreaty back and forward from the floor.

During this struggle Buck had been exhorting the clashing spirits to go away, but now he really became hysterical as he shrieked, "They're for you Gabby! A message for you! Ask them who they are - quickly, go on."

In this hysteria I daren't cross my friend, and with my mind in a whirl I complied.

Back came the answer, "A friend" - numbly I realised that it was I who was tapping out the answer.

"Ask again, Gabby! ask again," from Buck, and I couldn't stop now. Inspiration completely left me, then in my whirling mind came the thought of Bosun, our dead hero, who had died out in the Indian Ocean. With a touch of whimsy I followed up Bosun's name with Lofty Eastgate's, before I stopped, aghast at what I was doing - or was it I who was tapping out the message? Were my mind and hands, in which I could feel electrical tremors, actually possessed, and was I only the medium in a real show?

During the next hour I had plenty of time to wonder, when I shut down transmission and steadfastly resisted every tremor of the table, until even Buck reluctantly decided that we were finished for the night. He now loved me like a brother, and talked until dawn, giving me amazing insight.

John Reid's eyes were reproachful next morning when news of our activities spread. I avoided him until I had collected my scattered wits, then I told him everything. Later in the day Tiny and Lissy came over, and we thrashed the matter out. In the sane light of day it was easy to decide that imagination, atmosphere and strain were the ruling factors, but we knew it would be hopeless to convince Buck of this. He would swear that consciously or not I had been possessed and nothing would be gained. In fact, I would lose a friend and Buck would continue until his brain snapped.

We decided to work slowly, so for weeks I spent many weary nights round the table, waiting for results which I would not allow to come. Buck dropped Titch, then the other bloke, in the hope of eliminating a jarring influence, and even dropped me as a last resort, but by this time Titch had been reinstated, and he carried on my job for me.

Buck's enthusiasm cooled a little - fanned up again, then cooled and died naturally. He lost that wild look and on his wasted frame the flesh began to appear again, until at last he was once more the normal Australian of old. Meanwhile, we had assured the two bereaved members that they had no need to worry, and finally I managed to tackle my friend himself.

I got around to it one afternoon when we were lying out in the sun reminiscing and dozing. I exacted a promise from Buck that he would neither move nor speak until I had finished, and I gave him the full story.

When I had finished, he was silent for a time before he said: "I still reckon you are wrong, Gabby," and I couldn't shake him. I flung down a challenge to him to try and get in touch with his beastly spirits again, but sorrowfully he agreed that in sowing the tiniest of doubts, I had ruined his chances and we left it at that.

Among other things he had had a message from his own sister who had been killed by a car in Melbourne, and he even had the number of the car so I wrung from him a promise (for my own doubts) that he would tell me what he found out when he got home.

I have before me now a Christmas card received from Buck, or Ken Bryson in 1946, with no greeting except the scrawled words: "You were right Gabby."

CHAPTER THIRTY-EIGHT
THOUGHTS OF ESCAPE

Up to the end of 1942 there was always much talk of escape, but very few serious plans. We all felt there were insurmountable obstacles to any successful escape, first of all in the nature of the country itself, with its boundless jungle and swamps - secondly in the distance which separated us from allies - and finally in the attitude of the Burmese whom we regarded as the most treacherous race we had so far met. They had gone over completely to the Japanese and there was always a strong anti-British feeling. The average Burmese citizen came to hate the Japanese when they felt the yoke, but we never really felt that we could count even on passivity from them. Besides this they were mortally afraid of the Japanese and dare not cross their masters, who hadn't the qualms or scruples of the British in their application of measures to enforce respect.

At one period a party of seven of us including Lissy, Tiny and Lofty, had everything set for an escape and had developed our plans to such an extent that we awaited only the first black and stormy night to get out, but just at the crucial period we got red hot news of a big push towards Rangoon and the excitement was so intense and the news so real that we felt liberation could only be weeks away. By the time the rumour had fizzled out four of our party had been killed in an air raid and I was down with dysentery, and we never got round to active preparation again.

We had a raft made and ready in a timber yard, we had a work party there daily on the river and had a bamboo and wire ladder with grappling hooks inside the prison and even had a cache of food. The acquisition of the wire was almost the cause of my undoing, but it had funny aspects and illustrated perfectly the inability of the average Japanese to follow more than one thought at a time.

I had gone out one day on a work party to a Japanese barracks and as they were new to us we had a flag day for looting; I had got into the quartermaster's stores and had pounced on a substantial coil of this wire and later in the day pinched a pair of brand new army boots.

I wore only a loin cloth on this day, but borrowed a boiler suit from one of the Americans so as to conceal my loot. The boots were of new leather in its yellow rawness, and I only had time to hurriedly rub in mud

182

and dirt on the part that was showing before being marshalled ready to return to jail.

When we got back to the prison I was horrified to find that the guard on duty decided to search us, and as we were right in front of a sentry I had no chance of swapping ranks as the search progressed. I forgot all about my wire in my breast pocket and prayed only that my new boots would not be noticed, and was therefore totally unprepared when the searching sentry pounced on my coil of wire, and as the others came crowding round I could see that they felt they had got something.

A cold sweat broke out when I thought of the grappling irons in my bedding which a further search would produce. I knew I'd be shot and frantically tried to explain that the wire was for binding and repair work, but my Japanese at this stage was not equal to the task, and even though they tried to comprehend I was getting nowhere. In desperation I took the wire and went through imaginary motions with a needle and on inspiration I pulled my trousers up and did the motions on my brand new boots. I could have collapsed as soon as I had exposed my further theft but the light of understanding broke out on the face of the sentry, and with a drawn out "ah-h-h", of comprehension, he replaced the wire in my pocket and passed on leaving me almost collapsing with relief.

It was in 1945 that conditions began to improve a little in the camp. Rations were the first item dealt with and in the end we were given a full scale Japanese soldier's allowance officially. This did not quite work out in practice, as we were still unable to produce the ample stews and curries enjoyed by all troops with whom we came in contact. This was probably due to the inroads made by the prison staff on our allowance.

The time even came when we were given the job of killing our own beef and pigs, and dividing the rations throughout the jail, between Indian, Chinese and Whites. Certain sects of Indians would not have pork so we got that, and others would not have meat which had not been killed by themselves, so until they changed their minds we got extra here also.

However, we didn't always kill our own livestock and it was then we got a bad deal in receiving rotten meat. We used to cut off parts which were really putrid and cook the remainder, but on one or two occasions even the most optimistic of our cooks had to reluctantly bury a whole consignment. We stopped buying meat at this stage as a waste of money, although by that time it was pretty hopeless trying to buy anything.

The Japanese had flooded Burma with their currency and inflation had created an impossible situation. Cheroots for example had gone up from one rupee per hundred to one hundred and twenty rupees and later the price soared still higher. The 'pay' we received from the Japanese was scarcely enough to buy a morsel of food from the few natives who braved

Japanese wrath and traded with us through the wire, and most people had long since bartered away all their watches, rings and anything remotely valuable for food and smokes.

Besides an ostensibly better deal in food the general attitude of the Japanese changed. In the old days any one star private who felt liverish could work off his temper even on our Brigadier. One or two sentries used to come rampaging through our compound looking for the slightest chance to vent their spite on someone. A sentry would thoroughly beat up some unfortunate, put him in the sun to stand at attention or with his arms raised demanding complete immobility. Some of the sentries used to hide and pounce on anyone who, not seeing them, hadn't bowed. I have seen a whole row of officers and men lined up in the sun for invented slights.

By 1945 this situation had changed. On one memorable occasion when a sick man collapsed in the sun and was kicked to his feet, one of our medical orderlies remonstrated with the sentry. When the same treatment had been meted out to him he had gone stalking round the prison to find the Japanese doctor to lodge a complaint. In the old days the plaintiff against any of our captors would have had the beating of his life, but on this occasion it was the sentry who got his beating. After this we started lodging all kinds of complaints.

Our quartermaster, who was a sergeant or 'sojo', used to come and ask us for complaints or suggestions, but he was treacherous and it was impossible to work out his reactions.

The Japanese second in command 'Yagi San' was the best Jap in the jail. He made no fuss or fine speeches, but was the personification of justice. Although his stern demeanour made him a little feared he was also very much respected. He was a stickler for etiquette and demanded a proper salute from everyone, but would stand at rigid attention and bow, just as politely to the meanest British private as he would to the Brigadier.

He also addressed our officers with proper respect and Lissy, who could speak Japanese with an unbroken and even flow, was the light of his life. Every Japanese in the camp knew Lissy by name and even the meanest of them used to come to Lissy for a social visit and a chat. It was intriguing to see Lissy gabbling away and even heatedly arguing points. He only once got a beating, and then his other Japanese friends swore that they would beat the offender in turn.

W.O. Richardson was almost as fluent as Lissy and I myself acquired a large vocabulary. I began to regain my strength a little and Len White and I made a big effort to get fit, which succeeded to such an extent that we were finally allowed to go on work parties. For us, after being shut up for almost two years, even to see the outside world was a terrific thrill. I overdid it, however, and although I clung to my place in a work party tenaciously, was taken off eventually and ended my time as orderly sergeant in our sick compound.

The sick compound was no longer for sick men only, but was filled with Americans, Australians and New Zealanders and even included one West African, Peter.

In the early months of 1945 it became obvious that the end of the war was in sight - for Burma at any rate. Rumours which had always been rampant became too persistent to ignore. The long familiar phrase 'They're coming down' was becoming a reality. As each batch of fresh prisoners came in they brought heartening news of progress and what was more wonderful, they had a contempt not seen before for the Japanese forces.

For the Japanese the turning point had been their failure in March 1944 to capture Imphal, just across the Indian border, and it was here too that the Allies finally reversed their policy of retreat and decided to stand and fight. Now, in March 1945, they had beaten the Japanese back; they had crossed the mighty Irrawaddy and recaptured the Japanese stronghold of Mandalay. Suddenly, the war in the jungle had become almost a game for the Fourteenth Army. They were diving into the jungle to oust the remnants of scattered forces with all the zest of big game hunters.

The airmen, too, were having their heyday and British fighters were flitting with impunity over Rangoon. The whole population had become raid-conscious. At the first sound of a plane all work ceased and the inhabitants of Rangoon went cowering to their shelters.

The prison guards took on mournful faces and started reading up the provisions of International Law, instead of the Brand New Order instituted by the Japanese.

The Germans in Europe were receiving a beating and the end there was definitely in sight. The time was arriving when the Rising Sun of Japan would be left alone against the terrific forces of the West. Even so, we didn't really feel that the whole war would end for many years yet. The Japanese themselves completely accepted the idea of another 100 years of war before the allies were conquered. However, it would be over for us in Burma, or so we thought, and then a fresh bombshell fell.

By the middle of spring Rangoon was beginning to look as Singapore had done, three years ago. The native population were fast departing to their jungle relatives. Work parties had ceased and we were left very much to our own devices. Rumours of local naval and air landings were strong, and it became clear that the Fourteenth Army was not far away.

Rangoon in its position to the west of the Gulf of Martaban looked as if it would be cut off from the coast at any time. Then came the blow.

On April 24th the Japanese interpreter came to our compound and told us that we were to be moved from Rangoon to the safety of Siam. Visions of further captivity could be seen. This was heartbreaking when we had built up such wonderful hopes of release within weeks, and the whole camp was seething with the desire to escape. One enterprising party even boldly asserted that in a very much depleted Rangoon we could seize the city and either hold it or make our escape on the steamer down river to the sea.

The Brigadier firmly stamped out all such talk and ordered everyone to submit to the proposed horrible journey. He promised everyone that later on our overland journey he himself would properly organise a mass escape and would see everyone shepherded to safety.

The jail authorities now asked us to split our personnel into two groups - those who were fit to march and those who had to be left. There was a rush of those who wished to stay until the Japanese told us that these would be evacuated by sea and the rush stopped. Then the chances of escape would be nil apart from the far greater danger of bombing.

I was placed on the sick list but with my mind made up that I was going to get out of this at any price, I changed places with an Australian sergeant who wanted to stay.

It was about the 24th April when we were finally marshalled and the great trip began. We had already been fitted out with clothes, mostly Japanese uniforms including caps, and from a distance almost looked like a Japanese column.

The full force of the blows by the Americans and RAF were apparent as we passed through the streets which were completely deserted. Then the column was straggling northwards.

CHAPTER THIRTY-NINE
JUNGLE ESCAPE

We were to march north to Pegu to get to the head of the Bay and then move east away from the war towards Siam. It was generally felt that a break must be made before we passed Pegu and got too far away from our own troops. As the miles went by and nothing was heard of the Brigadier's plans, many of us became uneasy and wondered if his talk was not just a put-off to hold us together until it was too late to attempt escape. We knew he was capable of thinking himself justified in such a move to avoid deaths or hardship, but when he was tackled about his motives he produced a plan of escape just east of Pegu.

This decided me and I determined that even if I went alone I was not going past Pegu with the column, and accordingly set about forming a gang. I dare not tackle the escape alone with my poor vision and my old comrades scattered.

Lissy and Dicky were sick in Rangoon, Tiny was in a different part of the column. I seized on my remaining friend, Titch Hudson. Physically I was less than half a man now, and although my mind was still clear I needed someone else to lean on.

Titch and I soon got recruits as the legend of our adventures from Singapore was impressive and Len Coffin of the Kings, Dinger Bell and Bill McMurran, both of 17th Indian Infantry Division, joined us. Titch got shifted on the column and we lost him, but the remainder of us kept together by volunteering to manhandle en route one of the bullock carts which held our stores.

As the miles went by we systematically looted this bullock cart during each air raid and gradually filled a sack with rice, matches, candles, water bottles, peas, tea and sugar.

These air raids were real shoot-ups by questing Spitfires and Hurricanes. They became so persistent that by the 26th we were pinned down in a copse and couldn't move from it during daylight. Even here there was no respite, and the thicket was bombed time and again during the day. These raids were really a godsend to us as the Japanese and everyone else were pinned down in ditches and trenches and we were able to make unobserved visits to our vehicle for loot.

It was decided to make a break during the first raid that night. But when we were startled into activity by a roll call we found that Pete Wilson,

187

Lofty Eastgate and two other Australians, Ron Hadden and Harvey Boasby, had already made their escape and we realised that now the Japanese would be on the alert. A council of war left us resolved to watch for the first opportunity, night or day, and we sat down to wait for the next raid.

It wasn't long before a batch of Spitfires were merrily shooting up and bombing our copse. With shaking hearts we gathered our gear and started to walk away. Three years previously I would have had the confidence of fighting manhood and there would have been excitement and zest in the adventure, but now I was sick and trembling, and ready to panic if we were spotted.

We got almost to the edge of the copse when we saw the nearest Japanese sentry in his ditch between us and freedom, and we almost gave up there and then at the sight of him. However, the thought of freedom in the next few minutes against that of captivity for the next few years was too much and I could not let one Japanese soldier stand in my way. Back we went to our resting comrades and managed to get an invaluable cook's knife, long and sharp, from one of the cooks - and we stealthily made our way back to the sentry.

I was going to go up to the sentry, who only I knew. If he challenged my right to be away from the centre of the copse I was going to make a plea of fear of the bombs until I could get close enough to him to plunge my knife into his heart.

But something had happened to me in prison and even when I was sitting down, with him lying beside me on his stomach, I could not bring myself to do it. I had gone soft in camp and was no longer a man, and could not even bring myself to hurt him. Besides I liked this bloke, as I had grown to like many of the Japanese.

The situation was only saved by the man himself getting up and going on his patrol. In a few moments my gang were with me and racing across the open paddy field to the jungle and freedom 200 yards away.

The jungle swallowed us without sound, but we continued to run, wildly and hysterically, until we had to stop and lie panting.

We stayed only until our breath returned and then we were off again always to the west, and our allies, until at last the sun went down and we had to wait for the stars to appear and guide us. Dawn, and waiting for the sun gave us our first rest and then on again until the sun high in the sky had made west indistinguishable from east, north or south. Here we cooked our first meal and rested again until the waning sun gave us our direction and on we went again.

We slept for the first time since our escape that night in a bivouac of branches and took our time moving off next morning. We were weary even after a night's sleep and were hungry also, although we dare not use too much food. We had decided to have only one meal per day when the sun was high.

There was at least fifty miles of jungle between us and the next road running north and south. We were unable to cover more than a maximum of seven miles a day through the thick jungle and deep chaungs (gullies) of Burma. Apart from the natural obstacles we were all in bare feet and progress along the thorny bush was very slow.

There was not enough water to cook our rice at mid-day, and we wasted two hours following a dried stream bed digging at intervals before we finally found a spot where the earth was damp. In an hour we had a muddy but thirst-satisfying mixture in the bottom.

Our meagre supplies of food were very low by the fourth day, and we began to toy with the idea of approaching a village. So far we had avoided even small tracks which might lead to habitation or to a treacherous Burmese village. Even at night when we heard dogs in the distance we made wide detours.

After this we stayed on the first track we found and followed its meandering path through the whole of the fifth day, starting on it again on the sixth day. By mid-morning the single track had merged with a bullock cart track and before mid-day we heard the dogs in the distance.

We got to the edge of the village quietly and looked from cover at a quiet and peaceful scene with a background of six or seven huts. Some women were cooking by a fire and we could see not only that Japanese were absent, but that there were no men at all in sight except an old patriarch.

I left the others in the shrubbery and walked up smiling to the women and greeted them with the Burmese salutation. There was no understanding but they smiled and answered in a strange language, kow-towing vigorously all the while. I called to the others who straggled out, keeping close to the jungle and ready for headlong flight.

We stood round chatting and indecisive for some time and then I took the plunge and asked for some rice which stood in a pot away from the fire. Our intentions of taking it to the jungle and away caused a wondering discussion and then the old patriarch, grinning and toothless, came to us and vehemently insisted by signal that we sit down and wait. He pointed to the cooking food and we were sorely tempted, but memory of capture three years ago were strong and I didn't know what to do.

Our hunger conquered eventually and we squatted down well away from the entrance to the village on the very fringe of the protecting jungle.

A savoury chicken stew with hot rice made our wait worthwhile, and then we heard the dogs start barking again. The women reassured us and signalled to us to sit still, which we did, with our eyes glued on the trail until a group of natives appeared walking towards us. Warily we watched them approach until the leading man spoke, "Greetings master! Hello!" and we faced him.

He informed us that he had been a government clerk in Pegu until the Japanese came. We told him how we had escaped and were heading west towards the Prome road and safety. He shook his head at this and informed us that there was a concentration of Japanese forces between us and the road through which we could never pass.

This information was followed by a query as to why we should not stay here until our troops had won through. Again we were on our guard. This sounded too much like the familiar detaining subterfuge of the Burmese and eventually I gave it to him straight, pointing out our dilemma. To our surprise he became indignant when we spoke of the Burmese attitude towards the British and informed us in no uncertain terms: "We are not Burmese master, this is a Karen village," and we could have embraced him in our glee.

The Karen loyalty to the British was a tradition in Burma. Time and again we were regaled in Rangoon with stories of the unceasing guerilla war raged on the Japanese by Karen and Kochin tribes.

In fact the only other East Surrey in Rangoon, or rather ex-East Surrey, was an escaped POW called Corporal Pagani who had lived and fought behind the lines for two years in a Karen village. This Corporal Pagani had eventually set off on a mission to India and had later been speared by Burmese and left for dead, but had been picked up by a Japanese patrol and miraculously won his way back to health and strength. Lying in a Japanese prison he had not dared to disclose his name which was too well known to the authorities. He had maintained a dumb silence until an American crew, minus their dead pilot, had been brought in and after a thorough briefing Corporal Pagani had assumed the pilot's identity and was paid an officer's pay under the name of Lieutenant Malvern, until he came out of their hands.

As a fellow member of the Surreys, 'Malvern' had told me much of the Karen and I had no hesitation now in placing myself in the hands of those who warred on the Burmese and Japanese as much as we did.

We lived in a hut on the fringe of the jungle for two days until increasing Japanese patrols and flights into the undergrowth made our life one series of alarms. Then the whole village manpower turned out and made us a hut deep in a swamp some distance away, which was not only invisible at 20 feet, but could only be reached by a single unseen path through the swamp. We were given a puppy which sounded the alarm even when the villagers approached, and our days passed in unbroken serenity.

The monotony was only broken by constant visits from our original friend, the old patriarch, who set us smiling whenever he appeared. He took a delight in materialising from the jungle and, as even the dog didn't warn us, the first inkling we had of his presence was the rustling of the leaves as his toothless and grinning face was poked through the bushes. He would look cautiously round and then emerge with his hands behind his back, and then suddenly produce bananas, dureen, jack fruit, mangoes or even a chicken, although we already received more than we could eat. Our friendly interpreter also kept us going with news and a mass of information on the disposal of the enemy forces in the vicinity.

We had been there about five days when startling news came to the village. The British had re-occupied Pegu on 30 April and were patrolling the road from which we had escaped. This meant that they were nearer to us there than on the Western Prome road, and obviously our best plan, if the news was true, was to retrace our steps.

We could have waited in the village until the fact of British arrival was clearly established but the Karens had no doubts and were eager to deliver us to our friends, so we settled for movement on the morrow. Once again as on so many previous occasions, we lay down to sleep that night wondering what the morrow would bring. Under the tropical stars, we thought of home, of the past and of the future.

There was a long line of pictures from the past and a veil of sadness in those pictures. There was an infinite sadness in me for what could never be again; the tramp of marching glory, the camaraderie of the barrack room, the brotherhood of the corporals and 'sergeants' mess. All was gone forever.

There was misery behind me in the prison camp. The bones lying in the shallow graves in Rangoon, the lonely dyings far from home, and with all of this there was a great compassion and sadness for the Japanese who now wallowed in their own misery.

I wasn't sad for the warlords, the leaders who'd led a nation into poverty and desolation. The leaders who'd given license and encouragement to the beast lying dormant in every nation. But I had an overwhelming pity for the poor little coolies who'd been bundled into ill-fitting uniforms, torn from their loved ones and indoctrinated with the hate of the west before they were sent against us. Hate is fear and they had feared us. Fear comes from misunderstanding and they could not possibly understand what they didn't know.

They were being hunted even now out of their holes and corners to be shot, bombed or bayonetted. To be killed because they were ashamed not to die fighting. They'd be lying in their thousands in their far away scatterings, lying unburied with the pitiful photographs of wives who were now growing old and of babies they'd not seen.

They weren't so very different from us after all.

And what about tomorrow now? I almost had a fear myself of going back to the world. Not quite blind, not quite deaf, not very steady on my feet, what was I going to do, what kind of place would there be in the world for the hundreds and thousands like me, the armless, the legless, the sightless and the sick. The Smiths, the Browns and the Jones, Yank, Anzac, British, Japanese, Black, White and Yellow. If I wasn't such a pagan I'd just about turn Evangelist.

The bullfrogs in the jungle answered my thoughts, "Awk! Awk!"

I used to visualise them as monsters as big as my hand when they "awked" at the world, until one night in Malaya during a routine picket duty in camp, I tracked one down by its croaking. It had been raining, it was dead of night and I got right to the puddle from which the loudest bellowing came.

I shone my torch and there with its little throat pulsing as it croaked its challenge to all the other bulls in the world was the monster, about as big as my thumb nail. I wondered if I'd be leaving all jungle noises behind me soon and the sadness was back again.

I wondered if Lofty was lying somewhere else in the same jungle and I wondered if Tom, Tiny and Titch were lying somewhere with the Japanese column which was bound for the east.

Lissy and Dicky might be in Rangoon or they might not. As it happened they weren't. The naval landing that we'd dreamed of for years had taken place on 2 May after the Japanese had fled leaving the prisoners in Rangoon jail to take over.

Even now they were all free.

So were Tom, Tiny and Titch. A British column had rescued the lot and even now they were on their way to India. They were all free, all of our original gang were safe except for Lofty and me, Lofty was in another Karen village not far from us and the Karens took us back safely all right, straight back to the road from which we'd escaped and we lurked in our cover trying to identify the trucks and tanks on the road.

We moved closer and came upon an Indian patrol under the trees cooking food. They regarded us curiously and we looked at them dubiously. We continued on our way to the road. A truck full of British soldiers sped past us and some waved. Other trucks passed, none stopped.

ANGRY SEA

An Indian patrol passed and gave an ordinary salutation.

We looked at each other and took a tally.

Six Karens armed with knives. Armed allies maybe? Four bearded nondescripts! In Japanese uniform? With bare feet? What the hell did we look like? A patrol from the guards or Fred Karno's Army?

I stuck myself in the middle of the road determined to attract attention somehow and a lone driver pulled up. I explained who we were and could he take us to local intelligence. He was a bit doubtful and then I remembered I was a sergeant as I got a lift for myself. I couldn't manage it for the others but I sat them all down at the seventh milestone and told them to wait.

I had much to do for my Karen friends yet.

The truck pulled into the trees south of Pegu and the driver led me to Intelligence Headquarters. Intelligence was stretched out in a deck-chair under the palms with a sunshade and cool drink.

I smoothed my Japanese tunic, I marched forward and I tried to click my bare feet!

"Sergeant Gavin Sir!" I reported.

"Sergeant Gavin! Second Battalion, The East Surrey Regiment."

POSTSCRIPT

'YOU CAN'T LET GO'

One day in 1945 after four of us had successfully escaped and were safely in Chittagong in Bengal I got a bit of a headache. It was no more than that, with a slight temperature of course, and the only effect it had was to quieten me somewhat.

This was unusual for me in the observation hospital where we were receiving full VIP treatment, and one of the nursing sisters playfully put her hand on my forehead with the chiding remark, "You must be sick sergeant."

She let out a startled whoop, grabbed a thermometer which she rammed into my mouth and then fumbled for my wrist and pulse. Her eyes bulged, and she must have stared in disbelief at the thermometer reading. Then she acted. "Nurse! Nurse!" she called and two of them came running.

"Get him into bed!" she ordered. "With hot water bottles." Then she was off to get a doctor.

The first doctor got another one and they looked at me as I grinned at them gleefully. This was the life all right. Plenty of attention and fuss even for a headache. I knew what the headache was, I was in for a mild dose of malaria but they didn't think it was mild.

I was whipped into a private ward, I had a nurse to myself and I lay there luxuriating in the joy of being a bit off colour without having to will myself to get up to go to the benjo, or for a drink, a bath, I didn't even have to get up for tenko. All I had to do was lie there passively and leave my well-being in better hands than mine.

I learned afterwards that a hurried conference the following day resulted in the Red Cross machinery being set in motion to get my mother and father flown out from England and that the project was only abandoned because I couldn't possibly last long enough to see them.

I knew I was supposed to be really sick and it tickled me pink. The staff must have thought I was mad when I was grinning at them all the time. Then I got past the grinning stage and just dozed my days and nights away in a glorious half-conscious peaceful lethargy. The job of getting me better was still in their hands, and I was certainly not going to be robbed of the pleasure of doing nothing about it myself.

ANGRY SEA

Then one day, long, long afterwards it seemed, my barely conscious mind registered the fact that a doctor had raised one of my eyelids. I thought I grinned at him but I couldn't have done because he took a mirror from his nurse and held it in front of my nose and mouth.

They eventually departed and for the first time doubts came to me. I'd heard the doctor say, "There's still life in him," as if he was just a bit surprised about it, and later I recalled other little snatches of conversation from nurses who at various times had occasion to move my carcass about.

It took a long time to register but it finally did. I'd let myself fade away until I really was just about gone and with this realisation came an overwhelming disappointment. The doctors had failed me, they couldn't look after me, the long promised treat of letting myself go was not a treat after all. I was going to be stuck even now with the job of pulling myself round.

It never occurred to me that it couldn't be done, two years of struggle against dysentery, malaria and beri-beri had given me a complete realisation of what could be done. Then I began to wonder how long it was since I'd had anything to eat or drink, I'd lost count of days but obviously I had to start on my stomach first. I didn't realise then that they'd been feeding glucose into a vein in my foot for five days.

Anyway, much later, the next time somebody came to raise my eyelids I set my whole will into the task of winking at whoever it was. I must have got some life into my eyes because the nurse whisked herself off for a doctor. I'm sure I winked at him, I thought I asked for a drink but that may have been imagination.

However I got my drink, a drink of champagne of all things. Drop by drop they put it down my throat and against all the waves of nausea and repugnance I managed to hold it. This was mid-afternoon and by evening, I had moved my head and had managed a grin at the nurse. I was fully alive by morning with my mind made up. I was going to get up. The nurse thought I was delirious when I asked for my clothes so I bided my time.

It didn't come until next morning when the staff were dashing round getting the ward ready for doctors' rounds. My bed had been fixed and I was ship-shape and tidy behind the bed screens, so I had half an hour, and I used the time to struggle to get up. It took me all of it and I would love to have been standing up for inspection when the screens were parted by the ward sister and the doctor, matron and cortege looked in.

I had at least managed to get to the chair and I summoned up a grin. "Hello doctor," I said, "How are you?"

CIRCULATING STOCK	
WEXFORD PUBLIC LIBRARIES	
BLOCK LOAN	
BUNCLODY	
ENNISCORTHY	
GOREY	
MOBILES	W/D 8/01 M.S
NEW ROSS	
PROJECTS	
WEXFORD	
DATE	

J.K.